T0305708

I know I will read this again. And again. I need it as a reminder in the work ahead....

– **Trygve Aasheim**, Lead Architect,
Technology and Digital Channels, Corporate Banking, DNB

Bankers Like Us is about love and innovation at the FinTech Frontier of an inhospitable industry: banking.

– **Ronit Ghose**, Future of Finance Head, Citibank N.A.

An insightful read, based on lessons learned over a long career driving change in and outside the banking industry. Leda dives deep into the plumbing – systems, processes and culture – in large organisations, uncovering legacy tech and legacy mindsets with humour and humanity. These are real-world problems with real-world solutions from an expert in digital transformation.

– **Joy Macknight**, Editor, The Banker

In banking, we are in that rare moment of time where worlds are colliding. As Leda writes 'The challenge is that up until now, the industry has evolved. Now it has to transform.' As a long-time banker and newly-minted digital transformation leader, I know too well that years of 'existing' in banking created strong muscle memory that now thrashes against the pace of change. It pulls us back to what feels familiar and comfortable. This opportunity for transformation isn't about new ways of doing the old things, but more about completely new models of how serve the customer, and how we do so with completely new profit schemes. This book will resonate with anyone no matter where you reside on this journey, whether newbie or old guard. If you want to be part of this change, you need to understand all about the messy middle that Leda so expertly describes in this book. If you read this book and it doesn't resonate, then I suggest you think about stepping aside. As Leda explains, this change will need all sorts of talent and skills all the way down to the "friends in low places," but the one big thing to remember is this transformation is coming and won't care if you don't buy in.

– **Curt Queyrouze**, President, Coastal Community Bank

With personal and professional experiences beautifully weaved throughout, the book shares – in the most relatable way – that you don't need to compromise your principles to achieve business results, and that you don't need to sacrifice business aspirations to be a decent human being. Leda's narrative exquisitely captures so many of the industry's ideas and its participants' contemplations.

– **Tanya Andreasyan**, Editor-in-Chief, FinTech Futures

Bankers Like Us

This book will resonate with anyone no matter where you reside on this journey, whether newbie or old guard. If you want to be part of this change, you need to understand all about the messy middle that Leda so expertly describes in this book. If you read this book and it doesn't resonate, then I suggest you think about stepping aside. – Curt Queyrouze, President, Coastal Community Bank

The world is going digital, and so is banking—in fits, starts and circles. Why is it so hard? Why is the industry constantly getting in the way of its own technological progress and what can we do about it all? This book looks at the human and structural obstacles to innovation-driven transformation and at the change in habits, mindsets and leadership needed for the next stage of the digital journey and argues that this change will be brought about, not by external heroes and saviours, not by a generation yet to be born, but by people just like us. People who understand the industry and its quirks. Bankers who have the grit, determination and energy to drive change. Bankers like us.

This book celebrates and chronicles the shared experience of bankers like us. It starts with a 'this is who we are' piece, including the author's trench credentials. It then presents an overview of corporate culture (this is what we deal with and a few ideas on how to handle it), as well as a piece on why transformation is so difficult and so many get it wrong; a piece on the challenges our lack of diversity brings or compounds, and a hopeful look-ahead on what a team of principled, dedicated folks can do despite everything.

Bankers Like Us
Dispatches from an Industry in Transition

Leda Glyptis, PhD

CRC Press
Taylor & Francis Group

AN AUERBACH BOOK

First edition published 2023
by CRC Press
6000 Broken Sound Parkway NW, Suite 300, Boca Raton, FL 33487 2742

and by CRC Press
4 Park Square, Milton Park, Abingdon, Oxon, OX14 4RN

CRC Press is an imprint of Taylor & Francis Group, LLC

© 2023 Taylor & Francis Group, LLC

Library of Congress Cataloging-in-Publication Data
Names: Glyptis, Leda, author.
Title: Bankers like us : dispatches from an industry in transition / Leda
Glyptis, PhD.
Description: First edition. | Boca Raton, FL : CRC Press, 2023. |
Includes bibliographical references and index.
Identifiers: LCCN 2022038925 (print) | LCCN 2022038926 (ebook) |
ISBN 9781003364436 (ebook) | ISBN 9781032202037 (hardback) |
ISBN 9781032428154 (paperback)
Subjects: LCSH: Banks and banking—Technological innovations. |
Financial services industry—Technological innovations. | Bankers.
Classification: LCC HG1709 (ebook) | LCC HG1709 .G59 2023 (print) |
DDC 332.10285 23/eng/20220—dc23
LC record available at https://lccn.loc.gov/2022038925

ISBN: 978-1-032-20203-7 (hbk)
ISBN: 978-1-032-42815-4 (pbk)
ISBN: 978-1-003-36443-6 (ebk)

DOI: 10.1201/9781003364436

Typeset in Minion
by codeMantra

To my parents, for believing writing is the noblest of

past-times. Maybe after reading. Perhaps.

To Tanya, for getting me to write a book.

To David, for making sure I wrote it, without totally missing out on life.

To my tribe, for everything.

Contents

Foreword by Brett King

FinTech, like every other disruptive industry, has an incubation period where early adopters or believers are annoyingly passionate about the fact it is going to change the world. With FinTech impacting individuals and businesses in every corner of the globe today, those of us who witnessed and celebrated the birth of FinTech feel validated by these developments.

Dr. Leda Glyptis is certainly one such voice; a true believer that FinTech is changing the world for the better. In chronicling the emergence of the FinTech phenomena and the changes it has thrust on the banking and payments industry, we see the insights not only of a front-line practitioner frustrated by a slow-moving, intractable, outmoded industry, but also a philosopher debating the pros and cons of these changes at a human and personal level.

The global FinTech industry in aggregate is valued at more than $7 trillion today, and just in 2021 alone, venture capital investments reached a dizzying $210 billion for the year, with 1 in every 5 venture capital investment deals going into the FinTech sector. FinTech has spawned a bunch of major specialisations too such as Challenger or Neo Banks, the Cryptocurrency and DeFI industry (with a total market cap approaching $3 trillion), Mobile Wallets, Blockchain, RegTech and InsureTech, and much more. We also have the "TechFin" space – technology companies that incorporate next-gen financial services technologies to enhance their business – with players like Ant Group/Alipay, Tencent, GoTo/GoJek and Uber as exemplars. But just 10 years ago, most bankers (and certainly consumers) had never even heard of FinTech.

Today, the fastest growing financial services players in the world are FinTech. Some of the largest banks in their respective markets are banks that are less than a decade old, like WeBank with 250 million customers based out of Shenzhen; NuBank, the largest bank in the Latin American market with 50 million customers and a market cap that is 20% larger than its next biggest competitor Itau Unibanco (a 94-year-old incumbent); or N26, the second largest bank by market cap in the German space. Today, mobile wallets that didn't exist 10 years ago account for roughly twice the combined number of daily payments made via credit cards, debit cards and cheques globally. Ant Group, the largest FinTech company in the world, has almost 2 billion customers globally, and has the world's most successful and one of the world's largest savings or deposit pools in the world. This has all happened in the last decade.

Leda started this journey during the earliest days of the FinTech boom, working with a small network of likewise passionate players distributed around the world fighting to bring banking into the 21st century. Over the time since, she's spoken at conferences around the world, she's lent her voice to podcasts, she's built and consulted on technology transformation and she's regularly tweeted, written, blogged and posted on her thoughts and noteworthy developments in the space. This book brings together those experiences into some of the core themes of that disruptive decade.

The book tackles what it takes to lead in the face of fundamental changes thrust on an industry that often appears diametrically opposed to the inevitability of technology reform. Leda identifies many of the bad habits, processes, policy, systems and thinking that get in the way of real, material progress. But she also inspires the change we need, individually and collectively.

Prior to the global coronavirus pandemic, there was still a half-hearted debate in some areas that the whole FinTech thing might be a 'fad' that would come to an end as soon as these 'start-ups' faced a real economic crisis. The pandemic, however, demonstrated that the 21st century will reframe our economies to rely on technologies in every core aspect of society, whether it is the way we store or move our money or the way we access healthcare, education and services in general. In this way, FinTech was largely inevitable, spurred on by the internet, ecommerce and automation.

As we adapt to these broader economic changes, we must ask the tough questions about whether this is investment in technology for technology's sake, or are these changes actually making the world a better place? Is technology really lowering the cost and increasing access for those at the bottom of the economic pyramid, or does it inevitably lead to an increase in the wealth gap between the world's richest and poorest? Do devices like smartphones, that enable you to get instant access to credit, help you become financially healthier, or do they just accentuate existing financial problems? Is FinTech good for the world? Leda believes it is, and argues as to why that is.

In many ways, the FinTech phenomenon that is reshaping the way we think about banking, payments, investments and money is just in the foundational stage. The Metaverse, quantum computers, digital money and assets, decentralised systems, robots and artificial intelligence are just some of the elements that are still likely to reshape our future world. As Leda takes us on a journey through the birth and growth of the FinTech sector, we are granted a unique insight into how this happened, but more importantly why these changes are important to talk about, and what we can learn from the process.

While FinTech has shown it is inevitable, there's still much about the future that we are yet to define that needs this sort of conversation. I hope you enjoy her new book as much I did.

Brett King
Bestselling Author of Bank 4.0, Host of Breaking Banks
Podcast and FinTech Hall of Famer

Foreword by Antony Jenkins

Like all Barclays management trainees in the early 1980s, I began my career at the South Kensington branch.

In those days, a branch served everyone from students and waiters to the local accountants and lawyers up to larger businesses located in the area. You could get cash, buy foreign exchange, trade securities and prepare a will. It also processed checks, filed statements and performed a whole range of operational tasks. Over 30 people were employed in what was a medium-sized branch and we were part of the community, we knew our customers and they knew us.

Back then, I gained a key insight that has stayed with me throughout my career; banking is all about people. Customers are of course people, for most of whom banking is a necessary evil to enable something important to them in their lives. As I always say, nobody wants to go through the messy bureaucratic tedium of getting a mortgage, but everyone wants to buy a house.

In the branch, we had the time and the tools to solve the customers' problem, and there was nothing more satisfying. As an inexperienced banker when a customer came in with a problem I couldn't solve, I asked a colleague or consulted the 300-page product manual. You learned fast, and it was rewarding to have someone enter the branch worried, confused or frustrated and leave with their problem solved.

And of course, our colleagues are people too. I experienced then that happy and motivated colleagues led to happy customers and successful branches.

I do not hanker for those days through the glossy mists of nostalgia.

But I do believe that over the years in the pursuit of growth, revenue, cost cutting, profits and bonuses our industry has fundamentally lost sight of this profound insight around banking and people. Digital has only exacerbated this trend being seen as both a panacea and an obstacle, and it risks further alienating customers and colleagues.

Something must change.

This book is a timely exploration of an industry at a crossroads and where the only option is to undergo radical customer-focused transformation driven by digital technology. It asks the central question of how to engage and motivate colleagues to execute such transformation when there are strong cultural and psychological forces blocking change.

It is above all a call to action for bankers like us to embark on the journey of change with passion, courage and grit and to put people at the heart of everything we do. This is the path we must take now if banks are to much better serve their customers, colleagues, shareholders and above all society.

Change starts and ends with us. So get reading and start doing!

Antony Jenkins CBE
Founder, Chair and CEO at 10x Banking

Preface

SO MANY WAYS TO BEGIN: AN INTRODUCTION BY THE WAY OF INTRODUCTIONS

This book is about change.

Transformation of the deepest kind.

How it affects us all. How it complicates our lives and how, in turn, we make our own lives more complicated without necessarily meaning to, as we go through the transformation journey.

This is a book told from the vantage point of banking and the financial services industry, but it is neither just for bankers nor just about banks, as the experiences are universal in shape, if not in their particulars.

The book is about the people in the midst of change. Those who fight it and those who fight for it.

It is about radical change, intricate and complicated, affecting every aspect of a complete and complicated industry that, in turn, affects everyone's life because, like it or not, money is ubiquitous.

How do you kick off this kind of storytelling?

When telling the story in sequence is actually not the aim.

When you want to tell stories in the detail of this elaborate canvas and the canvas matters but isn't the story itself.

Where do you begin, when it is vital that you honour this complexity and context but when your story is about the people in the midst of it all, and the rest is backdrop? Vital, but not the main event.

How do you open a door into, not only a complete and complicated world, but a complete and complicated world in the midst of a radical and complicated shift, and do all that from the vantage point of a rather complete and opinionated worldview? A worldview comprised of experience, scars, stories and passionate convictions all held together with the sticky tentacles of 'oh and another thing'.

Where do you even start?

The beginning doesn't seem like a good place frankly. It will take us forever to get to the here and now and the things I actually want to write about.

The end is out of the question as we are not there yet and that's the point: we are in the middle of change, we don't know when or how it ends and this book is part of the work we are all doing to drive and manage and understand this change. To drive it towards a good outcome for all.

And the middle? The middle of the story is (I confess) my favourite part. It's the hardest and most important part of any endeavour. But I can't start the story there, or you won't know which bits are important and why, not until you finish the book, and that's no way to make you feel this early on in our friendship.

My friend Bradley Leimer said that starting in the middle will make people feel like guests at a party, where they know nobody else. Not even you, their host, he said. You want these guests to enjoy the party, so make them welcome, he said. Show them around, introduce them to the other guests.

But first things first, he said: start at the very beginning. By introducing yourself.

Where are my manners? He's right. Welcome, my name is Leda and I will be your pilot.

And Who Am I?

Why should you care to read what I have to say about things, you may ask?

And ask you should.

And I should answer.

I should earn the right to hold your attention for the hours it will take you to read these pages. Although admittedly, in my head, you are reading this section standing in a bookstore trying to decide whether this volume is for you, when, in reality you've already committed, and you have the book at home and I thank you and hope you enjoy it.

Still, the fact remains that we should not take our platform and pulpit for granted.

Who the hell are you is a question I (mostly silently) ask every time I walk into a meeting or conference and someone is waxing lyrical on a subject. I ask myself that every time I get sent a recommendation for a book or article. Who are you, speaker, author, pundit, whose opinion on this deserves my time? It's a genuine question and one I recommend asking as a filtering mechanism at a time when social media gives everyone a platform, in an industry that seems to enjoy generating influencers who have often never been practitioners.

Yes, please do tell me all about the thing I spend my life doing and you have never ever done yourself, I am all ears.

So asking is fair. Asking is encouraged.

I wish we asked and challenged more. We would get to the finish line a little faster if we spent some more time saying 'hold up, wait a minute, who the hell are you and what the hell is this and what does it do and why do I need it?'

So. Who the Hell Am I? And Why Should You Listen to Me?

I am a recovering banker.

I have been in FinTech as long as it has existed and in banking a wee bit longer (just).

I crossed the low fence from 'incumbent' to 'start-up' a few years back, building software *for* banks rather than building it *in* banks. I know how the industry works mostly by throwing myself against its boundaries to find if I could push them. It's not subtle, but it works.

You can push them more often than not, it turns out, but at a price.

I have 'done it' both on the institutional side and on the entrepreneurial side. I have also worked across retail, institutional and transaction banking and to complete the set, I have held roles in IT, ops and client-

> I know how the industry works mostly by throwing myself against its boundaries to find if I could push them. It's not subtle, but it works.

facing work. If I had a bingo card, I would be shouting HOUSE roundabout now (if this book makes it to the hands of someone outside the Anglo-Saxon tradition, it's just a full set of things and there will be no more bingo jokes, I promise).

What Would My Younger Self Think of This?

My teenage idealistic self would *not* have been impressed with me becoming a banker, truth be told. The level of complexity would have appealed to her. I've always enjoyed a challenge. The geek has always been strong in this one. But becoming part of the grey establishment, less so. Becoming an instrument for the perpetuation of structurally restrictive socio-economic forms? Not so much the stuff of dreams. My teenage self totally shared the dubious view of the greedy, cynical banker where creativity and humanity are not vectors of decision-making.

Not for me. Or so I thought back then.

I feel I need to declare that I never have been a very *predictable* banker even when I was on the inside and before the wave of transformation had gathered the tsunami-like pace it has now. So, my teenage self would have approved of my slightly rebellious ways, pushing boundaries and winning small victories in the name of logic under the banner of 'and we do that, why?'.

You'd be amazed how far that gets you, by the way.

Far, albeit not fast, because *not asking why* is pretty common inside a big corporate. Careers are built on *not* asking why, and I was never that person.

My teenage self would have approved of that too. And she would have liked me being part of the FinTech wave (by accident as well as design).

But let's be honest, my 19-year-old political scientist firebrand self would have reserved judgement until I crossed over to the side that rolled up its sleeves and says 'ok enough already with the experiments. Let's build something'.

Because with That Everything Changes

I have been across the spectrum of activity we are trying to change and that gives me some knowledge and many scars. They are both useful and if you have them, cherish them. Not just because getting them was hard (although, also that).

Knowledge helps us not break something important in the process of change. It also helps us navigate the resistance of those who hold the knowledge and use it as a deflector shield: oh no we can't possibly modernise mortgages, they are *complicated*. Oh no we can't possibly change the way we think about credit-scoring, it's *complicated*. And so it is. And understanding the complexity is key to the change, *not* where we stop.

But the only way to be able to move away from the resistance is to have the knowledge yourself. And the way to get the knowledge is experience. So part of the reason you should listen to me is that I have done this work for 20 years. So I can tell you these stories and face any resistance with some credibility.

I have sat in front of risk committees that believed messaging platforms such as symphony or slack were the devil (if you have never heard of either symphony or slack, let me just say: they are not the devil).

I have sat in front of budget review boards that told me I could have money for APIs or data governance but not both (no I am not exaggerating, it is a verbatim quote. Yes, it was a while ago; and no, not as long ago as you are hoping; and yes, it was in a big bank that is still thriving; and no, I didn't manage to persuade those guys that an API is like a pipe for data so one without the other wouldn't get me far; and yes, I found money for both in the end, because Compliance needed some help with some regulatory projects and that's what you do in big banks or small FinTech trying to get the big banks going: you make do, you find a way, you get the job done).

I can say to you and my younger self that I am someone who has built things and made change happen within this industry and have the scars to prove both that change is possible and that we make it harder than it needs to be. Everything I have done and learnt so far has brought me to this place, where I can join other humans, similarly inspired, and drive change that hopefully and bit by bit makes our industry better aligned with the wider economy. And makes money fairer. More accessible.

So I am a long-term, recovering banker. And this matters. Because all my stories are personal. All my observations derived in the trenches. All my convictions tested.

But that is not all I am.

I Am Also an Immigrant

And this matters for a few reasons.

Firstly, because I want to be clear about my politics from the get-go.

The book is *not* about politics and yet politics is everything.

One's view of fairness and humanity colours what you think is right, so although politics won't come up at any point as such, my own politics will keep coming up directly or indirectly in the pages that follow. You will find that doing good and trying to reimagine our relationship with money is inexorably linked to how we perceive humanity, society and entitlement. What we consider right.

We are in the tech business, for sure, but values determine the problems we choose to solve and the boundaries we set. The lines we are not prepared to cross. What right looks like, to each of us.

How we programme our algorithms and how we design solutions reflect our values.

And my own personal story moulds my values.

> We are in the tech business, for sure, but values determine the problems we choose to solve and the boundaries we set. The lines we are not prepared to cross.

Plus, there is a parable in there for the industry at large. So indulge me for a minute.

WHO AM I?

I am someone who lucked out and was standing right there as the FinTech magic started happening, creating a new reality for us all.

And when is that?

The Beginning of FinTech

Opinions are divided on this, but I start the clock in 2005 when Zopa first appeared in the UK, introducing the concept of peer-to-peer lending to banks that had had that game sown-up for a very long time. But also representing a different way of doing business with an expectation that a small company could have credibility and access *and* a future. They were not alone. They were not the first. But they stand out at a symbolic and pivotal moment in time.

It's an arbitrary event, for sure, much like the assassination of Franz Ferdinand didn't start the Great War, but it is a stark before-and-after moment, *after* which things that were previously percolating picked up speed and became irreversible. You can pick another moment if this doesn't cut it for you. I bet it will be very close to mine, in time, and that is important.

From roughly 2005 onwards, we saw creativity in tech proliferating and maturity accelerating, helped by the advent of the iPhone and some inspired regulatory moves in the EEA, Singapore and Australia with others following suit. We saw *FinTech* becoming a thing ... first a curiosity and getting air time and breathing space provided and curated by institutional players who didn't mean for it to acquire a life of its own, but by the time they realised this thing was bigger than they had originally thought, well, it was too late. We saw entrepreneurial pioneering spirit and folks jumping in to be founders and take on all the drama and uncertainty that comes with it. We saw new ways of working and voices shouting 'there must be a better way'.

But we didn't see a stampede. This hasn't been as quick as this narrative may suggest. Still, we saw incredible change and I, by luck and choice in equal measure, was there from the very beginning.

What Is FinTech May Be Hard to Define. *Who* Is FinTech Is Easy

There was a time, around say 2010, when we could hold everyone that constituted the FinTech community in the UK in one room. And we often did just that, courtesy of Swift and innotribe and some of the early innovation initiatives in the industry.

Have you got any idea how much you learn that way? And how fast?

We sat in a room imagining and then charting a path to a world that departed so radically from everything we knew as to seem preposterous. But there we were, and nobody was actually stopping us. And to us, the folks charged with changing the industry by the industry itself, representing our organisations with titles such as innovation lead and transformation champion: it all seemed possible.

We didn't know then that our very bosses would fight us every step of the way.

To the founders it all seemed manageable. To the banks it all appeared containable.

We Were All Wrong

The room kept getting bigger. The community and everything that flew under the banner of 'FinTech' kept getting bigger, encompassing technology, business model innovation, new ways of working, new ideas, new ways of making money and new companies in a large variety of combinations. And it was global. And as if that wasn't enough, the 'FinTech space' started engaging both with regulators and with customers without the banks' blessing or intervention. The banks soon discovered that this thing was much bigger than they had originally thought and not theirs to control. The founders soon discovered that success was heady but not as common as they may have originally hoped. The path was long, arduous and full of pitfalls, and the kumbaya atmosphere of the early days of mentoring sessions in open-plan offices with tea and biscuits and the word 'partnership 'bandied about with reckless abandon, as, after all, slightly misleading. Sure, the community was there and eager to help, but the market is competitive and survival is not a foregone conclusion, a good idea does not a business make and luck is a fickle goddess.

And as the journey started getting harder, those of us hellbent on staying the course became more determined. We worked harder. We just kept going even when, frankly it didn't seem like the obvious choice. Or the smartest one. And in so doing, we became trench buddies and those of us who survived can now say: well look, this is what we were talking about all along.

This is what we can achieve, if you get out of our way, if you don't get blindly protective of the way things used to be and if you let us do what is needed and possible and useful.

And weirdly, this is where my immigrant status comes back into the mix. Stay with me, you will see what I mean.

Immigrant Is Not a Dirty Word

I was asked recently in an interview what I mean when I describe myself as an immigrant.

The interviewer actually had a nifty little intro ready, teeing me up to talk about digital nomads and figurative migrants into a land of increasing complexity where our skillsets (as bankers or as digitally native disruptors, respectively) are 'other' and therefore sometimes met with resistance, 'in-group 'reflexes, mockery and attempts to belittle the newcomer and their value. Full marks for effort. And full marks for capturing the daily life of an immigrant.

But no.

I don't mean I am a digital nomad. I mean I left my home, my family and my country with two suitcases and a lot of hope to go to a country other than that of my birth in pursuit of greater opportunity. Dictionary definition of an economic migrant, that. And yes, it was legal. And yes, I remain legally in London (I have settled status and everything). And yes, I have always been here legally and no, I never crossed in a dingy and yes, I have always paid my taxes. But you see what's going on here, right? We all knew these are the first questions to be answered. Not what opportunities did you avail yourself of, and, more importantly for the community here: what value did you add? Did you generate income? Did you expand the economy? Did you create jobs? Further education? Did you make things a little bit better than you found them? Yes, yes, yes, yes and yes again.

Mine is a very common immigrant story, by the way, especially in FinTech where there are a lot (and I mean *a lot*) of immigrants just like me. And yet we live and work in environments that still use the word as an insult. Just as we live and work in environments that view change with suspicion and change agents with barely disguised irritation.

They don't wish you didn't exist per se. But would rather you weren't *here*.

See what I mean? There is an awful symmetry there.

Not You, The Other Ones

I got that a lot, living in London particularly after Brexit. People telling me they voted out because of 'immigration' then realising who they are speaking to as the speech bubble is halfway out their mouths and saying 'not you though, the other ones'.

There are no other ones.

We are it. I am what we look like after the experiment has worked. After we were lucky enough to get what we came here for: the opportunity to work hard and contribute. The opportunity to show *that* we can contribute. A bit like the change we champion. It looks different from the other side of the hard work. But it's not.

Look at me. This is what we look like. And to quote Hamilton (the musical, not the statesman): we get the job done. Often despite the folks we serve.

I got a note last year (you know who you are) that said: 'Thank you. I have been observing you from afar. You helped me believe that a woman with an accent, far away from home, can carve a path. In this city. In this industry. In this climate.'

I won't lie.

I had a little cry. And then I sat down and wrote my column under the title 'I am an immigrant'.* Just to say: *Look at me.* I am not saying my run is over. I hope, frankly, I am no more than halfway – not much unlike the transformation journey we are on: not that early, nowhere near done. But I haven't had a bad run so far.

I have been an educator, a volunteer, a writer, an entrepreneur, a banker, a Non-Executive Director and a teacher. I have created things and teams. I have built things with teams. Net net, I have not been a burden to the country I live in or the industry I am a part of. So I wrote my article to say: *Look at me.* Not to admire. Just to see. I am an immigrant. This is what we look like. When you let us. And the analogy is not lost on me. A lot of what I preach every day of my life is about what the industry can become if we let it. If we get out of our own way, take stock of what has been achieved, built and learned, and stare ahead with a determination to do better and a conviction that it is not only possible but also necessary.

---

* https://www.fintechfutures.com/2021/12/i-am-an-immigrant/

Acknowledgements

This book wouldn't exist without the help and encouragement of so many people.

A huge thank you to Tanya Andreasyan who, back in 2016, thought my style of writing needed a regular home and a platform. Without her, #LedaWrites wouldn't exist and by extension neither would this book. In her, I had a supporter, an editor, an advisor and, through our years of collaboration, I now have a friend for life. She is the buddy at the end of the phone, no matter what goes on in my life. She is the woman who doesn't just mention my name in a room full of opportunities: she goes hunting for them.

Thank you to my amazing early readers, friends and supporters who pored over the manuscript and provided encouragement and invaluable advice. Any remaining errors are my own.

Thank you to the fierce and kind Theo Lau, the thoughtful Brad Leimer and, Curt Queyrouze the coolest banker I've ever met, and the nicest man. Thank you to my favourite Viking and fellow digital believer, Trygve Aasheim, and to Kevin Johnson, the biggest heart in our industry and beyond. Thank you Ronit Ghose and Joy Macknight for your help and support with this project, and your friendship over the years. And thank you to Brett King and Antony Jenkins for their support and for taking the time to pen a few introductory thoughts for this book.

Thank you to #mytribe: all of you who have cheered me on every step of the way, who have clamoured for this book to be written and who are just magical, magical creatures.

Thank you to innotribe, past, present and future: Innes MacLeod, Nektarios Liolios, Matte Rizzi, Mela Atanassova, Peter Van, Ioanna Guiman … thank you for being there at the very start, thank you for bringing us together and keeping us together in so many ways. Thank you for those heady early days and everything since.

Thank you Adriana Pierelli for opening that door when others wouldn't even though they could.

Thank you to my team. You are magical, and I am honoured to serve alongside you.

Thank you to everyone at Taylor & Francis, particularly John Wyzalek. You've made this feel easy without ever leaving me feeling exposed. Quite the balancing feat and one I am grateful for.

Thank you to my mum, who taught me to love words and fear nothing (other than disappointing her. That's terrifying). Thank you to my step-dad, who has shielded me with the most perfect love since the day he met me over 40 years ago.

And thank you to David, for his gentle laugh, his support and patience. Writing a book while having a demanding full time job was mostly done at his expense: the time we would be spending together was spent writing. It would simply not have been possible without his encouragement, full endorsement and unique ability to see through the noise straight to what matters. A superpower if there ever was one.

Author

Leda Glyptis, PhD, is the author of the LedaWrites FinTech Futures column and regular contributor at industry events and publications. She is a lapsed academic and a recovering banker, having worked in 'incumbent banks' across various geographies and functions including innovation, IT and Operations. Most recently, Leda works as an executive with challenger banking software providers, rewriting the fabric of financial services. She is chief client officer at 10x and has served at 11FS Foundry, QNB, Sapient and BNY Mellon. She holds an MA from King's College Cambridge and an MSc and PhD from the London School of Economics.

1

FinTech, Bad Habits and Great People: The Main Ingredients of the Story Ahead

SNEAK PREVIEW

The best things in life may be free, but the essentials are not.

Money is important and inescapable … and for those of us who work in finance or banking, we are, in one way or another, in the money business, which means we are in a business that affects and impacts everyone. A fact folks in finance often forget.

As we now operate in a fully digital economy, the way we impact people's lives is shifting. And the fact that we are grappling with the transition from analogue to digital is, itself, also impacting people, communities and the economy at large.

So our work matters and not just to us and our shareholders.

In this chapter, we will be unpacking what this means, what it entails, who are the teams that persist at this work, what sets them apart and what any of this has to do with FinTech.

THE ACCIDENTAL BANKER

This is a good time to come clean about the fact that, although I am a banker, I am an accidental, incidental and highly reluctant one.

I wasn't always going to be a banker.

I fell into this, sideways, like so many of my generation coming out of 'good universities' and being courted heavily for careers in the City and pretty much little else. Although getting into a bank or a consulting firm was highly competitive, trying to find an 'in' to anything other than that was up there with unicorn-chasing. Next to impossible. And in fact, even for those of us who thought we had escaped, all roads led back to banking.

The Blair Witch Project of career choices.

Resistance was seemingly futile.

And believe me: I resisted.

No matter.

I fell into it eventually. I didn't choose it, and it didn't choose me. It just happened. But then I stayed. Because, much to my surprise and chagrin, I discovered I was good at it ... and I found it much more fascinating than I was comfortable admitting. So I stayed. For the love of plumbing and the fundamental belief that money makes the world go round, and that isn't a good thing in itself, but it is a true thing, a fact of life we have to accept and then can work with to make things better.

Let's unpack both of those things.

First what do I mean by plumbing, because I will refer to it a lot in the pages to come.

Plumbing is my catch-all term for all the things that happen *under the hood* (below the glass of a digital user journey on your smartphone or behind the banking outputs consumed by clients). Plumbing in real life is by definition designed to connect bits together and transport liquid stuff to the right places, places that know what to do with it. Your plumbing system will take fresh water to your tap and waste to a treatment facility. Similarly, the plumbing I speak of will channel data between places that know what to do with it (store, process, dispose).

'Plumbing' is not a technical term, in case you are wondering. It's just a useful one.

It works as a name because it captures the mechanics of what we are talking about perfectly. But I also like it for another reason and that is that the connecting bits are usually thought of as unsexy. They are not glamorous, and they are not talked about as exciting, enabling or interesting. They are a hygiene factor, a thing you need and rely upon, all day every day, but you are not excited about it. Until it breaks. Then you miss it like all get out.

That's why I fell in love with this job.

Weird, I know.

That non-sexy but absolutely essential part that needs to scale and be robust and reliable and ubiquitous? That's my favourite bit of banking. The pipes.

Don't you look at me like that.

Have you ever wondered why you can't set up a new payment on your banking app but can do it on the website or why you need to go in branch for a payment over a certain amount but not to pay your tax bill for exactly that amount, in the app of the very same bank?

Pipes my friend, that's why.

Pipes and the way they are set up.

That's the bit I like.

Because without pipes our precious digital innovations will never leave the lab and money will be hard to access, hard to store and hard to exchange. And in a digital economy, you can't have that.

Pipes make money go round so that they can make the world go round in turn.

It's such a trite and familiar phrase, isn't it?

And yet. That doesn't mean it is any less true.

MONEY MAKES THE WORLD GO ROUND. IT'S NOT A STATEMENT OF PREFERENCE. JUST A STATEMENT OF FACT

I am not channelling Phelps here.[1]

I am not saying I like it. I am saying that it is true: money is a step in pretty much everything you may want to do in life at an individual, collective – be it community, enterprise or country – and global levels.

The best things in life may be free, but the essentials are not.

Money fuels most activity, and although I don't think it is a good thing, I think it as a *true* thing.

Human activity (from the food you eat to the infrastructure projects, and your mother's hernia operation to global trade) invariably entails money changing hands directly or indirectly. Even in a country with universal healthcare, where you may not be paying for your mother's hernia operation, the doctor still gets a salary, the hospital gets funded and you pay taxes, so.

Access to money is key to everything and part of everything.

And if it's key to everything, and we work in an industry that deals with money, we have a choice to make as to how we perceive our role vis-à-vis the ubiquitousness of money.

Stay with me here.

---

[1] Nobel laureate Edmund Phelps offers a bizarrely upbeat and die-hard capitalist view in his book *Mass Flourishing*. If only I shared his optimism.

4 · *Bankers Like Us*

We all need access to money (be it our own or someone else's in the form of a loan or other form of credit) and we need means of exchange (payments, disbursements, etc.).

We need all that in order to live.

Banking or financial services more widely are often seen as an elite, corporate industry that doesn't deal in or deal with the common man, but really it's the industry that affects all of us in ways big and small. No matter what you do in life, where you do it, what you believe in or what football team you cheer on a Saturday night, money is part of your life.

So.

Those of us in the money business have the responsibility to think about how it operates. And make it better. That is a moral imperative. But we also have the responsibility to make it better in a practical way: the economy as a whole is digitising much more rapidly than the banking services that support and fund it do. So making banking better, in this sense, is not about lofty morality. It's about fitness for purpose: making banking better at doing what it's meant to do: i.e. move money within and around the economy as people go about their lives, commerce, trade anon and so on.

The way we do this work may be unglamorous, but it beats a clean path to highly relevant work and if you are that way inclined also potentially a slightly fairer world. So. Whichever way you look at it, it matters.

Ok. So how do we do that?

So glad you asked.

First we need to understand, truly understand, what we do today. Which is why experience matters.

Then we need creativity. And technology. To change parts of what we do today (pipes and connectivity: the systems, the structures as well as the habits of the people that perpetuate those).

That sounds like meaningful, impactful and heroic work, right?

Wrong.

Because in the day to day, what we need to do first, foremost and for a sustained period of time is change habits. And it's slow work. Painful work. But essential work.

Everything from day-to-day behaviours inside the industry, individual or team incentives, accepted truths and established wisdom needs to be challenged daily and consistently.

It is exhausting.

And all this has to happen *while* demonstrating the art of the possible to the folks resisting us, alongside the spectre of the inevitable. If we can't inspire them into collaboration, then we might as well scare them into it.

To do all this work, we need to understand in intimate detail what 'here and now' entails for folks. Why they resist and how: what they hide behind.

ALMOST HALF OF OUR ACTIONS ARE HABITUAL

Wait a minute, I can almost hear you say. You just spent 10 pages telling us the book is about change and those who champion it and now you are going to delve into all the people who are *not these people*? How does that even make sense?

Sadly it does. Firstly because the resistors and their habits are in large part what makes this work hard and what undermines its chances of success. So a lot of the work we do, a lot of the work ahead of you, if you are just getting started, will be around understanding and breaking these habits.

Secondly, equally sadly, the starting point of the industry is our problem even if we didn't cause it. The sins may not be our own, but that doesn't mean we are without obligation, if we decide to champion the change and do the work. And why would you be reading this if you hadn't already decided to do the work?

So. Habits.

Studies suggest that anything between 40% and 95% of human conduct is habitual. The American Psychological Association[2] published a study in 2020 that found 43% of everyday actions are enacted habitually *while people are thinking of something else.* That means that humans will slide into habitual behaviour that goes against the change you are trying to embed, without meaning to resist. People may want to support the change and still undermine it by habitually 'sliding back' to old ways of doing things. Unintentionally, unthinkingly. Repeatedly.

Although we deal in tech, all change is fundamentally human change. Change in the habits of those making the decisions to allow us to get on the journey in the first place. Change in the habits of those doing the work so we can get where we are going and not end up chasing our tails or back-sliding back to where we started.

If we succeed in this first cycle of change, more change is possible and that is just as well because more change is needed.

---

[2] https://www.apa.org

Change in the habits of those who will function inside in the new, *changed* operating models and business models and who will use the new tools without reverting to whatever they did before.

That is a lot of change needing to happen and take root at once. And I haven't even mentioned the tech itself yet. Because the first and foremost thing that needs to change is human behaviour and the habits that stop us from even starting on the road to change.

If that sounds exhausting, it is because it is.

Although transformation often comes with a rousing speech about strategy, the journey doesn't actually start until the realisation dawns that you can't take the first step before eliminating the excuses (familiar, trite and well worn) that people hide behind to avoid change. And that's where the fun begins. Because some resistance is habitual but a lot of it is not. So as you are going about trying to break people's habits, you will be met with people's attitudes in a rather special combo. People will look at the comfortable and familiar and push back on you and the change you advocate. They will tell you it's not possible. It is naïve. Expensive. Dangerous. 'Not for us.' They will use knowledge of how things work today to poke holes into your plans. They will use the very thing you are trying to change in order to block you. They will and they do and they have for a long time. And it has succeeded in slowing us down, if not stopping us. The arguments tend to be cyclical, tautological and fundamentally designed to shut the conversation down. And yet we persisted. In fact, we have spent a decade and a half persisting.

WHY DO THAT TO YOURSELF?

Our own habits, I guess.

There is a particular personality type that is attracted to this work. And the habits of these people meant we wouldn't take no for an answer. So a more useful question, for those of you also on this journey is less *why* and more *how* did we do it?

And the answer is, at first at least, by indulging the nay-sayers, frankly.

We went with it, engaged like we believed they were raising legitimate concerns on the way to change rather than trying to sabotage it altogether. And for a while we did actually believe that their concerns were, if not actually legitimate, at least truly held.

Endless proofs of concept (POCs) and experiments taking their objections at face value. Going through the motions of proving technology was real.

Of furnishing proof as requested trusting that once reality was established we would move on.

Which technology's reality was being challenged varied. The process did not.

At the start of my career, I once spent a full working day (9 long hours in an airless basement) with the compliance team of a huge tier one German bank (go on, guess which one) on whether Open Source software was 'safe'. I've had the same meeting about APIs, OAuth 'handshakes', the cloud. Yes the cloud. The verdict was 'the regulator would never approve' if you must know. Oh how we laughed.

Over the last two decades, the technologies we mistrusted, as an industry, have changed. But the meeting itself hasn't. The bank's starting point is to question the very reality of anything that was not 'invented here'. It's so much fun, you have no idea.

And what it looks like, up close, is endless conversations with people who know very little about the detail of what their organisation does now in the guts of their systems, but need to be convinced that the alternative you are championing is better. Yes. Better than the thing that they don't know much about at all. So, as they don't have a real benchmark, the comparatives become absolute. Things don't need to be better. They need to be good. They don't need to be safer. They need to be safe. And in the meantime ...

Tests and more tests.

Pilots and POCs. And endless business cases to show that the new technology of, say, cloud-based, containerised scalability (or whatever else is being challenged) is actually cheaper than the stuff it replaces. And infrastructure is possible to build as a scalable utility for all market participants. And as time passes and by hook or by crook we get to do this work, bit by bit. But we don't get to change the way we face into it. The process, the habits, are yet to be changed. We still have work to do.

That's the space I live and work in. Because I am a glutton for punishment. But in truth, I love it.

Partly because I like big problems and partly because, as a lapsed political scientist, it was drilled into me early on that civilisations rise and fall on sanitation, roads, irrigation. Long-term, long-range infrastructure. Pipes for the masses. I can get pretty fired up about this too. And I am not alone.

The passion blazes through a small community of like-minded people. I call them my tribe.

I told you I am not alone. This is a party, after all. And there are folks I need to introduce you to, notionally. Folks who fight the good fight and do the good work.

Be it leveraging technology to create inclusive identity assets, equitable credit structures or accessible pensions and loans and mortgages, *we*, our small but mighty global community, sit alongside the cynical banker. But as the poem goes 'we travel not for trafficking alone, by hotter winds our fiery hearts are fanned'.[3] Passion. Commitment. Creativity. Innovation, if that is what you must call it. And a lot of love. A hell of a lot of love. For people, for change, for the community, for each other, for the art of the possible.

It is out of love for this group and the work we do that I want us to stop indulging in the excuses. It is out of love that I write a book designed to fire up and arm more of us in the fight against, frankly, us getting in our own way as we try to do this work. This is what the book is. A call to arms. And our story. This is a book part celebration of our tribe, part reflection of what we've learnt and part handbook for those following in our footsteps. You will be pleased and relieved to hear it won't be all about core banking and pipes. A little, maybe. But mostly it will be about the humans that make the change and the humans that block it and what we are learning every day on this journey that may make the next step a little bit easier. So this may be a good time to introduce you to yourselves, to my tribe, to a hashtag (#mytribe) I am now seeing used by people I've never met and that warms my cockles.

ASKING WHY, AND NOT ACCEPTING 'JUST BECAUSE' AS AN ANSWER

I want you to think back to 2007–2008. FinTech is not yet a thing but a double dip recession is.

The setting: a Very Large Bank.

In some ways the biggest: holding and moving trillions in assets every day, clearing for the Fed, doing the most grown-up of banking possible: custody. In many ways, this was one of the best places I've ever worked. The culture was inclusive and gentle at the time at least (a lot can change in a decade and counting), the work was lost in the deepest recesses of financial services and far away from the consumer and *yet* there was a strong sense of mission: people had a sense of where they fit into the cycle of money and what their role was. The motto of the bank at the time was 'who's helping you?' and it resonated deeply with all of us.

---

[3] The Golden Road to Samarkand, by James Elroy Flecker.

But. A big bank is a big bank and the industry comes with its own foibles no matter how good your own culture. A lot of people in this industry just say *no* before you've even asked a question. There are rules that nobody remembers the origin of, the purpose of or the intention behind them so they go on to not only constrain everyone's life but are often venerated in a 'it has always been thus' manner.

Example.

We once found that the bank did not service ERISA accounts.[4] We found it as part of a process lifecycle efficiency project, and it was not something that was raised as an improvement area. Just a fact. Frogs don't fly and we don't service ERISA accounts. And that could have been the end of it. But it was not, as I had a colleague back then who never stopped asking why. Like a toddler with a PhD in theoretical physics. He asked 'why' even when he had no real expectations of an answer that would illuminate him. Not immediately anyway. But he asked anyway. And then unpicked the thread. And asked again.

He didn't like mysteries and didn't believe that 'it just is' is an adequate explanation for anything. We discovered many weird and wonderful things through this insistence of his. We discovered teams working hard at meeting regulatory requirements that no longer existed (the banking operations equivalent of the Japanese soldiers in the jungles of Borneo still fighting World War II, decades after it ended because how are they meant to know it ended if nobody tells them?) and we also discovered ERISA accounts and the fact that we were apparently free to ignore them in our work because the bank didn't service them.

Why, he asked, reliable as anything. 'Because we don't' was the answer.

That was not a good answer for him. So he kept asking. Was it a regulatory thing? Research. No.

Was it a profitability thing? Research. No.

Was it a systems thing? A competition thing? Research. No.

No.

---

[4] What ERISA accounts are is in no way relevant to the story, but I suspect some of you may want to know so here it goes: The Employee Retirement Income Security Act of 1974, or ERISA, is a US-specific federal provision protecting the assets of millions of savers so that funds placed in retirement plans during their working lives will be there when they retire. ERISA sets minimum standards for retirement plans in private industry. If you are dying to read more about this, there is more on the Department of Labour website of the US Federal Government and you, my dear reader, are a creature of strange hobbies but then again aren't we all. Knock yourself out here: https://www.dol.gov/sites/dolgov/files/ebsa/about-ebsa/our-activities/resource-center/faqs/retirement-plans-and-erisa-for-workers.pdf

What was it then? Sure yes it was a policy, but who made it a policy? Who said *this* was what the policy should prescribe? Who wrote the policy, who signed the policy and why? He didn't stop. He found the person who wrote the policy. And the reason why they wrote it.

And that reason was that a few years prior, a team needed to get some paperwork sorted by a certain date realised at the 11th hour that they hadn't accounted for ERISA accounts in their research for that particular submission. When they were faced with the decision of delaying their paper or submitting without ERISA accounts, the then head of that division said 'leave it for now'. She said this coming out of a lift on her way to a meeting apparently, a quick solution to a small oversight. She did it to keep things rolling, not expecting it to keep a whole chunk of business off the table for a decade. Nobody went back to the work to complete it. She didn't ask. Nobody wrote it down. So nobody did it. The fun doesn't end here as, by the time we discovered this incident this lady had one of the most senior positions in the bank. So I tracked her down and asked about this (like the insistent Rottweiler that I am, at your service). She didn't remember the incident. But could totally believe it.

Why? Because banks.

So.

Just imagine me, young and ambitious and inquisitive and profoundly uncertain about being a banker. Imagine me in the context where the bias towards rule-following inertia is strong, where regulatory limits are revered and people

> In a context where people default to 'no', how do you find the people who are willing to find a path to yes? The short answer is: by accident. But once you've found them, what you do next needs intent.

will default to 'can't be done'; in *that* context, I was trying to be me and trying to do the best work I could, first in a revenue protection process re-engineering function, then in operational and process redesign and then in client-facing technology innovation. All these functions by the way boil down to 'if I show you the money and the fact that the tech is possible and the fact that the regulation doesn't say we can't, will you let me fix some of the stuff that's broken?'. And the answer was mostly 'oh I am not sure'. And yet. I found ways. We found ways. I was never alone. And we found ways. We also found each other.

THE OPTIMISTS

In a context where people default to *no*, how do you find the people who are willing to find a path to yes? The short answer is: by accident. But once you've found them, what you do next needs intent. In my case, it started with friendship. And then someone gave it a name.

We are back at the Very Big Bank.

After a particularly bad couple of days, myself and a couple of trench buddies were grabbing a coffee in the office cafeteria. It was at the bottom of an atrium and when we came back up to our desks, a very, very senior man took us aside and asked what was going on down there.

Now.

Think: school. We thought we'd been busted. We hadn't done anything wrong but we felt busted anyway, so we started prevaricating. I mean … nothing … we just … a coffee break. But he insisted. He said he saw animated faces. He saw laughter. He saw scribbles on a whiteboard (we used to have these little adhesive sheets of A4 that we took everywhere with us, to turn any surface into a whiteboard). He saw energy, he said.

What was it?

So we told him.

It was nothing. We were just trying to help each other not to go crazy in an organisation that always says no first.

And how were we doing that? By asking each other for help, by breaking the problem down, by not considering things impossible till we had at least tried them. Big and small. It didn't always work. But at least we tried to keep our 'moan conversion ratio' trending to 1: if you are complaining about something, do something about it (the fraction being moan over action and the man who came up with the concept is called Ben Tucker).

He liked it.

The very senior man, I mean. He liked it a lot. So he told on us: he took it to the Chairman. Now we're in for it, I thought. But the Chairman *also* liked it.

How did you find each other? He asked.

I said well, it's a tap on the shoulder really. I know who I trust to be humble enough to ask for help when *they* need it and generous enough to offer it when *I* need it and there is nothing in it for them. And they know someone like that. And that new person also knows someone like that, who we didn't know.

So. You know. Like that. A chain of helpfulness. And what are you called, he asked. We are not called anything, I said rather baffled. We are just friends, colleagues, trench buddies trying to get through the day without burning the building down (my diplomacy skills needed work then and they need work now, I won't lie to ya). But true to the spirit of our group, my friend Matt Newman leapt to the rescue and named us on the spot: we are the Optimists, he said with a smile.

And that was it.

Within a year, the Optimist Group spanned the globe and had thousands of members literally just helping each other out. It was unofficial. It was informal. It was magical. The group is still going. I don't know if they are still true to the spirit, I left the bank many years ago. But I know they still exist as a group and I trust that they don't know my name or Ben's or Matt's and that's amazing. That's as it should be. I also know that the experience taught me a lot. It taught me to look for my people, not to create a group as such, just to find it and call it out for what it is and then bask in its glory. That group made the hard days easier, it made the work easier, it made life better.

ENTER LEFT: THE TRIBE

When I started writing for FinTech Futures circa 2016, the magnificent Tanya Andreasyan said we should make my column weekly. She said there was something in the way I saw the world and spoke about what I saw that was missing from industry publications. She said there was a community for it.

I won't lie, I was excited. But I didn't believe her.

Who wants to read these 'dispatches from the front' every week? I went with it but half expecting that the experiment would fall flat on its face.

Turns out, a good few thousand people agree with Tanya, for which I am eternally grateful.

I have never been happier to be wrong in my life. She was right, I was wrong, and there are thousands of you each week reading my words not because you are discovering something new (I don't think), but because you are recognising something heartfelt. #LedaWrites, as my readers call it, didn't create the community that consumes it. They were there already. The column was just my way of finding them. And this is what I found.

WE DIDN'T BECOME A TRIBE, WE JUST FOUND EACH OTHER AND REALISED WE ALREADY WERE

My weekly column has allowed me to find kindred spirits spanning the globe. It has uncovered for me a community that is not afraid to call things out, in plain accessible English, and say *hey this isn't great. We should be doing better than this.* A community that is unafraid to ask for help even though admitting you don't know it all isn't exactly glamorous and doesn't help with traditional ideas of status. A community that is willing to offer help, be it an introduction for a job, a reference, advice, a platform, a sounding board. The outpouring of support, actual material meaningful support not just retweets, that I have seen from this community has been humbling and consistent and reciprocal. So I started calling them my tribe because I felt the group was united by values and behaviours, even if they didn't know they belonged together.

When I was looking for a new role, the tribe came to the rescue with referrals and introductions without me asking. Dozens of folks offered help. I will never forget it but then again I hear of similar support every day. I was not special and that is the point.

When lockdown started and the tribe worked out I lived alone, flowers, chocolates, books, funny t-shirts and bottles of wine started arriving at my doorstep with notes from folks who had their own lives and their own problems. But they wanted me to know I am not alone.

When I need to hire folks, I turn to this group. When I need advice, I turn to this group. When I need support, I turn to this group. When I need a reality check, I turn to this group.

We don't co-exist in time and space and yet we are everywhere. We do not have a leader and a boundary, everyone who behaves in a certain way belongs and is welcome. Maybe a different name is more appropriate, maybe each member of my tribe thinks of the group in a different way and by a different name. It's part of its beauty: it doesn't need to play by any rules because it only exists by sheer choice. Its members turn up and behave a certain way. If this is your thing, then welcome. You are already home. And you can call us whatever you like. I call us #mytribe and I don't know how I ever did anything without you. Because the time is nigh. The moment is now. And, to paraphrase John Lewis, the moment has chosen us. And the thing that tells the tribe apart from other folks is that they rise to the occasion. And let me tell you, the rise of FinTech and everything that has come in its wake has been an occasion and a half. But in the beginning, we didn't even know we were part of something big, momentous and industry defining.

IN THE BEGINNING WAS THE WORD, AND THE WORD WAS WITH THE BANKS AND THE WORD WAS FINTECH

'What's the dress code?'

I have had many a strange conversation with Ali Paterson, editor of FinTech Finance, in the decade or so I've known him, but discussing outfits was a first. And frankly me talking clothes with anybody is not a thing that happens in the natural flow of life, as I tend to have an 'as it comes' approach to fashion and a 'does it pack small?' approach to shopping.

But this was not just another day.

Ali had organised an awards evening and the instruction when it came to clothes was 'think movie premiere'.

Geek chic. I got this.

And he was true to his word as, later that evening, we walked onto a bona fide red carpet. A room packed full of bankers, entrepreneurs, journalists, VCs and techies. Familiar faces in numbers I had not seen in such a long time. Because the timing of the event was just as special as the guy organising it. It came after almost two years of enforced separation due to COVID restrictions. And on this night, here we were again, together. In person.

There were hugs.

Now, if you are a banker, you know that *shi-shi* awards events are very common in our industry. Big ballrooms, ill-fitting tuxedoes, standard roast beef-and-a-limp-carrot dinners and free-flowing wine. I won't lie. Nobody ever got excited about those events. They were mostly pay-to-play 'corporate citizenship awards'. Standard, nothing-wrong-with-them affairs that represent a familiar industry dance of being part of something that doesn't mean as much as we would all like it to.

Let's face it, award-giving is not objective. Winning the Best Bank Award doesn't mean you are indeed the best bank out there, it means that the judges liked your submission better than the other three who also nominated themselves. That's not nothing. But it is not what it says on the tin, either. That said, we all acknowledge that in the spirit of 'you can't win a game you are not in', you can now *say* you were voted the best bank and that's not a fact, but it's also not nothing, and if your competitors want to wrestle that crown away from you, they are welcome to apply for the award next go round. So these awards serve a purpose, even though nobody ever got excited by them. Not even the people who won, because they sort of knew it was coming before they bought a table at the event for their staff.

After two years of working from home in our pyjama bottoms and bare feet, however, even the bog-standard industry event would have been exciting for most of us, to be fair. A dinner cooked (and paid for) by someone else? Actual clothes? And shoes? And humans you are not related to? A bit of glitz and glamour? Yes please.

So everyone was in a sparkling mood.

And to top it all off, this was not a bog-standard industry event and not just because the organiser attended in a kilt and Marvel t-shirt. This was in many ways the party I invited you to with this book. If you looked around you would see the pieces of this industry coming together, the bankers, the reformers, the regulators, the techies, the entrepreneurs and those who bring them all together. You would see so many of my tribe there, representing different organisations but a very similar way of doing things. The people who enjoy the awards but don't mistake them for the outcome we are all working towards. Because unless we transform the industry fully, nobody wins. And the industry is still plagued with folks who feel they can win at this with an app here and a partnership there, acting as if the digital economy would wait.

It didn't.

FORGET DIGITAL BANKING: IT'S THE ECONOMY THAT'S DIGITAL

The world changed when the iPhone hit the markets, didn't it?

And yes, the world was on its way to changing already.

The amount of technological infrastructure needed for you to be able to play Words with Friends and fight with Susan from Saratoga over vaccines on Twitter is mind-blowing and goes way beyond the device in your hand.

We can debate what came first, what started what and where intent lay. What needs no debate is that, if you look back, we live in a radically transformed world, a world that is digital, connected and real time and that this transformation is 10, 15 or 20 years old. No more. We can debate the exact moment but not the range and frankly I don't care to agree on the exact moment it all started: that's not what is important plus it is not relevant to my work here today. We can agree that it happened somewhere between 10 and 20 years ago and it has moved us from analogue to digital, from distinct pauses between things happening to a possibility for real-time connectivity in everything, from a visa application to enter a new country to seeing the tanks roll into Ukraine on your screen as events unfold.

The ubiquitousness of digital capabilities reaches, touches and transforms all aspects of our lives. From healthcare to friendship, citizenship to flirting.

The *economy* is now digital.

That also we have to agree on. It's not just amazon and Alibaba.

It is your local supermarket. It's the busker on the London Underground with his iZettle terminal.

It is everything.

It is the implicit assumption that *it will be so* and the expectation that everything, from identity authentication to payment rails, and online security to physical distribution, will just *work* and your brand new banjo will be delivered to *your* door tomorrow, *your* card will be charged the correct amount and your social media feed will be strangely replete with country music recommendations. That is when you know 'digital' is mainstream. And that is where we are, no matter whether it started with or before the iPhone.

And let me tell you, whenever it started, banks were sort of looking at the emerging capabilities right at the beginning of it all. We were looking at these emerging technologies and what can be done with them.

WE WERE NOT TAKEN UNAWARES BY ANY OF THIS

Contrary to what the current state of your high street bank may lead you to believe, digitising banking as a conversation that has been unfolding for a while and it has been engaged in in earnest for 15 years. And by that I mean 'people had it in their job titles' not just 'we were vaguely aware of it'.

What's been stopping us, I hear you wonder? So glad you ask. Keep reading. This book is mostly about that.

It's fair to say none of this journey has been linear and it has not always been pretty, largely because the industry worthies thought we had longer to work out what we needed to do. I can tell you for free that when we first spoke of APIs and real-time payments inside banks, we didn't expect that the economy would become fully digital, not any time soon anyway. We thought we were going to be leading this thing and, as such, could dictate pace, sequencing and timings. But we were overtaken. And this is important. Because banks have been slow to work out what to do with this digital malarkey for reasons we will unpack. But before we do, we need to flag that this very slowness has created a set of huge problems that make 'getting on with the programme' even harder. Again, we will address all those in the chapters to come.

For now, this is important context as we think back to the awards evening. Because in this context, it is clear to see that 'success' never comes cheap and it is never linear. For every highlight, every photo finish, every award-worthy bit of output, years of hard work have taken place in each company standing up for an award (and many who aren't) but also *between* companies and across the industry. For every success celebrated with an award, there are countless false starts, mistakes, things that never saw the light of day, broken dreams and broken promises. And across and between it all, there are people who kept going. And this awards ceremony was nothing if it wasn't a roomful of people who kept going through the journey of our industry's digital transformation.

A decade and a half into 'the era of digital transformation', there is a community of survivors,[5] practitioners and commentators who have gone the distance and are chomping at the bit to keep going. As you looked around the Awards Event in London that day you'd see the people invited to my figurative party too. The one I should make introductions to. These people are special to me and special to the industry because they are the reason we keep going, despite it all, despite our worst demons, hesitation and excuses. There is a lot of passion and fierce commitment to the work we do, more than you would expect in Finance, truth be told.

---

[5] There is no exact science as to when the 'FinTech' era begins. If pushed to give a date, I choose the arrival of Zopa in the UK in 2005 not because it changed something in itself but because it is as good a place as any to start the clock on a wave of transformation that involved new technologies (both software and hardware as the iPhone came soon after, in 2007 changing 'digital' forever); new business models; and new ways of working were soon to follow, exploring the art of the 'recently possible'.

Passion and commitment to get the work done.

In this industry that touches everyone's life whether we want that or not.

In this moment in time when digitisation is deepening and widening and transforming our relationships to each other, to our societies, to labour, to news and, inescapably, to money.

This is important work that needs to be done.

And we are here, ready to do it.

To paraphrase John Lewis, we may not have planned or chosen this but the time is now, we are here and it appears that the moment has chosen us.

2

Why This, Why Now and Why Working Towards a Big Dream Doesn't Feel Big and Dreamy

SNEAK PREVIEW

FinTech has become part of everyday language, but do we really agree on what it means? Other than 'all things digital, start-ups and hoodies'.

'Digital' is another word bandied about very much, both in our industry and more widely. More often than not, it is used wrong. Digital is not an app. Digital is not about design thinking, start-ups or FinTech. It is not about UX or channels. It is about all of it and quite a lot more. Digital is a configuration of capabilities that transforms everything we do. Digital is what the economy is. Digital, however, is what most financial services organisations are not. So, in this context, what is 'business as usual' in an industry that isn't quite digital, serving an economy that is?

How do we understand what this tension between the economy and our organisations' state of digital readiness means and how can it be resolved, once we've stopped trying to claim that separate rules should apply to us?

A BANKER'S STORY IS NOT JUST FOR BANKERS

Chris Skinner, in his book *Digital Human*, references research that 'banks believe they are two-thirds along their digitalisation path while the research team felt that they weren't even a quarter of the way through the journey'.[1] They are aware they are not done but they seriously underestimate how much

---

[1] Chris Skinner, Digital Human, Wiley 2018, p. 69.

DOI: 10.1201/9781003364436-2

they've got left to go and still they are scared of the road ahead. Because they know the journey to-date has been extremely hard and they can imagine what comes next.

Why am I telling you this?

Because if you are a banker, this applies to you.

If you are not a banker but sell into banks, this is relevant to you.

And if you are not a banker, but picked this book up because you are interested in digital transformation, *have no fear*. This almost certainly applies to you too. Because what makes this work hard is humans. And humans are similar no matter what context you put them in.

It is true that the examples I will use throughout the book are bank-y through and through but, for the non-bankers among us or the bankers who have skipped some of the classes, I make a point of explaining all pertinent detail, not least because banking is so complex and obtuse that seasoned bankers who have never worked in a particular vertical would find it as obscure as an outsider. And this, in itself, explains a lot. But more on that later. When it comes to the challenges with driving large-scale change, I am confident that the shapes and wider narrative will be universally relevant. And I hope that the anecdotes will still be funny or at the very least absurd enough to help highlight the human obstacles on the way to large-scale change.

And if you *are* a banker who doesn't feel like you are one of those heroic rebels still standing, stay with this and you may find that you have more in common with them than you originally thought, that you belong with them in a way you hadn't

> I think of the FinTech phenomenon as a window of time: a fleeting moment when technology innovation and human endeavour meet to change the economy and societies we live in.

previously imagined, or can do, if that's what you want. A lot of this book is spent on ideas, big and small, that help us all drive and sustain change from where we are each day. So if you want to be part of our tribe, the book gives some practical ideas to get started, and may trigger more. Our tribe is always keen to welcome members who didn't know we existed until now. We'd love for you to join.

WE INHABIT A SMALL PART OF A NICHE INDUSTRY

Some call it 'FinTech'. And you can call it that if you want.

I think of our work and the FinTech phenomenon, overall, as a window of time. And this is our luck: we inhabit a *moment in time* that, when it's all said and done, will span a decade (or three) but, in the grand scheme of things, it will be but a moment in history. But what a moment it is and what a place it is, to be found in: this fleeting moment when technology innovation and human endeavour meet to change the economy and societies we live in. And here we are, with the opportunity to re-think the way we do things in the industry that underpins all others. Because whatever you think of finance as an industry, access to money touches everything we do as individuals, families, communities, businesses and countries. Some see that as power. I see it as responsibility. And this is the moment where we can face into that responsibility with new tools at our disposal.

That's how I define 'FinTech', not in terms of the start-ups that flourished in this time or the capabilities built or the fact that design thinking[2] is now part of an average banker's lexicon, but rather in terms of the moment in time when all of those things and all the concomitant changes came to be and interact with each other, to produce a shift that is so total that there is no choice as to 'going back' to a time before. That is what I mean when I speak of FinTech.

Because let's face it, finance (or your industry whatever it may be) may in itself not always be exciting. But finance, at the very least, is always *essential*, as access to money is always required to fuel industry, commerce and science.

And finance is always, in turn, fuelled by all the discoveries and growth it gives rise to. This interdependence becomes even more significant when we reflect upon it during an era of digital acceleration across the economy. 'Digital' is not the banker's playground. It is the fabric of our emergent economy. Whether a bank likes it or not, the world is real time and interconnected. The ubiquitous availability of smart phones, e-commerce, digital distribution of media, entertainment and, increasingly, government services means that this thing we speak of is happening around banks as much as it is happening inside them. It is happening *to* them as much as it is being done by them. So in this context, and since money makes the world go round (literally, as nothing in life comes free), the potential for the use of new technology and ways of working that underpin how money behaves, moves and

---

[2] If you don't know what that is but would like to get a taste, have no fear and have a look at https://www.ideou.com/blogs/inspiration/what-is-design-thinking if you find this is of interest, the sky is the limit and there are countless resources available for free, through books and, by all means, courses galore!

is understood is surely the most exciting place to be at that moment when all is poised to change.

Or so I think.

I won't lie to you. This excitement I feel and describe here is yet to catch on with the general population. When I sit next to people who are not in our industry at dinner parties and they ask me what I do for a living, their eyes glaze over if I say I am in financial technology, banking, tech or any permutation thereof.

Recently, FinTech as a word or vague idea has entered the wider population's awareness, with a bit of a glitzy sexy 'I work in fashion' quality, but even those who go *hey yeah I know that one* don't actually know or care what it is we actually do and why we are so fired up about it. They may use Venmo, they may have heard of Revolut and carry a hot coral Monzo card in their pocket, but don't really care all that much about how these came to be and what comes next. And they don't think of their uber payment as 'FinTech' because they are using their Barclaycard, not a challenger, on that app.

And that's ok.

But also it isn't.

Exactly because they don't think of all this as (1) interconnected and (2) as 'banking'.

When people think 'banking' they still think of *The Colour of Money* and the *Wolf of Wall Street* and 'greed is good' and arrogant trader types making exorbitant amounts of money while the financial crisis destroyed hard-working folks across

> What is possible, for the bank, in terms of speed, accuracy, cost of processing and optionality needs to be explored in the context of what is true in the world around the bank.

the globe. Gordon Gecko is the stereotype that gave us all a bad name. And of course these people exist. But most of banking isn't them. Most of banking is cashiers and clerks processing corporate actions[3] and risk officers and people whose salaries are not too different to what they would get paid if they worked in your local bookstore. And most of banking isn't taken up with working out the next fanciful investment instrument or deploying creative new solutions, but rather with keeping things ticking over. Current accounts.

---

[3] Just in case ... these are events such as dividend payments or major events such as a merger or spin-off. They are approved by a company's board of directors and authorised by its shareholders before they are put into effect. Processing them is just admin. No maths or strategy involved. It's literally logging them and ensuring whatever needs to happen next, does.

And business loans. And a whole load of paperwork to make sure the money moving about is accounted for properly.

WHAT IS 'BUSINESS AS USUAL' IN A CHANGED WORLD?

Banking is mostly mundane and highly repetitive admin work.

All the things we do inside our institutions to 'keep the lights on' tie us to the way things are today by leaving no time or energy to think about what may not be working as well as it should. And by fragmenting the work too much for anyone to have enough of an overview in order to make real change. The 'ticking over' I mentioned above is way too restrictive both in terms of the time it demands and the attention it commands: it is all-encompassing. It's even called 'BAU': business as usual. And there is an implicit authority in this 'usual'. It is how we do things. It is tried and tested. And it intentionally implies 'more of the same', which wouldn't be a problem if the world was still *the same*. But it isn't. The art of the possible has changed. The economy and society any bank exists in is, to varying degrees perhaps but less so by the day, *already* digital. And this wider socio-economic reality keeps getting more and more transformed by technology. So what is possible, for the bank, in terms of speed, accuracy, cost of processing and optionality, needs to be explored in the context of what is true in the world around the bank. Choices need to be made. Only, people are busy doing BAU. And of course 'more of the same' is possible and it's not in itself bad. But as my mum will tell you the enemy of 'good' is 'better'. So more of the same is not ok when 'better' is possible.

This book is to a very large extent fuelled by the belief that we have the means, the technology and business model capability to do things much better. Faster, cheaper, smoother. It is also driven by the hope that there is enough will to both do *better* and do *different*. Not just more of the same but instead leverage human creativity, technical innovation and a different set of values to drive change. This means that, for the large part, this is a book about denial: the denial of our industry over the past couple of decades to accept the inevitable and get on with the programme. This denial took the form of an absolutely irrational and firmly held hope that we, as an industry, would be an exception to the wider economy, that we would have time, that we could selectively opt out of the digitisation avalanche. In short, that we would be ok.

DOES THAT SOUND TOO FLUFFY?

Ok, let me bring it to life for you.

When COVID hit and most governments issued a payment holiday for home loans, interest rates needed to be frozen and automatic payments needed the option to be suspended in order for that to happen. Sounds simple right?

And it could be. If banks had already spent time working differently, allowing teams and colleagues to ask different types of questions around what problem we are solving, who for and why, and encouraging their teams to leverage technology designed for information-sharing and connectivity. Changing interest rates was indeed easy for the banks who, for the past 10 years, had been trying to both do better and do better *differently*. So the banks that had leveraged all the technical and creative bounty the last decade and a half brought us, had digital capabilities at their disposal, when the crisis hit, and they could therefore make the interest rate change or mortgage payment freeze in a matter of minutes. Enter information, press 'submit'; second pair of eyes checks, clicks 'approve', away you go.

The others, the BAU types, the 'we have time' types, the 'digital is not quite how we do things around here' types, had to bring COBOL[4] engineers out of retirement to update systems dating back decades, in projects that lasted 6 weeks of long hours and sleepless weekends.

For the same outcome.

An interest rate change.

6 weeks' worth of 10 people's time vs 10 minutes of one person's time.

That's what I mean by 'we can do better'.

You'd think it's a no-brainer. And yet.

Two things are obvious in the example above.

---

[4] COBOL is a computer programming language designed for business use (it literally stands for COmmon Business Oriented Language). The main thing you need to know about COBOL is that it appeared in the 1950s. Right. That's all.

So when we say that mainframes are still COBOL based, we are saying that they were designed in and for another era. And although financial institutions still maintain COBOL systems because it feels cheaper to do so than to start from scratch, the opportunity cost of trying to function in a real-time economy with technology that is almost 80 years old is mind-numbing!

The type of change we mean when we speak of 'digital transformation' is *possible*. It is real and scaled and some of your competitors are benefiting from it.

But getting there is not quick. You can't jump in and 'transform' when you need it. When the building is already on fire. You need to invest time. And not just 'doing' time but also 'thinking' time. In order to drive digital transformation for your business, you need to understand your options and work out what you are trying to achieve, learn, try, adjust and build.

It's like saying you want to remodel you house.

Great.

A whole host of choices need to be made next. Do you want an open plan kitchen? Will you rip out the bath and install a shower? Carpet or wood floor? Wallpaper or paint? And how about a new bedroom set?

Choices upon choices. Not to mention all the weird and wonderful things you will find as the work begins. Strange plumbing choices made by the previous owner, a partition wall that falls out as you try to prize off the old bathroom tiles, walls not being as straight as your carpenter assumed when they built your fitted cupboards.

It's a lot of work, a lot of stress, a lot of curve balls.

And this entire process is the necessary journey, the necessary pain if you will, to get to the desired outcome of a beautifully renovated home.

The process, the detail of deciding what you want, what you don't want, what you can afford, what you like and what is possible given the size of your house, is how you get to the desired outcome.

Digital transformation for your bank or business is actually very similar.

Deciding to do it is when a whole host of follow-on decisions begin in earnest and you need to do the work, before you can move into your new home.

You need to do the work.

It sounds obvious, but when the rubber hits the road, wishing you had done something ages ago is a bit thankless and deciding not to do now what you should have done before 'because it's too late now, we need to put out the fire not fix whatever is on fire' is actually borderline stupid. And yet.

My friend and colleague Mark always says that the best time to have planted a tree is 20 years ago. The second best time, however, is now. And although we could and should, as an industry, have done a lot more in the decade and a half we've already spent staring into this, there is still time.

This, in fact, is the second best time to act in order to make banking better. For everyone it serves.

BANKERS ARE NOT A THING APART

In the money business, the often unspoken truth is that *everything* we do affects how money is accessed and exchanged, so everything we do touches and by extension has the power to change people's lives. Inside the finance industry we rarely think of our work this way and even more rarely treat this as an opportunity, either because the industry attracts cynics (fact) or because looking at endless Excel spreadsheets makes it hard to visualise the links to real humans (also fact), hard to imagine how we can do our jobs well and make real lives better, but that doesn't mean that link and opportunity isn't there. There may be little romance in pensions, but I wish my grandmother had had one. There is no righteous poetry in mortgages, perhaps, but coming from a country of inaccessible loans towards home ownership, I can tell you how it can be the stuff of dreams. The same applies to student loans and business starter loans and bridging finance. Most dreams shatter at the feet of lack of funds, not lack of conviction. So facilitating access to funds is not as exciting as whatever people do with it. But it matters. And that's our job.

FinTech was the moment in time when we felt we could actually say that out loud.

And of course that was helped by the advent of digital capabilities that made it possible to build and distribute systems cheaper, to design products and interfaces that were accessible, both in terms of usage

> If it takes 10 engineers 6 weeks to make an interest rate change, flexibility has been historically seen as a very expensive premium.

and in terms of cost. FinTech was the moment where we could think and say: we need to re-think money.

THERE'S MORE THAN A 'COOL APP' AT STAKE

The work we are discussing here is complex because we are not fixing a single issue. So when you think about digital transformation and FinTech, you may think about the shiny apps and you won't be wrong. But you should also be thinking about all things behind the apps that make them work. It's where the magic comes from. The seamless, effortless, secure, scalable connectivity.

It is also why it is so hard for the banks to know where to begin. Because there is so much to change, so much to learn and it goes deep and it goes wide. Both in terms of reach and in terms of its potential impact.

The way you make changing an interest rate quick and easy and the way you make servicing certain communities (such as the poor) financially viable is actually through fixing the same set of ubiquitous problems: pipes. The way you make instant point-of-sale lending possible and micro-lending financially viable is by fixing the infrastructure that is as old as me and makes the work slow, ponderous and expensive. If it takes 10 engineers 6 weeks to make an interest rate change, as we saw, you can see why flexibility has been historically seen as a very expensive premium.

The economics of looking after the vulnerable when our technology was heavy, clunky and cumbersome was a commonly acknowledged balance-sheet liability and, although we will be coming back to challenge this idea later in the book, it is important to say out loud that all of it comes back to the same set of solutions.

What we can do right now is fix the infrastructure that drives costs up and creates risks that make it impossible *not* to look at the margins as a zero-sum game. What we do right now makes it possible to look after marginal issues and small communities and not hurt your profit margin in the process. We are transforming the infrastructure that has long been the reason or excuse for leaving people behind.

And does it matter?

Does it matter, to be able to have access to the system, to be on the grid, to have a bank account? Hell yes. Does it matter to have access to affordable loans and credit products? Hell yes. Does it matter to have options that align with your values and what is good for the planet? Yes and yes. And that is the point: the same infrastructure that makes it good business to serve the poorer segments of society *also* enables us to create a highly personalised set of services. The same infrastructure that makes it possible to do micro-lending allows us to create liquidity management dashboards for corporate clients or allow your bank to ping you the day before you go overdrawn to say your credit card bill is coming up and there are insufficient funds in your checking account. Do you want an overdraft, a loan, a sweep from your savings or click here to phone a friend and borrow some cash.

They don't do that last bit. But the point is: they could.

The plumbing that permits connectivity, data parsing and secure scaling is indifferent to what problem you point it at. We are building the infrastructure to suit our aspirations. And we are dreaming big. This is what the moment in time has allowed us to do: this is FinTech.

Every day, I walk into an office or flick on my laptop and I feel a little proud. Proud of the team I work with and the wider community I am part of, proud of our partnerships, proud of the dream that drives us. Exhausted a lot of the time, don't get me wrong, and annoyed about so many calorie-burning distractions that add nothing to journey, but proud to be trying to do what we now know is possible. Frankly I feel proud but also humbled. To be lucky enough to be here, in this moment in time when the inflection point materialises and the choice gets to be made. And it's never one thing. And it's never one person. But it is always a finite moment in time when things can change. And this is ours.

VERY SPECIFIC MANIFESTATIONS OF UNIVERSAL EXPERIENCES OR THE CUSIP STORY

Many years ago, my supervisor at the mental health unit where I volunteered said to me it's important to remember the purpose and the greater cause of our work. It is important to remember that what I do with my life is important. Because what I do with my day sometimes doesn't quite cut it.

So now that I've built up the big vision we are serving, I need to bring you crashing back to the reality of what doing the work looks and feels like day to day.

Because if you were thinking Braveheart at the battle field, think again.

We are not united in this heroic effort.

Although picking a path to the future and doing the work of getting there is hard, what makes change challenging above all else is humans with their habits, insecurities and foibles. Organisational inertia on steroids. As processes, artefacts and structures that were man-made once become venerated and untouchable by a strange act of osmosis and man is not allowed to undo what man once did, because that's how big companies stay big. That is not a banking trait. That is a 'big shop' trait.

The digital capabilities we are trying to introduce and leverage, and the challenge they represent is not industry specific either. Because what the technology does for you may be very specific, but humans being afraid of change is as universal as it comes. People holding onto what they used to know and behaving badly in the process is, sadly, not industry specific.

And folks obfuscating or hiding in highly complicated detail in the hope that the challenge will fall down on a technicality is not industry specific.

So if I tell you a complicated story about that one time when I worked on a programme that spanned two continents and lasted half a year, trying to rationalise a bunch of systems used in a bank before part of it was sold off … and, during that work, we found that one of the systems was being used by a team as a library, a repository of data of sorts … you will probably be able to relate with a story of your own, regardless of the detail.

So here is what happened.

We were in the process of sunsetting a system. We did the work we needed to do to minimise disruption and then flicked the off switch. And that is when we found that this one team in Oriskany were using the system (that cost millions of dollars) as a place to look up information. It was not designed for that. We didn't know they were doing that. They weren't meant to be doing that and when we did our pre-work of identifying all the users of the system and all the uses of the system so that we wouldn't leave anyone without the right access and tools when the change kicked in, they didn't appear anywhere because they were not *using* the system by anyone's definition. They had 'read' access, which you don't think of as important. But when the system was switched off, they had a meltdown.

This is where this gets boring for the non-banker. You can skip through the detail or read through and learn some weird banking apocrypha.

Securities are identified by standardised alphanumeric codes. An ISIN is an international securities identification number for, you got it, securities traded internationally. A CUSIP is a different code used for securities traded, cleared and settled in North America and helps uniquely identify a company or issuer and type of financial instrument. As a company can trade internationally, a CUSIP is entirely contained in an ISIN.

Simple enough and you could probably work it all out if you had that kind of time or inclination. But the team in question didn't.

The system in question offered an easy way for this team to double-check and cross-reference those blasted codes and we took it away from them because we had no idea they were relying on the system that way, and since we didn't know they were doing it, we didn't realise we needed to provide an alternative for them. This happens inside banks every day, by the way, and it's one of the scariest things about tech change. You never know what you don't know about the systems that have been in place longer than I've been alive.

It doesn't matter that you didn't know what an ISIN was before now or that you will forget it by the time you get to your next meal. The problem is familiar. That thing where humans develop habits and practices that are neither recorded anywhere nor are they necessarily the most sensible way of doing things, but they work within the constraints of their circumstances and the resources of their organisation and together they create a web that needs to be untangled before you can go 'TA-DA we have gone digital'.

CUSIP or no CUSIP, this problem is familiar and even if my examples are weird and wonderful, you will be thinking of your own industry's foibles by now or your own version of this story. You may also learn some very strange things about what passes for normal in banking. Even if you are a banker. The industry is huge and complex and chances are if you have spent your life in, say, retail banking all my examples from corporate cash management will sound as strange as if you came to us from manufacturing. But the recognition of organisational inertia and humanity getting in its own way is universal and the point I am trying to make. So banker or no banker, if you are a change-maker, if you work where old habits and new possibilities converge, you will find things to enjoy in these pages. Or at least I hope you will because this book is very much for you too.

NO-ONE IS AS SPECIAL AS THEY WOULD LIKE TO THINK

Change is always uncomfortable and radical change is plain scary.

The reflex of trying to find reasons why something scary doesn't apply to you is human, understandable and universal and a topic we will return to later in this book. In fact thinking our industry is unique, special, exempt and inaccessible to all laypeople is a default position, not just cultivated to resist transformation but one historically resorted to in order to justify the status often associated with banking jobs. Frankly, our 'special' status is one of the biggest defensive lies manufactured to keep the critics at bay and defend the aura of serious professionalism. Also, one of the most frequently used arguments in favour of slowing down innovation inside our organisations.

But.

We are not that special. Banking, as an industry. Not that special. And each bank? Unique in its history and acquisitions, is actually convoluted in the same way, albeit differently in the specifics. In order to do our jobs (the change agent job), we need to respect that feeling of uniqueness that each practitioner has but also see the patterns between institutions and between industries and not be dazzled by the Special Ones.

Actually moving away from *'that doesn't apply to me because'* is exactly why I am a firm believer that the messages in this book and the pain and what it takes to drive this kind of transformation is universal across industries. And let me labour this point, using a banking example that I trust resonates across all of us: despite what type of bankers we are. Even if we are not bankers.

So. Here goes.

Big corporates are all the same.

Banks are all the same. But in pro-

Banks are all the same.

But in profoundly different ways

foundly different ways. For real. Stay with me: banks are fundamentally, painfully the same. And so are big corporates. If you've seen one, you've seen 'em all. And of course, there is a good reason for that. They evolved and developed in similar ways, survived similar challenges, aligned to create markets under parallel circumstances. They went after the same business opportunities.

They were regulated in the same ways. Competed with each other. Emulated each other. Acquired each other.

Fundamentally, banks are all the same. They are the same in their very guts and purpose. They are the same in the way they make money. In the way they capitalised on opportunities and leveraged technology as it became available decade after decade. In the way they standardised, collaborated, pursued efficiency and negotiated best practices. It stands to reason. They do the same thing in the same environment, follow the same rules and largely fish in the same client and talent ponds. So, you know. They are the same. Writ large. And that means that when you go from one bank to another, as a banker or as a vendor, you recognise shapes. You recognise colours and hues and problems and narratives.

It's very tempting to go 'ah yes, seen it all before'. But you shouldn't. For two reasons. One is, if you say it, your banking stakeholders, the very people you seek to influence, will stop listening because they don't believe you. They believe their organisation is different, their regulatory environment tougher, their conditions harsher and their circumstances extenuating.

The second reason is subtler but equally significant.

Seeing a pattern isn't the same as recognising the detail beyond the pattern. Because all banks (or big corporates for that matter) are the same, yes, but in profoundly different ways. To drive transformation, you need to break through the 'special status', work to the patterns and solve at the level of the most idiosyncratic detail. Otherwise whatever you do won't take root.

So how do you navigate that and how do you get something usable out of this witty aphorism that currently leaves you exactly nowhere? You keep your eye on the ball that is the big big vision we serve. But you live out your day and do your work in the minutiae of what is real where you stand.

WHERE DID YOU GROW UP?

I spent a big chunk of my career at BNY Mellon and I have a deep, enduring love for that company.

During my early days at BNY, someone asked me 'where did you grow up?' and I answered 'Athens', and they laughed. Good-natured laughing, before you get upset on my behalf. They didn't laugh at me. The question was esoteric, and they explained. What they meant was where did you learn your craft. Where did you get to know what you know so we don't assume the wrong things about each other. It's a good question. I wish more people asked it. I wish more people recognised that we are all the same but in different ways and helping flag those similarities and differences saves a lot of time and heartache.

The colleagues I served with answered their own question in two ways: they would say I grew up in operations, in IT, in sales. And they would say 'I am legacy Mellon, legacy BNY, legacy JPM'.

What do those two things say about you? They say: these were the things I learned first and therefore the things I know most viscerally and they are the things that may inform my mental starting point for how big a problem seems to me ... or how important a fix appears to me ... or where I will probably think we should start the fix, for that matter. All the mental models I use may be coloured by those things I learned first, things you may not know much about.

Just take a moment to appreciate how helpful and self-aware that is, even when the information wasn't necessarily offered with that in mind. Even when the information was used as a trump card, it built a bridge. Intentionally or not.

The second identification declares the wider estate people learned their craft in. The systems, processes and administrative choices. The policies, rules and incentives. The culture. The tech. The products. The lot. Banks grew by asset swap and acquisition. We didn't all grow up in the same part of the map and there are parts we know better than others because, you got it, we grew up there. Be it the department, the geography or the business we did our learning in. When I first heard people putting their credentials on the table like that I was a little confused, I confess. Is it a pissing contest? Is it a divisive act, aligning us more with our past than our desired shared future? Turns out sometimes it was used to rub other people's faces in one's superior knowledge, of course it was, we are humans and the playground is never far. But the net effect of this habit was the exact opposite.

You know what this thing did for us? It allowed us to be vocal and upfront about the differences in our vantage points. It allowed us to be active in finding ways to navigate the highly complex combined tech and human estate of a post-acquisition hangover. It allowed us to staff teams with enough background – by department or legacy and usually both – to ensure we minimised our blind spots. It allowed us to be smart about our own challenges so they wouldn't become dysfunctions. It wasn't a strategy by the way. It was an organic thing people just did. And it worked. And it will work again, if you want to try it, no matter what the legacies being negotiated are. No matter what industry you are in.

See? Not just for bankers.

And of course bankers and non-bankers alike will, and can, and did get defensive and protective of their own way or overly keen to safeguard something that was known to work for them and their clients, even if it didn't work for anyone else. And of course we didn't end up with a magical unicorn level of perfection. Because *humans*.

But it helped those very humans navigate. And that is not nothing.

Why am I telling you all this?

Because if you are here reading, you are either a banker trying to solve some of the common problems our organisations have as we face into our digital future, or someone trying to help this journey from the outside-in, as an adviser, vendor or partner. Or you are someone who is trying to solve similar problems in another industry and want to get ideas of what worked and what didn't from the veterans of the trade. You may want some tricks, tools and practices that have helped. Maybe you want to learn from our mistakes and our successes and maybe you want to feel that you are not alone, that others are struggling through the same journey.

That's why I am telling you.

Because no matter where you sit, you know that strategies are devised at the plane of reality where all banks (or insurance firms or corporates) are the same. They all have legacy infrastructure and bloated hierarchies and paper-based solutions coexisting with state-of-the-art tech and work-arounds and talent gaps. And they have business models that still mostly operate in a pre-digital economy. And they want to transition into the future in the least disruptive way possible.

Slap their logo on the front of your PowerPoint and tell them these are the areas that need to be addressed for a successful digital transformation and you will be right. For all of them. For any of them. And then you will get the job and on day one they will ask you where you grew up. What's your answer?

THE CHALLENGE IS UNIVERSAL, BUT THE SOLUTION MUST BE SPECIFIC

We think in generalities, but we don't live in them.

There is nothing wrong with a strategy that is generic and universal as above, before you get upset with me. And you can sell that plan in good faith to every bank on the planet if you are that way inclined: even some of the digital ones. They don't have all the problems on your laundry list, but they have enough of them as they balance scale, operational efficiency and business viability while maintaining capital adequacy and compliant services across the board as to matter very little. At that level, banks are all the same. And it helps, when drafting a plan, if you've seen it all before. But plans are executed in the specifics. Plans are executed where banks are drastically, dramatically different. Where habits, weird choices, different strategies are layered upon each other like a microcosm of the earth's own strata ... where all the things that are very different by department, geography or organisation live. That's where you execute. That's where your work takes place. In the detail of how things are today. Because where you are today is where your journey starts, whatever else you may wish for. And where you are today is a mess.

Decades – in some cases over a century – of layered policies, legacies, choices. Departments working in silo. Not exactly against each other. Not exactly together. Everyone likes your strategy. Everyone wants you to succeed. Everyone wants digital transformation. But if you go into that office thinking 'all banks (or corporates) are the same, how hard can this be?', I wouldn't even bother getting a coffee. You won't be there long.

Because yes. All banks are the same, but in profoundly different ways. And that's where you solve their problems and unlock their futures. So be prepared to ask your stakeholders where they grew up. Find the stories of how we all got here. To the specific 'here' of this department and this bank and this day. Not the generic 'here' of being on the cusp of disruption. Find the parts of the landscape that are not represented in the room you sit in. Ask why. Adjust accordingly. You don't need to be from around here to navigate the way out. You just need to respect the landscape and pay attention to what you see. Don't assume you've seen it all before. Because I can assure you, you haven't.

This is tricky.

Because most bankers (and actually most resisters to change) start from a point of exclusion. This doesn't apply to me because … You wouldn't understand, this is way too complicated … somehow trying to claim a special status of protection. That sadly won't wash. The challenge of needing to keep up with the economy doesn't care how special you think you are. Sadly, the complexities that you may think shield you from the need to do certain things are actually the very thing that makes doing what you need to do so much harder. So I guess you are special. Just not in a good way. The sticking point here is that, in order to make that case to a bank or any other specialist institution, you need to display your credentials. You need to show you understand them intimately. You need to show you earned the right to tell them uncomfortable truths. You need to be one of them, which is why, incidentally, a lot of cross-industry transplants fail so spectacularly. Not because the skills are not transferable. But because the 'host' rejects the implant by claiming obscure, apocryphal 'truths' that an industry outsider can't debunk.

The generalities can probably be seen from space, now. The detail, where we fight this battle, requires inside knowledge.

Driving digital transformation, our calling, such as it is, is not actually specific to the craft of a particular industry. It's just you are always better able to change things from the inside. And that's what we all try to do. Only the 'inside' of any big organisation is filled with traps: habits, rules and structures that seem and are treated like they are inevitable. Changing the game means challenging all of those sacred cows, all of those established structures and behaviours in ways big and small. And creating new habits and structures as well as new systems. Because without new habits and new structures, the new systems would be doomed if they ever materialise in the first place.

So our work is about people. And their foibles.

And it is those foibles we turn to now.

3

Bankers Behaving Badly

SNEAK PREVIEW

The thing about change is that it never starts with a blank sheet of paper. It always starts from where you are when it starts. And that means you carry legacy. Systems. Knowledge. People. Above all people. The heaviest legacy is not the technical estate you need to upgrade but the behaviours, habits and established wisdom of your teams.

What we value, what we notice, what we measure, what we forgive or tolerate in our organisations, forms a heavier burden than the tech we need to upgrade. And those behaviours, individually perpetuated and collectively respected, give rise to standards, practices and structures that are heavier to shift than mainframes.

For years we believed the behaviours were incidental and if we shone a light on the new tech, the rest would follow. We found out that was not to be the case the hard way.

So let's take a long hard look at the things we do inside our organisations that get in the way of the future.

THE NAUGHTY STEP

We wrapped the last chapter firm in the belief that 'better' is both possible and necessary.

This belief is not revolutionary, but neither is it universally held or, rather, it is not universally honoured. Nobody in their right mind will disagree that we should do better, at least not publicly. Some may bristle at the implication

DOI: 10.1201/9781003364436-3

that banking isn't already living its best life, projecting its best self (not a joke) and many have and continue to challenge that better is possible, refuting 'the art of the recently possible' in a corporate version of hand-wringing 'if only I could'.

You can.

We can and should. But it's not easy. It is not easy to implement large-scale change. The work itself is not easy. But often, it is equally hard to see a way through the here and now. What we now have and where we now are is so solid, complex and engrossing that it can become a trap of sorts. Navigating the status quo doubles the complexity that change work brings in itself and, more often than not, gets in the way of that work succeeding, or even starting.

So before we move onto our call to action on what needs to change in order for us to move forward as an industry and how we can go about making that happen, it is important to spend time on the things that hold us back, some of which would be funny if they weren't wasting human potential in offices the world over, across industries and verticals, day in and day out.

STARTING AT THE START: WHAT DO WE MEAN WHEN WE SPEAK OF LEGACY

The obvious place to start is, indeed, to state the obvious. Our industry is plagued by legacy technology. What does that mean? It means a few things actually. It means that most of the systems inside banks now are old.

Not 'ageing', but old.

Old in a way that corresponds to a different era of technology: a different way of working, processing and handling data, security threats and what 'fast' means. But it also means other things. It means that systems inside banks were developed in ways that are themselves old school. So it's not just the tech itself that is old but the thought processes and ways of working that got us to the tech are old. The systems we refer to as legacy are built in a world and for a world where connectivity and collaboration were not part of the normal way of doing business; where decision-making was rigid and organisations were command and control. Where navigating systems was an arcane art and UX didn't mean much other than a blinking censor on a green screen. Legacy speaks of systems before agile software development and service-oriented architecture were known terms. These are systems that were built in a time when banks believed every line of code should be proprietary because you never know what may make all the difference.

So when we talk about 'moving away from legacy', we don't mean giving people who are trying to work collaboratively the tools they are craving for. We mean teaching them to work in a different way *at the same time* as giving them brand new tools. So when we speak of legacy we mean the tech *and* the mindset that led to it. The tech *and* the ways of working all around it. And our industry is rich in legacy. Of course it is.

> Having a successful business today and wanting a successful business tomorrow, perversely, are at odds with each other because yesterday's success makes risking today's comfort for tomorrow's success a much harder proposition than starting with nothing or starting with something that has failed.

The industry has existed for much longer than any of the digital capabilities we discuss have. Our industry goes back to when the abacus was the bleeding edge of available tooling so, yes, as it enters the digital era, the industry carries baggage including systems built with the best technology we had when we built them. We call it legacy and not in a good way, but it is important to flag that it is the price you pay for successfully existing for a long time, and that matters. Legacy technology is of course a hindrance in the digital era. But the unspoken concomitant of having legacy is that you also have customers and revenue and proven business viability. These things are extremely important, positive and frankly need to be protected. If anything, why does a business try to digitise and keep up with the times other than to retain its customers and protect its profitability? To remain, in other words, a continuously viable business.

But it's exactly this current viability that makes the transition extremely hard, because the risks are high and the trade-offs not obvious. Having a successful business today and wanting a successful business tomorrow, perversely, are at odds with each other because yesterday's success makes risking today's comfort for tomorrow's success a much harder proposition than starting with nothing or starting with something that has failed. So the very fact that business was good up until now is part of the reason why resistance to wholesale change is often mounted. And understandably so.

We may all agree that the world has changed enough that technologies built before the digital era hold institutions back. We all agree that this 'legacy' holds them back. That is a commonly made argument and although it is a blanket statement that hides a multitude of sins it also is absolutely true. But given that legacy comes as a side effect of prior success, what do we actually mean when we lament legacy?

LEGACY AIN'T ALL BAD

If anything, the existence of legacy technology is proof that banks invested heavily in technology throughout their existence. That's both a good thing itself and, frankly, it represents the mindset that every digital challenger appeals to: you already know how to invest in tech, you already know how to use tech to further and reinvent your business, let's do it again!

The existence of legacy means that banks and financial institutions *get* the importance of technology and understand that sometimes building the right systems takes time, money, energy and vision. There was a time before email was deemed a good investment. There was a time when tools like slack and symphony seemed like so much noise. There was a time before algo-trading.[1] And although there may have been initial resistance, banks embraced all those technologies and more. In fact, banks had algo-trading before they signed off on universal use of email.

Digest that for a moment.

Banks had pioneered the creative use of technology in their businesses before some of the challengers' founders were even born. So don't patronise them. They know how to invest in technology. They know how to assess and deploy. This familiarity and track record should, in fact, make embracing new technology easy. And at times it has. Algo-trading is an excellent example of new technology coming in roundabout the 1970s, that fundamentally transformed the way banks did *something* and the banks themselves embraced the change. But the reason they accepted the change (and cost and disruption of going from one way of working to another) is as important as the adoption. Algo-trading or high-frequency trading came with investment

---

[1] Algo-trading, or algorithmic trading, is a process for executing orders utilising automated and pre-programmed trading instructions to account for variables such as price, timing and volume. Algo-trading combines complex formulas with human oversight to make decisions around buying or selling securities. These technologies enable high-frequency trading whereby the use of technology essentially enables thousands of trades to take place per second, a pace no human could manage.

in systems and fundamental change needed in operational and governance components around how the technologies were used. So there was some discomfort and grumbling an investment and period of transition. But the bank ploughed on ahead because doing so came with an upside they could understand so the cost and effort of building the tools seemed like a good investment and trade-off.

Hold onto that thought, we will need it later.

So. When we speak of legacy tech, what do we mean? We don't mean bad tech. We mean old tech tightly bound up with ways of working that are as old as the tech and as limiting. 'Legacy' has become an umbrella term that means the estate banks come with, accumulated over decades of doing stuff, building stuff, buying stuff … including other banks that often had duplicate systems … and then deciding that migrating data to one system was too much effort not worth the risk, cost and disruption. So 'legacy' also means this for banks: not only do they now have ageing technology, but they also have multiple versions of the same thing. Versions that don't talk to each other because they were not provisioned that way, not designed that way etc., etc., etc. And to add to this existing complexity (affectionately referred to as 'spaghetti' inside big organisations) people built 'bridges' to make doing their jobs easier as they negotiate these ever-shifting complex domains of technologies.

So 'legacy' just got a little more complicated by decades of folks trying to navigate complex systems and complex bureaucracies around them.

What does that mean?

It means that 'legacy' doesn't just mean the tech and governance structures but actually it also encompasses decades' worth of workarounds people came up with in order to get something done that the systems they had don't exactly do. It means little hacks (it's not meant to work this way but we found that if you press this after that, the system gets tricked into giving you what you need). It means the dreaded UDTs.

UDTs may sound like a sexually transmitted disease but for a bank CTO it is potentially worse. It stands for User-Defined Technologies and they are *everywhere*. A widget here. A hack there. And the endless spreadsheets where 'this guy Dave' does price verification off the system 'cos its faster'. Or where we track the breaks in a trade, that will need to be reconciled back up and downstream, before we enter it all back into the system for the fund accounting software to do what it does … or where we keep calendars of public holidays for 'exotics' (that's bank speak for all currencies that don't trade much. Many of those don't come from very exotic locations at all. If you are thinking 'beach and pina colada' you will be sorely let down). If you are not a banker the specifics of these examples will mean nothing to you, but even if you don't get what a break in a trade is (it's when information appears in more than one place and those instances don't match up, so the trade can't go through the process and reconciliation is needed to see who fat-fingered what where), your spidey senses will be tingling. You don't need to know the specifics to realise the examples I describe are a recipe for inconsistency, complexity and untraceable error.

'THIS GUY DAVE'

'This guy Dave' is a real person, though I've never met him.

Approximately two decades ago, he left his role in a major bank, leaving behind a lot of obscure voodoo in macros nobody could understand and mammoth Excel spreadsheets the bank needed for a lot of its middle office functions. Dave was a hero with me and a few friends who had a little start-up back then and we got the gig of turning Dave's spreadsheet into software. I wish we had known where Dave had gone to. Following him around would have made us a killing. But the reality is we didn't need this particular Dave. It turns out, they are legion.

Years later, while I was working for a different bank, our regional CTO told me that his UDT removal project had tacked in excess of 300 'home-grown' solutions and was nowhere near done finding all UDTs let alone eradicating them.

Daves everywhere.

There are still so many Daves inside banks, trying to get their job done in a complex operational environment where the technical tools provide an imperfect fit to the needs of the job. In the process of 'getting the job done' by the Daves of this world, who create tools and hacks and spreadsheets and workarounds, these Daves, unwittingly, add to the complexity of the landscape they are already burdened by. The Daves get the task done but, in the process, they create a little bit more legacy for their future selves to untangle.

If that sounds stressful and rather a lot, it's because it is. And we are not even done.

THE TIMES THEY ARE A'CHANGIN'

On top of all this, when we speak of the burden of legacy technology, we also mean technology built before real-time connectivity was actually possible. In many ways, legacy systems are designed to do the opposite of what we now need of them. This is technology built to hold information, not securely share it. It is technology designed to process information in batches, usually at the end of the day, and not in real time. Technology built to be a fortress, not plumbing pipes.

It's existentially different to what the digital era expects as standard, and that matters. All of these traits are foundational to how systems operate. What they were designed to achieve. What good looked like. What *normal* looked like. This is a fundamentally new definition of normal, nay: a definition of normal that is opposite to what you used to do, so changing systems and governance structure to fit this new normal isn't about a small uplift. You can't tweak these legacy systems to be digital, you have to replace them. But as the systems were core to how we did business, in fact they were developed to reflect how we did business at the time, that way of working is also foundational to the structures, operational behaviours, risk matrixes and bureaucratic hierarchies that were built to deliver and support the business.

So when we speak of legacy technology we don't just mean some old mainframes, which is complicated enough to replace in its own way. We mean *all of it: systems, processes, structures and ways of working*, because digital connectivity enables a new way of working that the systems now need to support. It's not just a systems upgrade. It's an operating model shift and that's before we get to the business model imperatives of the digital economy.

This is hard. Because in order to digitally transform, we must radically change the lot: the systems *and* ways of working that either led to them or were developed around them. It doesn't much matter which came first, what matters is that to change one you must change the whole. And that's a lot. And what you change towards is fraught with uncertainty. And that just makes it worse.

> Legacy technology is existentially different to what the digital era expects as standard, and that matters. Legacy systems are often designed to do the opposite of what we now need.

PLUS, IT GETS EMOTIONAL

One fine day in my late twenties (in the early noughties, if you must know), I was presenting some work my team had done on business process automation to a Big Cheese inside the bank. The work was solid. We had proven in a series of small projects that we could reduce time to market dramatically (from 18 months to 6 weeks) and produce all-green client key performance indications (KPIs) using this particular approach to our process re-engineering, essentially reducing human touchpoints and scope for error. We also found the possibility to reduce cost dramatically by decommissioning duplicate functionality across our tech estate. You'd think that's a shoe-in victory.

You'd be wrong.

To deliver this uplift, the CTO of that particular business line had to sign off (and yes, young padawan CTOs per line of business are a thing … it's the idea that you could or would have economies of scale across the estate that is still fairly new) …. So Big Cheese CTO looks at our work, nods his head and then goes aha … but to deliver the goods and get the saving and the accelerant you speak of, we would need to kill system x, is that right?

Yes, I said. That is true. We would 'grandfather' the system (that's a polite way of saying we won't put any new stuff on this system but won't aggressively kill it – the euphemism for active killing is 'to sunset'). We had found the system largely duplicated functionality and there was not much work to be done in order to ensure that the unique and non duplicate things it did were picked up elsewhere without needing to carry all that tin, add unnecessary steps to the process and all that jazz.

And why wouldn't you kill it outright, I hear you say? If it costs money to run and it doesn't add anything? Ah because of Dave, you see. You never kill a system outright in a bank because you know that for a few months … maybe years … you will be finding weird and wonderful ways the Daves of this world used the system in question that weren't the way it was meant to be used but now you have a whole team up in arms with no way of getting their job done. So you remove systems slowly and with a lot of process redesign work and endless consultations.

Is that what the Big Cheese said, then, I hear you ask.

Of course not.

Oh I don't like that, he said. I put that system in before you were born young lady.

That was to me. As if that was an argument. Because to him, it was. The system had worked long enough, was the logic, and it ain't broke so don't fix it. Plus it's not legacy, it's *my* legacy. If there is duplication in the estate, kill another system. Not this one. This is mine. It was invented here, by me. And that has a strong emotional pull at the best of times so you can imagine that, in the era of proprietary technology and senior bankers owning system like empires sticking flags in bits of land, this argument carried the day many times a day, in offices around the world.

THE HEAVIEST THING ABOUT LEGACY IS THE HUMANS THAT PERPETUATE IT

Legacy is the story of how we got to where we are today and why it's not just a matter of getting on with uplifting our existing systems to move ahead. Legacy is in some ways the cost of doing business. It bears the imprint of growth (acquisitions and mergers), success (workarounds and hacks to accommodate the pressing needs of business) and human ambition.

But legacy itself, perversely, also carries the stamp of innovation and creativity and that is equally important. Banks building proprietary systems was, for a very long time, seen as a competitive edge, a value-additive activity that spearheaded competitive innovation. And now we are telling them not only do your systems suck but your way of developing them is also obsolete. There is bound to be resistance. The tech teams inside banks want to continue building the cool stuff. That is what techies do. The 'not invented here syndrome' the business had may be weakening in light of innovations coming at the banks from within the open market, but the reality is that, for every pitch a tech vendor submits to a bank, the most dreaded competitor is not another vendor but the bank's IT team who will want to build the stuff themselves.

And why shouldn't they?

Why shouldn't they deal with their legacy in the same way that they acquired it? By doing new things for themselves? It's a fair question and one many banks grapple with.

The main problem with that, is that tech teams are bound by the same legacy governance, practices and tooling that is what needs to be changed anyway, so their chances of success are sadly tied closely to the bank's overall transformation.

Chicken, meet egg.

Bringing in systems from the outside isn't *just* a way of leapfrogging from where you are today to where the rest of the economy is without needing to 'build your way there', it is also a way of accelerating systems transformation *on the road to* helping the bank on its wider transformation journey. Breaking with the tradition of building most of our own systems inside banks (or buying from traditional vendors plagued with all the same problems we have described here) has the double benefit of bringing in new technology *and* accelerating the wider change we need by breaking a vicious circle of using old tools to solve new problems. In fact trying to transform a business by building new systems under all the constraints of the old business seems at best counter-intuitive and at worse mad. And yet. That's where we are.

Now, multiply this reality across banks, countries, continents, business lines and what you get is what we *actually* mean by the word 'legacy'. And we are not done yet. There is one more thing. Remember back at the beginning of the chapter when I said banks have historically been good at investing in new technology, despite its cost and complexity, when they could see the financial upside of doing so? And I said, 'remember that, we will be needed it later?'.

Well. Now is later.

And we need to remember that although the realisation that 'legacy' technologies and ways of working are 100% not fit for purpose for the digital realities we now inhabit and the future we expect, there is no corresponding certainty as to where banks should go next. Generic direction of travel is clear: you need fully digital capabilities, you need a dynamic approach to data, you need to understand that digital capabilities changed the economy not just the tools we use day to day, so you need to think about your purpose in this new economy: what you will do that is valuable, and how you will do it to make money.

Generically, we all agree that this is what needs to happen. Specifically though? Do you need hyper-personalised retail banking, AI-enabled fraud monitoring, IoT-enabled supply chain financing on the blockchain, API-first liquidity management, embedded payments, straight-through reconciliations and and and ….

And while you are grappling with all this, DeFi has emerged as a complex industry of its own, Web3 has landed *and* the economy is in a crisis that can only be technically described as 'the wheels coming off'. In this context, you need to make multiple, complex decisions on incomplete information.

Do you need it all? And if not, how do you choose what you need? And in each of the things you decide you need, what is the right focus, architecture and deployment approach? If there is no clear upside to anything and a clear downside to standing still, is it sensible to stall and buy time and commit a little effort across a lot of options, until answers become apparent or do you need to go boldly forth and take big risks?

HARD CHOICES MADE ON INCOMPLETE INFORMATION

If your head is beginning to spin a little, then you are facing the magnitude of the task at hand with empathy and may find yourself feeling a little more charitable towards the folks who are reluctant to start on this journey, go too far or too fast and keep asking *when is it enough*? And do we really have to go all the way?

Estates – technical, human, organisational – are cumbersome, occasionally esoteric, definitely not streamlined. All of those things stand in the way of transformation. As does not knowing what to chuck and what to keep. As do regulatory barriers (or at least the way we chose to address those), business imperatives and profitability drivers. It's not easy, this stuff. A lot of work needs to be done. Complicated, time-consuming, fiddly work that will require commitment and focus and effort. And that is hard. And if I have spent the best part of ten pages describing legacy, it is not to say 'oh well we will have to live with this' but to genuinely highlight that this is hard. And exactly because it is hard, it needs to be addressed in a way that is consistent, constant and sustainable. None of this is a quick fix. None of this is a heroic push over a hill. This is complex, long-drawn-out work that can fall down in a myriad of places.

And that is the topic we will turn to next.

Because above all else (and I mean, seriously, above all else) what stands in the way of our progress, in the way of changing what we have inherited in light of what we now know is possible, is *us*.

Humans. And our habits.

Some of those habits were developed in reaction to the directives and constraints imposed by the systems we now look to change, by the structures they imposed, the limitations they came with, the realities of the day-to-day work that pushed people in a particular direction. Habits, policies, structures and organisational hierarchies have a tendency to develop around perceived realities. And it works both ways. Maybe the way people did things determined what the systems looked like, as solutions were designed to add efficiency to the way things were done already, technology coming to make it better, not 'other'. So, in many ways the habits led to the 'legacy' in all its forms. And then were 'fed' by the legacy in a virtuous unbroken circle of positive reinforcement. So now the habits run deep. They become industry-wide, as folks go from job to job and from organisation to organisation, taking 'what they know to be true' with them. And so the habits are perpetuated as they are aped, learned, taught, chosen, tolerated or rewarded through hierarchies, and constantly emulated in a way that cumulatively sets the tone of what *Working in Finance* feels like and how *Successful Finance Professionals Behave.*

And the impact of these is not limited to processes adjacent to technology. Their impact goes beyond technology to all decision-making (that affects but is not limited to the decisions we make, pertaining to technology). These habits are pervasive and ubiquitous and designed to perpetuate a status quo that is static, bureaucratic, hierarchical and above all *set*. So if you look under the hood, you will find that seemingly unrelated challenges such as how we do requests for proposal (RFP) submissions inside banks, why we have so many blasted meetings in our industry or why certain ideas never seem to stick, actually have a lot of commonality. They all go back to ingrained bad habits.

In the next few pages, we will unpack some of those bad habits in the hope that you can't fix something you can't see but once you have seen something for what it is and understood it for the harm it does, you have no choice but to address it and, in doing so, minimise the impact said bad behaviour has on the future we are trying to build. Although the list below is not exhaustive, it paints a picture that goes beyond banking. And although the suggestions of what each of us can do to combat and stem these bad habits are specific, you will see a trend running through them that will, hopefully, help you fuel resistance to the many bad habits in our industry and others that are not listed here, perhaps, but they are ubiquitous, pervasive, damaging and in need of challenge.

BANKERS BEHAVING BADLY IN THE WILD

Exhibit A: The Cult of Busy

Wait, you may be thinking, you are going a bit too far left field. We were talking about tech here. And we expect to hear about habits on how we decide to build, commission and decommission tech, what's all this stuff about people being busy now?

You have a point. But. In this new digital era of ours, everything is about tech and nothing is about tech alone. And therefore the way we operate across the board affects how

> In this new digital era of ours, everything is about tech and nothing is about tech alone.

we approach those decisions about tech. And it is exactly this sort of habit that affects the quality of our decision-making that I want to surface over the course of this chapter. Starting with the default position of being always rushed and always cranky.

IF YOU ARE NOT ANGRY, ARE YOU EVEN SENIOR?

For an industry that prides itself on *not* being emotional, there is a lot of emotion in the average bank, or any place bankers normally frequent: in the Times Before COVID that used to include airports, commuter train stations during rush hour, sandwich shops in Canary Wharf on a rainy Tuesday lunchtime. Now that same type of 'unemotional emotion' is also manifest in one-line emails and snappy zoom calls. The settings have proliferated but the realities of life haven't changed much. There is still a lot of emotion, and that emotion is angst. A heady blend of anger, stress and White Rabbit levels of breathlessness because everyone is determined to be busier than the next guy and therefore they are always on the cusp of being late and on the wrong side of being stretched too thin.

If you haven't seen a suited and booted corporate droid losing their cool at the airline staff at 5 am at City Airport in London because their flight to Luxembourg is delayed and therefore they will be late to their meeting, you haven't seen ire. There is a lot to be learned about the industry sitting in an airport observing the suited crowds tutting at the slow-coach making their skinny latte in the airport's overpriced cafés, back when it seemed that half of London's bankers were zooming off to meetings on early Monday morning shuttles, all crisp shirts and sleepy faces. Filled with under-caffeinated righteous indignation.

My friend Sarah, an Arizona native, calls this slowly simmering anger the New York Frown but, frankly, you see it the world over. Its wearer usually carries a laptop bag and will not hold back when unhappy. Observing the businessman's anger targeted at the barista, at the security guard going through the drill and asking them to remove their shoes like we knew they would, watching them shouting down the phone at an assistant while their plane sits on the tarmac, you are not seeing an exception. You are not seeing one grumpy git or an otherwise lovely family man having a bad day. You are seeing the norm. You are seeing the default mental state of senior banking decision-makers, you are seeing the Cult of Busy in the wild.

Being busy is a badge of honour in a bank and the wider industry.

'Have you *seen* my diary?' is one of the most common laments in the industry and I am as guilty of it as anyone.

Back-to-back meetings with assistants valiantly squeezing 30-minute sessions in wherever they can. Sessions that you will be a few minutes late for, because no time was allowed to wait for the lift, say hi to a client coming out of the meeting room across yours, going to the bathroom or running over because, frankly, 30 minutes is not enough time for every type of conversation, it turns out. So everything runs a little late as you run from call to meeting, a little out of breath, flicking through your calendar on your phone trying to remind yourself what the next thing is about, flicking through the background material as the presentation kicks off, one eye on your emails, shooting off three-word answers to important questions because you can't manage to type much more than that while you walk or half-listen to a presentation.

AND IF YOU ARE THINKING, WELL THANKFULLY ALL THAT STOPPED WITH COVID, DON'T

The Guardian newspaper published a survey on 23 March 2002 saying that home workers napped on average three times a week and watched a lot of daytime TV.[2] I genuinely don't know who these people are because in my part of the industry, what I have seen is the opposite: we took the worst of our office habits, turned commuting time into work time and (since being busy is the only way we know to show value and 'you are home anyway') here's a 6 am call and a 9 pm debrief.

---

[2] https://www.theguardian.com/business/2022/mar/22/dozing-from-home-how-workers-have-perfected-the-art-of-napping-on-the-job

Things only got worse with wall-to-wall zoom calls with no time to make lunch, call your mum, pay a bill or stretch your curved back between the sessions. Attention fragmented by the constant context-switching and the fact that you are keeping an eye on email (just in case you can turn simple things around while on a call to avoid pile-ups that translate to late nights and weekend work), keeping an eye on slack to ensure the rest of the team get what they need from you and of course your personal device close to hand. Too much demand on your time and attention and the feeling that, if you broke into a thousand pieces, there would still not be enough to go around. And no, I am not going to take a stand on the Great Work from Home debate. I am trying to take a stand on the 'This Is No Way to Live' debate. Whether we do it from home or the office matters less to me than the fact that we have normalised 14 hours of meetings, 5 days a week with the weekend as 'catch up time'.

BEING TOO BUSY TO THINK IS BAD FOR YOU AND BAD FOR BUSINESS. AND YET HERE WE ARE

That's then you know you have achieved seniority in banking, you see. That's how you demonstrate that you care and work hard. When you run around like this, openly and unashamedly leaving yourself no time to do any work, any thinking, any team development, any learning of your own. Or have any bathroom breaks. Not to mention do any living. You work yourself to the ground, pile on the hours, the anti-social flights and late meetings, the weekend email clear-outs and late-night responses leaving juniors quavering in fear of the early morning inbox harvest. And wondering whether they are *also* meant to work weekends so now they do, to show themselves willing and capable of one day having your job.

You want to talk about legacy? Let's talk about this.

You are busy. You are rushed. You live on caffeine and the hope that nothing will require more than 30 minutes' worth of attention because, truth be told, you can't remember the last time anything required concentration and you are not sure you remember how to do it.

And of course and as a result, everyone is cranky. Because this is no way for a human to live, despite how many do, despite how we treat it as a badge of importance and proof of success. And forget for a second what it does to your mental and physical well-being. It's not even good for business.

It's not good for anything. And that in itself adds to the frustration and crankiness.

As a result of working like this, of course, nothing ever really moves adequately forward and that is frustrating in itself. And although half-hour increments every 3 weeks is really not how you solve complex problems, devise strategy, execute, build and develop teams, get things done, it is how we keep trying to do it time and again. We go on giving things inadequate time, with too many waits in-between, too many things all at once, none of them prevalent enough, nothing taking precedence and nothing getting really, fully, properly done. Until it catches fire. Then it gets focus. Otherwise we keep the plates spinning. And we know it's not great but this is how everyone is doing it and, for anyone trying to tell you otherwise, you have the moral high ground of hallowed banking tradition on your side. And often when you try to change it (and trust me, I have been trying for years) you get a refrain of 'but you are important, that is how it goes' as if we have all collectively conspired to forget what the word 'important' actually means or what type of work and responsibility and accountability comes with seniority.

The very people who are meant to be custodians of critical decision-making are living in a state of acquired attention-deficit. And we all accept that is normal because we accept that senior folks are rushed. They have no time. They have no bandwidth. We accept that as normal. Not an unwanted side effect, a lamentable state of affairs that stands in their way of being effective strategist and thoughtful leaders. We take the current situation and go 'that must be right'.

> The very people who are meant to be custodians of critical decision-making are living in a state of acquired attention-deficit.

This is tantamount to saying oh look the building is on fire. I bet it was meant to be because why else would it be on fire? Keep feeding the flames.

It's not exactly logical and yet we nurture the beast. And it sucks for everyone involved, the juniors trying to get some attention and guidance and the seniors wondering 'how many more years can I keep on living like this', but mostly, for the purposes of this book, it damages our ability to think about long-range change in two ways.

One, it strikes in all the places where creativity flourishes and complex thinking can unfold, leaving us with highly mechanistic working practices where the ability, space, time and impetus to be playful, creative or simply methodical and thorough are strained, stretched and chopped up too thin.

Two, angry people are not at their most creative. And neither are they the people you want to show your moon-shot ideas to. They don't look like a receptive audience for a work in progress. And yet, this way of working also means that the people who need to look at the options and make choices and decisions that will move their organisations away from the complex legacy we have discussed earlier give the matter no more than 30' at a time.

And there is more.

THE CULT OF BUSY INFANTILISES DECISION-MAKERS

Senior people are time-poor and you should respect that and work to that is what juniors are taught. So we all learn to refine the art of executive briefings and crisp summaries. High-level highlights and clear asks. We all know how to do it. And it is a very useful skill, don't get me wrong. It just doesn't work when you need to tackle open-ended complexity. In a changing industry where hard choices need to be made, taking into account technical innovation in other sectors itself moving at breakneck speed; in a context where technology and regulation challenges the way you have historically made money and the options as to what to do next proliferate, and the choices themselves have complex and often unknowable consequences *and* you need to spend some time thinking those through; in *that* world, in *that* industry, no executive summary can give you what you need to make decisions.

Complexity needs time and concentration. If you rely on Cliff notes and executive summaries, you rely on someone else's interpretation of what is important. Is that your idea of leadership?

But we make no time and arguably have no staying power for complexity anyway. The average human's attention span is reducing with every passing year and the ability to concentrate is notoriously affected by context-switching, interruptions, multiple stimuli and stress. So we are not setting ourselves up for success here.

But try saying that in an executive boardroom.

Try suggesting that the way we work is not conducive to making informed decisions or reflecting on challenges and opportunities. Try suggesting that working like this leaves choice to chance because the seniors can't see beyond the next half-hour interval and the juniors churn out PowerPoint, safe in the delusion that their seniors and betters will notice if something is missing, if something is wrong, if something is inadequate – and too distracted by half by a desire to be at the apex of business themselves: that magical time when they will be reading other people's badly thought-through slides, too busy to actually help them get the work right.

In the meantime, they simplify to make their slideware work. They make extremely important decisions

> Working like this leaves choice to chance because seniors can't see beyond the next half-hour and juniors churn out PowerPoint, safe in the delusion that their seniors and betters will notice if something is missing, if something is wrong.

around the spectrum of possibility they will feed to the layer above, in the interest of defensibility or a balanced presentation. Please digest this before moving on: the most important decisions about what will be considered as part of a bank's strategy are made by the juniors trying to work out what they can get into a deck without being ripped to shreds by their stressed-out supervisor trying, in turn, to meet a vague brief without getting into trouble themselves.

And each layer in the hierarchy streamlines a little more before passing their analysis up to the next floor.

I had a boss once who used to change the whole direction of the work we had done (including the recommendations sometimes) to make the slides work.

He went far, by the way, career-wise.

And truth be told, I didn't like him much. But he was not the problem. He was just playing the game he was in.

Expecting seniors to have no time or headspace to dedicate to really complex topics, disconnected teams present their view of the world in the simplest and punchiest manner conceivable, opting for obfuscation to avoid coming across as patronising. And all this is done in the sincerest of hopes that they will capture the

> Expecting seniors to have no headspace to dedicate to complex topics, disconnected teams present their view of the world in the simplest manner conceivable, confident that someone, somewhere has the full picture. But who?

imagination of their over-wrought executives and confident that someone, somewhere has the full picture.

But who?

When the uppermost echelons of the organisation consume information curated below them by the very people who trust someone else is in control. Meanwhile the meetings pile up, the hours stretch out. The sheer amount of things one has to understand, process and decide upon ever-increasing.

And in this context of stretched attention spans and sleep-deprivation, anger acquires insidious authority.

WE HAVE NORMALISED THE THINKING PATTERNS OF EXHAUSTION

The first time one of my team told me how jealous she was of my 'jet-setting' and 'how hard it is to get into my diary', I had just wheeled my suitcase and my weary bones into the office straight from the airport, for a bunch of meetings that could have been emails, before going home to swap out my clothes, shower and cat-nap before the next flight.

And before you say 'well covid rescued you' let me say two things: flights are back baby. And some of them are much needed as there is nothing as valuable as being in the room with people and I have been the first person on a plane to meet my clients and spend uninterrupted time with them in front of a white board when it became possible again. That is not the problem. The problem is that there is also no upside to 14-hour days of 28 30' zoom calls, just because you are at home in comfy jumpers and that was only made worse by COVID.

You don't want to live like this. Heck I don't want to live like this. But it's hard to break the cycle. If that's how everyone does it. And before you say 'if everyone sticks a pencil in the nose will you do it too' this is not about peer pressure in the playground. This is about people building careers and doing something that is *long term bad* for both you and the organisation you are in, but in the short and medium term it is the acceptable way to build your career. Choosing between the two is hardly an easy or indeed a fair choice to have to make on an individual level. If that's how senior, successful people pace themselves, to do it differently makes you entirely out of sync with your peers and the folks who measure success and commitment within the management food chain, not to mention out of sync with your clients and their needs. What's clever about that? What's useful about that?

So you join the ranks of the sleepless, rushing corporate zombies and, before long, you realise that the final trapping of traditional authority in banking, that slight aloof coldness, the short fuse, the fragile temper, is actually fatigue. And the dismissive sneer we see so often is the low-latency seething anger of overstimulation, sensory overload, stress and too much caffeine usurping the place of sleep and regular meals. And the odd walk in the sun.

Yes, people storm in and out of offices or zoom screens with faces of thunder and cutting remarks. Sometimes they do more than that: the odd shout and banged table is not uncommon and a friend of mine once had a pen thrown at his face, by his boss, in a bank, narrowly missing his eye. That has only ever been topped by the story of a girl I know whose boss threw a shoe at her, in the heat of a moment I cannot even begin to imagine. The shoe may be an exception, but the pattern is not. And don't ask me where the shoe came from. Women in offices used to keep several pairs of heels under our desks back when we used to go to offices every day and wore smart clothes to work. Those things look good on your feet but only the brave few commute in them. There has always been an abundance of shoes in corporate offices. The anger behind throwing the blasted thing though is another matter. And although the gesture is unusual, the tense and aggressive context is not.

As an industry we pay inadequate attention, we exhaust ourselves into a cranky distracted irritation, which often makes us bad colleagues and bad managers. And as we are stretched too thin, rushed and distracted, we become bad learners and weak thinkers. And no creative inspiration comes to a mind scratchy with fatigue and flammable with stress and irritation. Plus, feeling like this makes us resent all this work, to make it to the top, to simply have no time to do anything, which in turn makes us lose sight of why we are doing all this in the first place. And the hamster wheel reigns supreme.

Don't get me wrong. This has always been bad for the people involved. It has been destructive to the health of many an aspiring executive. Bur rather than changing it, we embrace it. We celebrate it as a tribal mark.

Every successful executive in Hollywood movies takes medication for their ulcer and is iconically constantly missing their kids' nativity pageant, baseball game or ballet recital. It's a cliché and recognisable because it's familiar and true. Plus it is telling of what we have collectively accepted as the Shape of the Thing. And this acceptance as well as the behaviours themselves have contributed to banking being generally considered as a soul-destroying place to work even by those of us in it.

This way of living and operating is bad for the humans inside the operations. It has always been and still is.

But now it is also bad for business: the things we have to think through and decide about cannot be done in the way we normally operate. This is not business as usual and what got us here won't get us where we are going to next. The world has changed. The pace of change has increased, yet our organisational learning pace in the last few years has been held back by meetings and action points constantly tabled for next week… and then again the week after that, while each working day is getting a little longer, so your hamster wheel can go faster, but not forward.

BANKERS BEHAVING BADLY IN THE WILD

Exhibit B: The Dark Arts of Planning and Measuring

Hating the Player, Not the Game

Just as you are beginning to think 'yeah this is bad', strap in. We are just getting started.

Because this behavioural pattern has, as you would expect, side effects that run deep. As if the behaviours themselves didn't have a profound impact on culture and conduct (which they do), they *also* create patterns that have separate and cumulative repercussions which *then* go on to create monsters of their own. And one of the worst monsters of banking resulting from the cumulative effects of these habits and patterns and feeding right back into them is the way we plan and measure things.

Let's start by saying that anyone who tells you their success results from faithfully working to a plan is lying.

I know that, from sport to Hollywood and self-help stories to entrepreneurial success, we love the narrative of 'set a goal, believe in yourself, work hard and you will make it by the end of the movie'. This is a fallacy even if you expect a curveball to the narrative about 45 minutes into the film. It is a fallacy both because the vast majority of folks who do just that will *fail* by sheer dint of numbers and because, even for those where the description is not untrue, it isn't the whole truth.

Life doesn't happen in a linear fashion, not even in fairy tales. Reversals, miscalculations, unforeseen consequences, lucky breaks and curveballs are part of everyone's story: from Rapunzel's to yours and the same applies to business ideas, ventures and companies. Nothing is linear, nothing works entirely according to your plan or your dream, no matter how much you believe.

That said, you need a dream or a vision to set direction. And you actually need a plan because in the act of planning you take stock of what you are trying to achieve and why, what you know about what you need to do to get from here to there. Planning helps you work out what you have in your arsenal that may help on the journey and what you need but don't yet have. Be it an expedition to the Sahara or a new business venture, these things are key so that you can assess whether something is a good idea and prepare for the road ahead.

Right out of the gate, however, the plan cannot be static. Right out of the gate it has myriad hypotheses in it. For instance, *what* you are trying to achieve and *why* are key to assessing whether the cost of achieving it is worth paying. Be it fighting a war, launching a new product or cycling across Africa (I don't know why you would, but people do) *why* you are doing what you are doing is a key

> Why you are doing what you are doing is a key benchmark to whether you want to continue doing it when the cost of getting there – material and otherwise – becomes known.

benchmark to whether you want to continue doing it when the cost of getting there – material and otherwise – becomes known. So if, for instance, you decide to cycle the length of Africa for health reasons, after your doctor warned you that your sedentary lifestyle is bad for you, you may find yourself reconsidering the plan, when the very same doctor suggests that you are not in any physical condition to endure the hardships of such an endeavour and maybe you should take out a membership in your local gym and attend a weekly spin class instead. If, on the other hand, the reason you are cycling across Africa is to raise awareness and funds for the real-life challenges to getting medication to those who need it most, then the hardship of your quest will probably actually be a help towards your ultimate success.

Why matters, always.

THE PROBLEM WITH ASKING WHY IS THAT YOU NEED TO KEEP ASKING

This sounds sensible, right?

Ask why about all things, keep asking why, keep asking that the reasons why we do things are still valid and the way we are doing things still aligned to those reasons. It sounds fairly straightforward and sensible.

But sadly that is not how we do things inside big organisations.

Problem one: inside a bank you are highly unlikely to ever assess whether the cost of doing the thing you decided to do is still worth it, once you have started doing it. Part of that is symptomatic of the way we supervise work in a way that fits the calendars of busy people. So short status updates every few weeks rather than holistic, existential assessments measuring impact against purpose and the original vision against a shifting world. Part of it is also symptomatic of the expectation that your executive will start each meeting angry and distracted and who wants to stand up and say 'we need to reconsider'? Not on your life.

So you will almost never find a bank asking itself 'is the way I am executing this thing going against the very thing I am trying to achieve?'. The answer would be almost always yes, by the way, but nobody asks so nobody tells. And without that reality check, a plan, such as it is, cannot generate meaningful metrics to help you work out whether it's all working. Whether the things we are doing are getting us closer to the thing we are trying to achieve.

For example.

A bank I used to work with about 10 years ago decided that the war on talent was getting aggressive and would not actually ever be less so (they were correct). They further believed that a learning culture was key to success in the knowledge economy (inspired, and also true) and that a lot of what they needed their workforce to know would:

1. Forever morph, evolve and shift, so this was not a one-and-done mission and
2. they could teach themselves (from tooling and ways of working to programming languages and design classes) and in the teaching also foster a culture where learning is part of how we work.

Brilliant. Actually brilliant.

Then the vision and the mission were handed to the learning and development team, who had to devise a plan against the vision and then execute against the plan, and measure progress against success metrics defined in the plan. So. They decided to build an academy, falling short of the implicit assumption that the whole point was to acquire knowledge the organisation didn't already have, so an in-house teaching machine wasn't exactly the way forward. Then, realising that assessing the usefulness of the things taught and the speed with which the workforce was getting up-skilled in-pace with the market were hard to pin down, they decided that success would be measured in terms of how many people went through the academy every year instead.

And to make that number big and impressive, so they could all get a bonus at the end, they made the learning modules small, static *and* compulsory. Success for the team, bonuses all around. Absolute flop in terms of achieving what it was meant to do.

Exception? Not on your life.

Banks have a command-and-control execution approach. That is also true of many large-scale businesses and it stands to reason.

You need to have mechanisms to ensure that work gets done with predictability and up to a consistent standard across populations of tens of thousands of workers, sometimes more. And largely the approach works. It helps standardise how we procure paperclips and how we ensure all software releases work to the same quality assurance standards. It's how we know regulations are adhered to and all the good stuff. The problem is that there are many a plan (transformation work is definitely firmly in this category but also all software development, by definition) that needs to be fluid and changeable and reactive to what we learn as we go. It's not the goal that is fluid and changeable, you understand. It is how we execute the plan towards it, learning as we go. But that goes against the grain of how the body corporate operates and measures success. Applying learnings as you go sounds obvious but try it inside a big bank and you will be accused of changing the goal-posts to reduce your team's accountability or hide something. So the instinct is, as we are demonstrating here, to force the new thing to fit into the old shape: to try and beat predictability out of fluidity, losing flexibility in the process.

CAREERS ARE BUILT ON NOT ASKING WHY

Think about it.

As a matter of course, in every piece of work inside a bank you are asked to commit to a concrete plan with timelines and specific deliverables at the beginning of the journey. That is when you know the least about what lies ahead.

The first problem with that is that you will guess a lot. The second problem is that you will focus on the things you know for sure, and you will also do that a lot. You don't know what the deliverable milestones will be so you commit to delivering updates at specific intervals. You don't know what you will find when you start the work, so you commit to a communication plan and dev days and things that you can measure, even if they mean nothing other than 'we are working here, busy busy'.

But of course the commitments create a schedule. You now have to produce what you said you would, even if it is a distraction, even if it is not useful at all. Even if it gets in the way of the work itself.

Plus, once you start the work, or any journey, you get smarter as you go.

You learn things about your assumptions, your team, yourself, what you are trying to do by doing it. So you should be able to course-correct as you go, based on the things you are learning as you are doing the work.

But no.

Course-correcting is seen as lacking in accountability.

Like you say one thing on one day and another the next, to suit your circumstances. And always the lurking suspicion that the team may not be trying hard enough.

So you stick to the plan.

And god forbid if, in doing the work, you discover that the destination you had all agreed upon isn't the best thing to be doing after all. That would be 'killing the project'. That would get chalked up as a failure. You would lose your budget and whatever you want to advocate doing next/instead would have to go through the annual planning cycle, with the black mark of failure against your name. Let's see you securing a budget in this context.

We talk about pivots and 'failing fast' inside banks, but we don't actually allow for that to happen. The path to success inside a programme of work is expected to be linear and follow a project plan. It is expected to. So it does. At the expense of both the work and the success that would have otherwise been possible, and because, let's face it, the destination may change or at least alter the smarter you get.

WHAT YOU MEASURE DEFINES WHAT YOU DO

Once you've thought about it for a second, it should stand to reason that anyone who asks you to devise a comprehensive not-to-be-revisited plan towards and for success, from a standing start, is delusional.

And yet that is exactly how banks do programme management because you need to be able to track progress in a way that is aligned with the way senior management works and we covered that in the section above. Now some of you may think 'you can't be right. Even if that's how we used to do things, surely we have changed: there are innovation departments with bean bags and people in hoodies, playing around with new technologies, learning and failing as they go, I have seen them'.

I have seen them too.

I have even built a couple of such departments.

And it is true, inside those departments, you can play. In fact you are expected to be seen to be playing. It's part learning curve part PR showcase.

But you can't fail, not as such.

Because failing raises systemic concerns, governance issues, compliance problems. Talking about failing and actually permitting it are two very different things.

Plus, if you want to take something you built in one of those departments into the main bank, the rules of the game change even further. Or rather, they revert. So, if you want your experiment, your new learning, your amazing discovery, to be part of the main business, you get to play like the adults do.

What does that mean in real terms?

Imagine that your innovation team built a widget.

It took 6 weeks to design, build and test, in collaboration with a client who is super excited about it.

Imagine this client is a pension fund and this widget pulls data from their portfolio and allows them to have answers to two questions their members have been asking: what is the carbon footprint of my pension (this is now a regulatory requirement in many EEA countries) and what does company X (whose stock is held in my pension) being in the news mean for my pension. Having easy access to this information allows the pension fund to design proactive communications to their communities around things that they care about. Imagine watching the news and knowing your pension is heavily indexed in, say, a particular car manufacturer and you hear that their CEO just stepped down or that the regulator slapped a fine on them. Should you be worried? Will this affect your pension? The pension fund we worked with used to get an avalanche of calls after such news events and they wanted to get ahead of the game and reassure their clients.

The widget was fun to build. The client loved it and we were sure that other, similar clients (pension funds are a pretty big demographic) would find uses for this application. Extending the solution to them didn't involve much work at all: no integration, just pointing the widget to the right portfolio data and letting it do its thing.

Easy-peasy, you'd think.

And yet going from 'lab' to production meant that we had to get in line and wait 8 months to get into a release cycle because there is a process. End of story.

End of a *true* story by the way.

Why would you take something that was meant to prove the bank's ability to be agile, responsive and creative and stick it at the bottom of a queue?

Because that is the process and how that team measures success isn't tied to how quickly they move things through the funnel, getting working solutions into the hands of clients. Their success is measured in terms of how closely they follow the risk protocols and how many things go wrong. If 0 things go wrong they have succeeded. Even if that means that 0 things got done.

Inside banks there are teams whose measure of success isn't tied to how quickly they get solutions into the hands of clients but to how many things go wrong. If 0 things go wrong they have succeeded. Even if that means that 0 things got done.

What you measure determines what you end up doing.

Do you want another example?

Another bank I worked with killed a core competency programme of work in its second year because it couldn't predict exactly when it would be finished, even though it was progressing to plan so far. That sounds strange, right? Two years prior to that assessment a plan was submitted: we will build a new credit card issuance system proving a new set of architectural principles. We will do this, they said, because the existing solutions are too inflexible and too expensive. So we will create a flexible solution that will be cheaper to run. Amazing. Go go go.

For 2 years, the programme measured itself against its plan (as you would expect, it entailed proof points and audits and hiring plans and communications plans).

At the end of the 2 years, all metrics were green, progress was good and, perversely, the hypothesis underpinning the strategy were proven. No acrobatics required. The thing was working.

All you needed to do now was double down and build it for use outside the lab. Extensibility, penetration testing, etc.

So all the teams whose success is measured in terms of things not going wrong came into the room and assessed the experimental core competency against what was already there, found that it didn't match up like for like, found the plan to finish the work was too open-ended and killed it for 'not being already done'.

On the very same day, the same bank agreed to continue funding a programme building a smart fridge, running its own Kubernetes cluster and able to take payments for drinks taken out of said fridge through facial recognition.

Isn't that clever?

If you are trying to reconcile these two choices in terms of budget allocation or a coherent perception of risk, don't. Each decision was made in the context of how that particular team measures success. The core competency needed to be measured against 'things not going wrong'. The innovation idea is measured against 'projects engaging with new technologies that we can talk about'. If it ever succeeds enough to contemplate leaving the lab, it may find itself facing the same fate as the credit card programme.

Neither of these initiatives, you will notice, is measured in relative terms (we have this much money to achieve everything we need to do, so where do we put our money, time and effort) and neither is measured in terms of impact. On either client well-being or the bank's bottom line.

WE MEASURE FOR ACCOUNTABILITY BUT END UP REWARDING INACTION

Inside banks, we all learned the hard way that, if you want to deliver work with impact you have to do it in the body of the beast itself. It can't be done in an innovation department. It can't be done as a side project. Even if the ways of working of the main bank go against what you are trying to achieve in the first place. If it sounds mad, it is because it is.

The bank realises its ways of working get in the way of innovation. So it creates an innovation function, unshackled from the habits and burdens of old. That's not crazy in itself. If it's done as a way of 'buying time' while fixing the things that get in the way of innovation. But that's not what we do. The innovation department is created and then the body corporate considers its work done. Nothing changes in the main bank and when the innovation folks start trying to feed their findings and discoveries and creations to the main bank, they find that they are not treated as 'real', 'robust' or usable because they were created outside the ways of working and approval functions of the main bank.

Oh the fun we have.

That boils down to: let's create an agile, highly responsive infrastructure for ourselves but let's make sure we work in the most command-and-control way possible to get there. What could possibly go wrong with that?

A lot. A lot can and a lot has gone wrong with that in all the ways I have discussed above and many in-between.

And yet we are still inching forward and transformation work is progressing. Despite this mad, back-to-front way of working, we are making progress. More slowly than we need to exactly because of these obstacles that have nothing to do with what we are trying to achieve. They are par for the course. But not part of it: they are entirely unnecessary obstacles of our own making.

It is also important to stress that, to my unsurprised dismay, this was how banks approached their mid-COVID-19 'take stock' sessions and their subsequent 'this pandemic is not going away' 2022 planning sessions: treating the global pandemic as an unforeseen delaying factor triggering a key risk indicator that now has its own RAG status on the plan we were working to.

In some cases that meant a bit of a replan. In *every* case it meant logs and dashboards.

In no case (please call me if you have an outlier here, it would do my soul good to hear about it) did it mean a radical re-think of 'our role as a bank and the tools we need at our disposal in order to fulfil this role in a changing world'.

Too big. Too complex. Too naïve.

So back to the hamster wheel with you.

We have delivery commitments that need to be honoured even though the world is imploding. Every banker I spoke to during the pandemic said that their banks had generated a 'tolerance level' that they overlay on their KPIs allowing them to deliver 15% less of everything and not miss their performance targets. Let that sink in for a second.

Meanwhile, and since we know that PR works, every bank under the sun went on webinars and remote conferences and celebrated how well their teams are doing and how strong their digital capabilities are. All the while folks had to go into the office mid-pandemic because 'not enough laptops' (true story). People were being called back from retirement to hack interest changes on COBOL-based systems (also true story). And consumers received text messages saying 'yes we know you may be entitled to a mortgage holiday but please give us a few weeks to get the systems working and we will call you' (yes, also true story. But you knew that).

The legacy systems that had not been updated for all the reasons we have been looking at so far and all the reasons we will be looking at in the rest of this book, and the processes that hadn't been challenges for all the same reasons we are looking into, meant that rising to the challenge set by governments, regulators and, frankly, circumstances was going to be done the hard way: human effort, task-based project management, pyrrhic small-scale victories but no long-term re-think and cheery PR, in case anyone is watching. Trying to turn one of the most disruptive global events into a Gantt-chart symbol.

THE MYTH OF INEVITABILITY

I can hear you thinking it's human nature, to try and bring things to manageable proportions.

From myths of origin to your mum compulsively making gallons of chicken soup while your baby brother has a high fever because she's frantic with worry and that's the one thing she can control: nourishment.

And you would be right.

It is true. But it's not the full truth.

The truth is we always try to treat the world as if it were static. Ours to interact with. The entire history of modern banking has been one of comparative success and relative stability for the banks (less so for the consumers). The complex finance system as we know it took a long time coming, wobbled more than once, destroying human lives in its wake and was deemed (sometimes in exactly those words) 'too big to fail'.

So it is big, it has been largely unchanged and, for generations of bankers plotting their careers, it seemed shielded from oblivion. Sure, things had to change here and there and regulation was always constraining but, largely, the idea that a day would come when banks as we know them wouldn't exist was inconceivable for decades. That feeling of being *inevitable* created profound habits, including the ability to run from meeting-to-meeting knowing things will keep till you have the headspace to look at them. However long that may take.

The feeling of inevitability came with the belief that change would wait for you to be ready for it.

This may not be how life works, but it is how banking worked for a long time, and the fact that digital transformation is not playing by these rules is a bitter pill to swallow. And a departure from what is known.

> The idea that a day could come when banks as we know them wouldn't exist was inconceivable for decades. That feeling of being inevitable created profound habits, including the belief that change would wait for you to be ready for it.

In fact, for a long time, it was a fact that was simply not accepted as true. The digital work was seen as another stream, another project that had to fit into the world I am describing here. Only it won't. It is a phenomenon that will transform the world we are used to. Not fit neatly into it. This game was never static anyway and with digital transformation being THE agenda, *static* couldn't be further from the truth. It sounds obvious when I say it now, but it has not been obvious from within the banking institutions for a long time and, in many cases, still is not.

Technology is moving rapidly ahead in adjacent industries. Businesses, start-ups and scale-ups, are maturing rapidly without the bankers' participation. And so is the regulator. For all the reasons discussed above and some that we will address later on in this book, the incumbents who represent the vast majority of financial infrastructure and activity are not equipped for either this pace or this complexity. They can do *fast* and they can do *complex* but they can't do both at once without overhauling the way they work.

And this is the crux of the matter: they would rather not.

So the digital transformation work that banks have accepted is now inevitable, inside banks, is managed in the Old Way: set a goal, make a plan, treat the plan as gospel and if anything doesn't go according to plan … well … we can work through the night and weekend to close the gap in terms of our metrics; we can ignore it and focus on the good stuff; we can whitewash it; we can chastise the project manager or; if it's too big for any of those remedies, if it's COVID big, we can just replan as if it was just a blip in the matrix.

So much for agility.

Agile is not a software development methodology, boys and girls. It is a software development methodology *that* allows us to not try and answer all the questions when we know the least about everything and encourages us to learn each day, together, and apply our learnings immediately because that is what the learnings are for. Repeat after me: That is what learning is for. To be used. Ideally immediately. If you find out the building materials you are using when building your house are highly flammable, you don't carry on building because now that you started you are committed, while the rooms you just completed smoulder. You adapt. You learned a thing. And now you are doing better as a result.

> Agile is not a software development methodology. It is a software development methodology that allows us to not answer all questions when we know the least about everything and encourages us to learn each day, and apply our learnings immediately.

Only, not in banks. And why not? They have some of the smartest people in their respective markets, they have some of the best kit and they can afford stuff. Why can they not do this thing that pre-schoolers learn?

Because banking decision-makers – and, sadly, decision-makers in a lot of other industries – have somehow learned that big girls don't cry, boys of any sizes don't cry, plans need to be infallible and approvals are irreversible.

Am I exaggerating? Of course. But not by much.

HOW PLANNING GETS IN THE WAY
OF APPLIED LEARNING

You are probably tempted to skip to the next chapter by now, thinking, *I got it, we do planning in a way that gets in the way of results ... move on already. I know you get it.* But we are not ready to move on yet, so please stay with me. I will bang on about this a little bit longer because the impact is so profound that to eradicate it and really affect change, we need to address it in all its manifestations and insidious detail. So.

In banks we submit a plan. We get approval. We agree on KPIs. And then the KPIs become our gods.

The RAID logs, RAG statuses and updates.

Example:

Say you are changing your go-to market strategy for a particular product or segment.

You accept it will take a couple of years before you know if the new approach is working. You are ok with that. But you can't leave things unsupervised till then.

So what are some of the leading indicators we should be keeping an eye on, in order to have a sense of whether what we are doing is working? Numbers of sales pitches done under the new requirements? Looks like a solid thing to measure. Only if that's what you measure, the team that wants you to know they are trying hard will go for volume and send proposals that they never have a chance of winning to hit their targets.

So not that.

Conversion pace? How fast conversations and deals are moving through the funnel?

That's a nice one.

So what should the desired pace be?

We don't know, this is a new approach.

We can talk to industry experts and read books and apply prior knowledge but the truth is we don't know what the conversion rate should be.

Now, in a start-up you go a'right, let's keep an eye on it and see what emerges. We know this is important, let's work at getting smarter.

In a bank that kind of heresy means you can't close your OKR, KPI or goal-setting system at the predetermined date and it won't do, not least because if you don't play by the rules you won't get a bonus and you will get passed up for the next promotion cycle. So you agree on *something* to measure.

And once something becomes the thing you measure, it becomes the thing you work to, right or wrong. And the assumptions we made are no longer allowed to be fungible as the things we were trying to achieve become secondary to The Plan. And The Plan is not just a blueprint for teams to organise their work. It is how Management expect their 30' of head space to be used, with updates against The Plan. And it is how individuals inside the team expect to be rewarded at Year-End: in terms of their success against The Plan. And if that doesn't actually deliver against the purpose for which we were doing all this malarkey anyway, oh well. That was not in their KPI, it's above their pay-grade. Someone else is surely thinking about it.

Imagine what pernicious impact this has on the work or selecting and rolling out new technologies to support new business models. Imagine, for a second, how thoroughly self-sabotaging this well-intended set of practices is.

> The Plan is not just a blueprint for teams to organise their work. It is how Management expect their 30' of head space to be used and how individuals inside the team expect to be rewarded at Year-End.

And before you say, why do I care, let me remind you that all this matters immensely because all these folks who trip over their own feet while trying to plan for complicated, new work, manage your money. Your pension. Your mortgage. Your business loan and the sovereign wealth fund of your government.

Although 'FinTech' has made room for neo-banks and challengers, new providers of pensions, mortgages and lending, the staggering majority of people's money, loans, credit cards and savings are with traditional institutions. And that number rises sharply when you look at who finances and holds the funds of businesses and governments, who clears and settles all transactions, who syndicates loans. So *it matters* that banks should get with the programme. It matters a lot. And it matters to all of us.

So. Back to KPIs.

I am all for trying to impose order on a chaotic world. Business is not static. Humans are messy and trying to plan and measure is absolutely the right thing to do. That's not what I take exception with. What I have an issue with is *the way* we plan (when we know the least about a thing), the way we don't replan when we know more about the thing and what this does when it comes into contact with the behaviours outlined above. It is inevitable that for many an individual and a team, the net result is that more effort is going into appearing like we are in control rather than actually ... being in control. And this is where it all gets very interesting.

WHAT YOU ARE NOT DOING WHILE ACTING LIKE YOU ARE IN CONTROL

Have you ever considered what you are *not* doing while you are busy trying to look like you are in control? The banks' pretence of invincibility has worked well enough, long enough, don't get me wrong. But have you ever wondered what isn't happening while bank decision-makers are busy pretending it's all in hand and it will all stay in hand carrying on pretty much as we are? And yes, before you say it, *yes* new technologies are introduced, and people wear jeans to work. But none of that will ever be more than the sum of its parts until the fundamentals become negotiable. That's what we're discussing here. A shift in has occurred in our civilisation so profound that it changes economic models and social hierarchies and law and custom. And our organisations still try to treat it as largely a distribution opportunity. The 'digital' challenge being about channels. Spare me with the narrative of 'this is smaller than it seems and entirely under control'.

In fact, have you wondered what *isn't* happening while we are so busy trying to project-manage the advent of digital technologies without facing into the overall impact of said arrival?

The first thing that *isn't* happening is active learning. Because learning is vulnerable work. It starts with not knowing (on a good day) or being wrong (on an average day). Neither of those things plays well inside a bank hierarchy on *any* given day. Even less so during times of stress (bad quarterly results), strain (a plan not going to plan) or full-blown crisis (enter left: COVID). It is not unreasonable to want to appear in control, especially when a crisis is looming or raging. Confident leadership is important. We all know that. And banking is an industry where careers are built on expertise and authority.

> A shift in has occurred in our civilisation so profound that it changes economic models and social hierarchies, law and custom. And our organisations still try to treat it as, largely, a distribution opportunity.

Marry the two, and you have folks striving to look in control even when they are not. And it can be reassuring. But it is also highly likely to hinder a lot of the learning, change the questions away from what we should be answering.

And what would those be?

Can we retain a hierarchical view of the world given the highly egalitarian nature of digital interfaces? Are our international footprints creating a global poor underclass that is nobody's problem and everyone's responsibility? How do we serve a changing economy? How do we retain relevance? How do we safeguard agility in a world that may hit us with another COVID-sized puzzle before long?

Instead, we are limiting ourselves to the questions we feel comfortable answering.

How many committed projects can still be delivered after our re-forecasting? Should we review our offshoring strategy? Should we revise our budgets in line with the loss of income the last few weeks experienced?

The first set of questions is baffling. Scary. Open-ended. They are the problems you need to stay with before you answer them. They are also problems that may lead you to the realisation that you are not inevitable and all your planning gets in the way of your progress and survival.

So instead, we turn the big questions into *problems we live with* while asking questions we know we can answer. And now we look and feel in control.

The second thing that is happening is we start drinking our own Kool-Aid. While we are pretending to be in control and acting like the Process is our Shield of Invincibility (yes, the caps are meant to make it sound silly. And yet you know it's true.), we start believing our own storylines. We start believing that the game we are playing is won by answering some questions. And if you answer them well and deliver against the tasks you set yourselves, all will be well. That is the ballgame. That is the test. That is what being in control looks like. Only saying it doesn't make it so. Choosing happy doesn't guarantee you a happy ending. It is just a statement of intent about how you live despite what the world throws at you. As an organisation, we pah-pah choosing happy and yet we try to Gantt-chart our way to the happy ending. Doesn't work that way.

How does it work, I hear you ask?

If you strip it back down to basics, everything we do in business (and that applies to any business) should be in pursuit of relevance. Revenue, profit and return on equity is how we measure that continued relevance. Is the thing I do/make/sell/produce/enact something my intended audience still wants to consume?

It is that simple.

Sure it has complexity on top but strip it down and you have the most basic supply and demand dynamics. Everything you do is in pursuit of maintaining and increasing demand. So the whole ballgame is relevance. The things customers come back to you for. And believe it or not, being in control is not one of them. It's a hygiene factor. But it is not all that you think it is. And being invincible isn't even on the list. Especially when appearing in control and pretending to be invincible is done at the expense of all the things that challenge your relevance in a changing economy.

> Everything you do is in pursuit of maintaining and increasing demand. So the whole ballgame is relevance. The things customers come back to you for. And believe it or not, being in control is not one of them.

Habits run deep, so deep that sometimes they become self-perpetuating in a way that isn't just self-sustaining but it becomes bigger than the business itself. But if you cut out the noise, relevance is what business is about.

Relevance is what the digital transformation journeys we started were about. It was not and is not about the digital capabilities themselves but about what they enable us to do in terms of building and asserting business relevance in a changing world. Relevance is what the conversation should be in boardrooms the world over as we come up for air post the first wave of COVID-19. Relevance is the ball game, even though the goalposts just keep moving on us. Get used to that. That's here to stay. You don't get to play the game you were playing before, just because you want to. And you don't get to fast-forward to the end by changing the size of the task to something you feel fit to face. And you most definitely don't get to win because you found the courage to play or defined some metrics that make you look like a champ. But unless you do find the courage to play, learn, adapt and answer the question actually being asked rather than the one you are happy answering, then you don't stand a chance of winning at all. And that is exactly what you are *not* doing while you are busy looking in control.

SO WHAT CAN EACH OF US DO ABOUT ALL THIS?

Creating Healthy Habits Inside Your Organisation Starts with You

Your descriptions of the endemic counter-productive behaviours resonate, I hear you say, and it's all good and well and true, and we agree, but so what? Not all of us get to hold the pen when it comes to plans and targets and approvals and agreeing with all that is being described here isn't going to do us much good if we work in organisations that set the tone just described.

Which is absolutely true but yet again, and this time thankfully for all of us, not the whole truth.

Because such behaviours are ubiquitous and cascade in ways big and small and we all have a chance to call them out for what they are and maybe challenge them through making a change without fuss but with consistency in our own behaviour. Doing so does not constitute innovation as such, but it will shield it where it is needed, protect and nourish it.

Part of how you nourish innovation is by creating time for it, nurturing a culture of learning from past mistakes, challenging 'the way we've always done things'. Accepting something that is counter-productive just because it is the way we do things is, actually, one of the earliest and biggest obstacles to innovation. And that is because it undermines the ability to believe that 'different' is possible, potentially beneficial and, anyway, *allowed*. So. Shielding your team from endless meetings or the transitional planning cycle may not be an act of rebellion, but it is an act of applied critical thinking and, as such, it is an act of resistance to the things that stand in the way of progress, innovation and that feeling of your soul being crushed by the grey establishment when you walk into the office every day.

There is another reason, other than getting the muscles of thinking beyond what is in front of you working. And that is the simple fact that time is the one thing we will never get back. The only thing we will only ever have less of. Is *this* (whatever it is you are being asked to spend time on) a good use of a resource we will never have more of, as individuals, as a team, as a company?

If not, then change it.

BANKERS BEHAVING BADLY IN THE WILD

Exhibit C: When Habits Breed Structures

Paper Monsters and RFPs

I know I have already harped on about how the way we plan and measure combined with the way we fragment our attention are fundamentally not conducive to learning, solving complicated problems or adapting to external stimuli in an agile and timely manner. I have harped on about it and I know you get it.

But.

I am not quite done yet. Because it is important to digest the fact that, the ubiquitousness of all this leads to structures and secondary behaviours developing to ensure the organisation makes decisions, despite it all. Decisions that are critical for survival but can't be made in the normal course of things because of how we have set ourselves up. If it sounds counter-intuitive, it's because it is.

So we create structures around our habits, rather than changing the habits, and institutionalise decision-making by committee, having already normalised that executive attention span is brief and furtive.

Yes, this is the stuff of horror movies. It is also how we do RFPs inside big organisations.

Did you get a little shudder of horror there, just by thinking of the process? Because you should. It is the stuff of nightmares.

Now I should confess that I have never worked in procurement. But I have dealt with RFPs all my life and from both sides of the table. I have sat in teams in many a bank that needed a thing the bank couldn't build themselves, so we had to go out to market for it and, of course, we did so in a way that took twice as long as learning and then building the thing ourselves would have done and 10 times as long as it would take our partners to build the thing if we went out there and described what we were trying to achieve and then asked people to prove themselves in a competitive POC.

And I know that because, in desperation, one year I asked the COO of the bank I worked in at the time, to let me do exactly that. Instead of an RFP for an RPA (robotics process automation) solution, we would engage three vendors to solve the same problem as part of a competitive, no-charge POC. They wouldn't pitch for the work. They would do the same 4-week POC in parallel instead of a 6-month procurement process. We would learn, we would see things in action and we would have proof points not problem statements. Then we would choose. Based on the things we learned in the process of doing the POC and the actual experience of working with the vendors.

It will never work but go for it said the COO.

It worked.

The vendors went for it. The teams learned a lot so, by the time we started the work in earnest, we knew a lot more than when we wrote the RFP and we were delivering against our first milestones before the original RFP process would have been completed.

Now ask me if the bank changed the way they did vendor selection on the strength of that evidence.

Like hell they did.

I have sat in committees inside a variety of banks, reviewing RFPs, both the drafting of and the selection post the drafting. So much reviewing. And when I have not worked for banks but sold to them, I have been at the receiving end of 2,500-line spreadsheets as a tech vendor and worked through them cursing my fate, especially knowing what I know about how RFPs come to be and how they are read once received.

And here is what I know. And here is where we are all complicit in perpetuating the bad behaviours this whole chapter is about. RFP processes are most often about risk-aversion and internal politics. They are about risk-mitigation and responsibility evasion. They are about creating a process whereby, if things go wrong, it is nobody's fault, *really*. They are about the fact that these two department heads over there are not aligned and, rather than working that out, the organisation uses the RFP process as a way of creating a time-box for resolution. Forcing them to talk and play nice in the context of a committee and an RFP. Or institutionalising the problem.

Ask me about that time that Channels and IT (yes they were different departments with different reporting executives) didn't manage to solve the issue they were fighting over (that boiled down to 'who gets to be responsible for this thing we need to build') and we ended up having two separate payments gateway *and* payments transformation programmes resulting in two RPFs I could barely tell apart and a bunch of vendors tearing their hair out, unable to understand what they were missing as they were trying to submit two differentiated proposals for two things that had different RFPs, different budgets and yet looked … sorta, kinda … the same?

And the selection committees sitting back to back with largely overlapping members going, 'wait, which one is this one'?

Don't ask me, you know the answer already.

We didn't even award both RFPs to the same vendor, making them rich but hacking through our own dysfunction Gordian Knot style. That would be way too simple.

THE TRUTH ABOUT RISK-AVOIDANCE IN PROCUREMENT

If you ever wondered why a new set of stakeholders appeared 3 weeks into a selection process or why there were 17 different people on the client side during your demo, now you know. If you ever wondered why there are three seemingly identical questions in the RFP, some questions that don't seem relevant at all and at least one

> RFPs are Frankenstein documents made of recycled parts of old RFPs, watered-down requirements and vague business objectives written by people who didn't fully understand them and reviewed by people who didn't read through everything.

question that seems to assume some technological advancements of the last 10 years have not actually happened, your answer is RFPs are almost always Frankenstein documents. They are more often than not made of recycled staple parts of old RFPs, watered-down requirements and vague business objectives written by people who didn't fully understand them and reviewed by people who couldn't be bothered to read through all the questions assuming someone else above (or below) their pay-grade had it all in hand; plus I am sure it will be fine, they thought, as long as our key questions are included it doesn't really matter what else is in there.

Only it does.

Because the vendor has no idea what is important but badly phrased, recycled but polished to great clarity over the years, trivial but written by a pedant or what. Word to the wise, by the way. If you are a vendor and an RFP reads well, is smooth, focused and doesn't feel like body parts stitched together, your competitor wrote it. You are dead in the water.

Is there no chance that you are dealing with a procurement department that has its act together, I hear you ask. Of course there is. In fact, I saw a decent, coherent, to-the-point RFP not so long ago. It was a marvel. I wanted to frame it. I will be telling generations to come about it. Like the duck-billed platypus, unlikely and yet possible. Which is what makes your garden-variety RFP so irritating and our duty to resist from our very own desks each day so poignant. Because a bad way of choosing tech partners is pervasive when the alternative is both possible and infinitely better.

I have another bitter truth for you, if you are a vendor.

Nobody on the bank side reads a full RFP end to end. Not when they are preparing it. Not when you submit it. People will review their bits. The bits they care about. What, to them, are the important bits. Only you have no idea what those bits are, and they are often not the bits you may think. Incidentally, if you are a vendor wondering how you write a document nobody will ever properly read, you won't like the answer. You answer it in sequence. You answer it in full. You answer it like every question is the only one anyone will ever read. Because it might be.

How do you produce a good RFP, may be a better question. And it has a short answer. You don't. You go back. Reshape procurement, the process, the risk matrix, the articulation of business value and your sordid office politics that play their own shadow theatre in your document and you shake up the review committee structure. You ask yourself the same questions we have been going back to, like a good innovator or at least a protector of creative thinking, only this time in a bigger scene. You ask: what are we trying to achieve and is the way we are going about it sensible? Do you really need a committee? Do you really need answers to 3,800 questions to make a choice? Do you know what you are trying to achieve, why, by when and at what price – monetary, opportunity cost and risk acceptance?

Do you?

If you do, that's the benchmark for choosing.

If you don't, then the RFP can't solve this for you, not even if you add a new set of 7,000 questions.

Go back. Answer the questions that matter. You will find knowing what you intend to do with a piece of kit makes choosing said piece infinitely easier.

Then, once you've achieved a small set of miraculous and much-needed changes, you back out to the market with your ask – and yes sure it can look like an RFP, if it must – and remember to treat your vendors with respect while you are at it.

Respect their time and intelligence, because one of them will be chosen to be your partner soon and you are teaching them what acceptable behaviour looks like by the way you treat them.

So, do all that and then make a choice that meets your needs and accept responsibility for your business vision and the choices you made to get you there.

You can do that and still satisfy risk and compliance by the way.
You can resist.

Bad habits and bad behaviours are perpetuated because people either engage with them or don't call them out when they see them. So don't take on the world all at once. Start from where you are. Challenge the process. If you are in need of a tech partner for your part of the business, resist going down a paper monster route and chart a path that actually aligns purpose to utility.

Start believing you can take a stand against the silly no matter how big it is. And it is big. And some of it is sinister. But the reality is the bad behaviour won't stop on its own. And we can't wait for the people doing it to come to their senses.

The only thing necessary for the triumph of evil is for good people to do nothing (it's a famous quote but it's not clear who first said it, some say Edmund Burke, some say JS Mill, I say it is its own truth, whoever may have said it).

This is a chapter about bankers behaving badly and although a lot of it is bad habits perpetuated by good people, let's face it, it's not all that innocent. So before we move on, let's address the genuine bad behaviour that goes beyond bad habits and inertia.

BANKERS BEHAVING BADLY IN THE WILD

Exhibit D: The Cycle of Aggressive Conformity

It may feel counter-intuitive to spend this long, this early in the book speaking about bad habits. And yet. They are what held us back before. They are what holds us back now. They are insidious, pervasive and extremely persistent. You may already get the picture and wish I would move on, but I'm afraid I am not quite done yet as this is the single biggest part of the problem we are trying to solve, the biggest obstacle to change. The behaviours, that is. But equally big a problem is the fact that we accept these behaviours as part of the furniture in this industry.

Time to stop.

If the last 15 years of transformation have been about anything, they have been about breaking the cycle of self-perpetuating assumptions of the 'it has always been thus' variety. We just haven't gotten to human conduct yet.

And it is time. Digitisation is just the means and catalyst and toolkit for a transition to a new socio-economic paradigm. Digital transformation has been about enabling our industry to compete in a digitally enabled economy, where the tools are the means to an end. And the end is participating in brand new economics. And the obstacle is *not* how proficient we are in using the tools, that bit is teachable even though, arguably, our industry is not. Teachable.

The obstacle isn't even how well we understand the economic models of platformification and digital distribution. We don't, by the way. But we can learn. If we are open to it.

But that's where the rubber hits the road.

The obstacle is our teachability, our attention span, our aggressive one-up-manship culture. The habits that block creativity, vulnerability and experimentation. Because it doesn't just affect our industry through pig-headed action and petulant inaction. It also affects it through *reaction*.

> The obstacle to transformation is not what we know about technology or platform economics. The obstacle is our teachability, our attention span, our industry's aggressive one-up-manship culture.

Picture this. It's early 2007 and I walk into a small meeting room in a large bank in London. It's a routine terms negotiation for a contract renewal. Or at least, that is what it was meant to be. Until I walked in and closed the door behind me and turned to face a man who looked deeply uncomfortable at my presence.

Where are the guys? He said. Cutting code, I said. It's just me big boy.

Obviously I didn't call him that.

But the rest is pretty much verbatim. We proceeded to have the meeting. The contract was renewed. A couple of points that needed raising were raised. We signed. We even shook hands. But the next day I was asked, by profoundly amused colleagues of above-mentioned man (let's call him Skippy), 'what did you do to Skippy? He said you were one tough cookie'. More giggling.

I never did find out, what I had done to Skippy, that was simultaneously so funny and so traumatic. This cookie thing, though, has been a recurring theme. For years, with every promotion, any new project, any high-stakes meeting, someone would look at me and go, after a moment's pause, 'ah you'll be alright, you are a tough cookie'.

Aren't you a bit young for this job? I hope you are a tough cookie. This is a hard gig, you've got. For your sake, you'd better be a tough cookie. You are *his* boss? Ah, you must be a tough cookie. Oh you got a promotion? Well, you are a tough cookie. Innovation? In this place? You better be a tough cookie. You worked in the Gulf? But you are a *girl*.... What a tough cookie. And my absolute favourite: a woman! How novel, but you are a tough cookie. You will be fine.

I AM NOT SURE WHO NEEDS TO HEAR THIS BUT *I AIN'T NO COOKIE*

What do these phrases even mean?

Cookies are by definition soft. A tough cookie is a terrible cookie. So what exactly are we telling someone, when we tell them they are a tough cookie? That they will make it through a situation that is expected to be hard for them by dint of being, unexpectedly, not what it says on their tin? Surviving by not being true to their soft cookie nature?

For many years, as the only woman in the room, I braced my shoulders and dealt with it with the distaste and attention it deserved. Both short-lived and limited. I assumed, for a long time, that it was a phrase people wheeled out to every woman they saw doing what they perceived to be a man's job and doing it well enough to not be easy to dismiss, enough to make the status quo defenders uncomfortable. For every person promoted before their hair went grey. For everyone championing new ideas and advocating change.

And I believed, for years, that it is meant to be insulting. It is meant to be demeaning. It is meant to make you feel like a circus freak. Yet the truth was I didn't care. There are few people whose opinion truly matters to me and they all have deep affection for baked goods. The rest can say what they like.

But as I get older, I am beginning to think there is something insidious about this kind of language and, although we will get to the demographic components of these behaviours in the next chapter, I want to stay with that dismissive language a bit here. Because it gets in the way of the dialogues we need to have to do the job. It creates tension and division and it comes laden with assumptions about what the industry is, what it expects, what is good, normal and likely to succeed. It paints a picture of a reality that is impossible to ignore. And it matters. Because language forges the context in which we operate and as part of the 'what can I do about all this'. I say you can start noticing it and calling it out.

WE HAVE NORMALISED SNEERING AT OTHERNESS. TIME TO STOP

Seriously and back to the cookie business.

Why do I need to be tough? Why might I not be fine? What do all these implicit statements, unspoken and universally understood, say about how we perceive our own industry? What are we actually *not* saying, in the second before we call someone a tough cookie?

Banking is an aggressive industry. And it can be a mean industry. There are no prizes for playing nice, there are no prizes for nurturing others and offering constructive feedback and no-strings-attached cooperation. Although in recent years, concerted efforts are being made to engineer an alternative industry-wide professional ethos, the road ahead is long and success to-date is patchy to say the least. So when we look at someone who is about to go forth into a meeting, into a new role, into a highly competitive setting what we are really doing is scanning them for vulnerabilities.

Your youth is a weakness. Your skin colour, your height, your face, your gender, your accent, the pitch of your voice, your demeanour and your sense of humour could all mark you out as prey. We scan for the things that may become targets, the things that may get the bloodhounds sniffing. We assess the size of the possible attack – some direct artillery fire, some stealth ambush and undercover tactics – and the ability of the warrior we are sending forth to withstand it. And decide that it will suck, but they will be fine. They are stronger than the nonsense that will be thrown at them. Or maybe we are surprised that they are, after all, stronger than the nonsense, despite the 'handicap' of not being middle aged and already there. Or whatever the baseline is.

So we learn to brace our shoulders. And we teach others to do the same. We know that being tough is required. Even more significantly, we learn that being tough is valued. So we toughen up. We learn to sniff out the nonsense and deal with it swiftly and decisively. We learn to move forward despite it all. But that is a terrible lesson to learn. Because it perpetuates the nonsense. And being tough becomes a laudatory remark. It becomes a badge of honour. You resigned! Why? I thought you were a tough cookie. You didn't find that meeting constructive? Why, aren't you a tough cookie? You really want to kick up a fuss over *that*? I had you down as a tough cookie.

It is very easy to lose sight of what is important. The reasons why the new employer was a better proposition; the ways in which colleague interactions could be improved; areas of organisational culture, operational efficiency and performance management that could be re-thought. Surviving in a hostile environment becoming its own reward is the surest way of perpetuating said environment. If being a tough cookie is so important the nonsense is left unchallenged because it now insidiously becomes

Surviving in a hostile environment becoming its own reward is the surest way of perpetuating said environment. If being a tough cookie is so important the nonsense is left unchallenged because it now insidiously becomes a test to separate the wheat from the chaff.

a test to separate the wheat from the chaff. If being a tough cookie is key, then we need to test ergo there is a retroactively-found purpose for all the bad behaviour, all tied up on a bow. Doesn't it help you be a tough cookie and demonstrate said tough cookie-ness, after all? Try bringing innovation into this environment. Try thinking out loud. Try being different. Try being young.

WHAT IS THE PRICE YOU ARE *NOT* WILLING TO PAY?

So in the spirit of making a change from where you are without leading a rebellion (yet, that comes in a later chapter, I am still warming you up to it) I say: how about starting with finding the price you, as a human being with your values and principles whatever they are, are *not* willing to pay.

Find the price *you* are *not* willing to pay. And don't pay it.

The answer is not the same for all of us as individuals. The playground bully is happy in this context. But surely that's not our moral beacon of choice. Many of us find our way, despite thinking it's all a little counterproductive. A little destructive. But many don't feel it is worth it. Many don't feel being a tough cookie is its own reward at all. Many exit. Not because they can't hack it. But because they don't want to, because to them the price tag is not worth it. So, off they go to do something else and we are left thinking them unworthy cookies.

And nothing changes.

And we lose talent and diversity and empathy because, hey this is what it takes to survive in the industry. As if somehow the ridiculous cultural tropes were intrinsically linked to innate abilities in mathematics or engineering or governance or sales.

For me, the price I didn't think worth paying was becoming as hard as some of the people around me. Sure, be tough. Take no shit. Take no prisoners. Just, whatever you do, don't harden. That's the price truly not worth paying. For me as an individual. Take a moment to find yours. Whatever it is. And just don't pay it. These are battles worth fighting, trust me.

But for the organisations we are in? For the body corporate? The price not worth paying, surely, should be the exact price we are currently paying: ensuring that we beat empathy out of our new recruits, ensuring we teach them to treat every encounter as a cockfight. Teaching them that, until you are part of the furniture, you need to fight for your right to be here, you need to earn your stripes, *by being tough*. Not doing good work. Not helping us get better. Just being tough. And the more different you or the thing you are trying to do is, the tougher you need to be. And while you are toughening up over there, we will sit over here and try to understand why all these soft cookies out there in the open market keep getting user-centric design and human-centric service right while we suck at it. Paying the highest price of all in the hard currency of lost competitiveness.

It's time to break the cycle of nonsense.

Put all this acquired toughness to good use.

By the way …

If you are nodding because the tough cookie thing was used against you and it sucked, but you have called someone 20 years your junior a snowflake, and bemoaned their entitlement because they challenged the way they are treated or the direction of travel Big Boss Man set out as gospel, then you have learned nothing and you are becoming part of the problem because you forgot that empathy may not be valued in banking but it is valuable for life and your tough cookie is their snowflake. Don't be that guy.

That's what you can do from your desk today and every day.

Don't be that guy you hated when the shoe was on the other foot. As advice goes it's simple to give and hard to follow because it requires consistency and humility, but there you have it. Consistency and humility is key to learning, and learning is key to innovation so although I am pointing out a million ways that we need to adjust they all ultimately point to the same place: creating an environment that is better for our humans to bring their ideas to make our business better.

> Consistency and humility is key to learning, and learning is key to innovation and both are key to creating an environment that is better for our humans to bring their ideas that will make our business better.

Your results are good, I was told once by a boss, but your team looks too happy (true story). You need to control them more tightly. You need to toughen them up. He even tightened his hands around his own throat, in a flesh noose, to demonstrate the point he was trying to make. Weirdo? Only because he said it out loud. Otherwise he was working to a theme.

Of course the truth is, I didn't *need* to do any of that. He wanted me to, sure. He wanted and expected more tough cookies in his image. He wanted to see their shoulders braced. He wanted to see aggression and anger and over-worked irritation killing creativity, teachability and their attention span. Like true bankers.

But that was a price I was not pre-pared to pay. And when it came to the nonsense ahead, he found I was one tough cookie. I knew it had to be good for something in the end. And I guess that's my ask of you, before we get to full-blown rebellion. If you are a tough cookie, because, how else would you have made it this far, use that tough cookiness to shield people from the nonsense. It is self-perpetuating and not good for much beyond that. Use your own knowledge of the game to shield people from the lessons you know were not worth the learning.

> Use your own knowledge of the game to shield people from the lessons you know were not worth the learning.

THE CLOSET OF SHAME

There are many ways of using your knowledge to help those coming after you.

Some entail calling out and stopping bad behaviour as discussed above. But there are less confrontational ways of making a change. In fact, one of the most powerful ones, especially as we are striving to create learning organisations that can innovate and create and reflect in a changing world, is getting rid of the closet of shame.

And before I go any further I feel compelled to say that although I am no longer a banker, I work with banks. And, hand on heart, I am not sure if I will ever fully *not be a banker*. It's a world I understand deeply and have come to care about both because I get how it impacts life and because I can see how to fix it, and therefore fix it I must. It's a space that makes sense to me, with all its failings and foibles. It's the industry that made me who I am and the cause I come back to time and again. And if I castigate, it is because I care. And if I flag its shortcomings, I do not consider myself outside looking in and making light. Far from it. Everything I flag, I want to fix, not mock. And nothing more than the closet of shame, an idea that isn't even mine.

It came from a former colleague, Bill, who had a sharp wit and a soothing sense of humour on a bad day. Well. Every day, to be fair. But it was most needed on a bad day. And we had been having a bad day. I can't even recall why. The details are lost in the decade between that conversation taking place and now and the multitudes of times the same circumstances have transpired since.

Are you a banker? Then this one is familiar.

A mistake is made. It can be a small one or a huge one. It can be a deliberate political manoeuvre or a genuine miscalculation. It may be that a person was given responsibility for a big deliverable and it is really not working out but nobody is willing to call it out. It could be a glaring error (like that bank I once worked for that forgot to accrue contractor pay for the month of May and would rather delay all projects by a month than go up the food chain and admit the boo-boo). It could be miscalculations in estimates, complexity, dependencies or you name it. It could be the height of stupidity or a minor oversight. It doesn't matter. Both happen all the time. What matters is what happens next and our place in it.

So that thing that I genuinely can't remember had happened and I am on the phone to Bill. He can't fix it any more than I can and, although he is as disappointed as me, he is resigned to it all.

Meanwhile, I am furious.

And why am I furious? Because that thing, whatever it was, had happened before. It was entirely avoidable and would have been avoided if only we had talked about it and learned from it the time before, and the time before that, when the exact same thing had transpired. That person doing a terrible job at stakeholder management has actually driven three more projects into the rocks of misaligned expectations. Why are we acting surprised? Why are we using the same estimation tools that didn't serve every other time we used them? Why did we repeat the same mistakes in the same way? Why can't we learn?

Because of the closet of shame, said Bill.

Everything that goes wrong in a bank, big or small, gets put neatly away in the closet of shame. Don't get me wrong. Consequences are real and, for big mistakes, financial repercussions, fines and folks losing their jobs are not unheard of. But even then, subsequent reflection is minimal.

The organisational learning non-existent. Because, once the dust settles, the incident is put in the closet of shame never to be talked about again. Never to be learned from. Or not quite. We actually do learn. But we learn all the wrong things. The things that will help us navigate the world I have been describing for the last few pages. We learn that the closet exists and therefore you take things out of it at your own peril: if you have ever mentioned past failings in a big meeting and were enveloped by the awkward silence in the meeting room you know what I mean.

If you want to know what is actually inside the closet of shame, don't ask in the meeting room, don't ask by the water cooler. Don't ask in the pub, don't be daft, that only happens in movies. Ask on plane rides and train journeys (the in-between places where everything is possible), ask during time out of time moments when you will receive an answer human to human, not colleague-to-colleague. But be careful not to use that knowledge and betray the confidence. For the unwritten rule is that we know of the closet but do not speak of what is in it.

Only the non-bankers are laughing by now.

Because they know this is true. And they also know there is one more truth we all quietly learn in this process.

───────────

THE SPACE BETWEEN ACCOUNTABILITY AND DENIABILITY

We learn that responsibility and accountability are slippery things and if you retain deniability, if you produce enough paperwork to show due process, if you have a risk log and close your Jira tickets, you may fuck up, fail at the work and still person-

> To make sure the learning is passed on is not an act of rebellion. But it is an act of resistance that, done consistently, will create a clearing where talent can thrive.

ally triumph. We know that there are tools and paper trails that can protect you and consign your failures, should those occur, directly to the closet. And although nobody sets out to fail, everyone protects themselves just in case. That's why half your life as a banking junior is spent filling out templates and producing documents that have no purpose: no actual usefulness and no apparent use. They may be apocryphal but the closet is real and the survivors know what they are doing. That's why the 6-week build for the widget mentioned earlier had to go to the bottom of an inexplicable queue. It was being closet-proofed.

As you grow and learn the skill of creating a project plan, and pre-agreeing KPIs and milestones, and communication cadence models and risk logs, you realise *nobody is trying to arm the team to do the work through these tools and artefacts.* That comes after, if it comes at all. And you know what I am going to say here: to use that knowledge to protect the team, to make sure the work comes and to make sure the learning is passed on is not an act of rebellion. But it is an act of resistance that, done consistently, will eventually create a clearing where talent can thrive without spending all its creative energies, all this effort, all this work, all this toil on a possible one-way ticket to the closet should things get bad.

Failure isn't talked about if it's neatly wrapped in logs and reports, updates and Gantt charts.

So what if we never learn to estimate?

So what if we never learn how to measure performance in ways that will, god forbid, improve it? So what if we never give people a chance to fall, get up and learn from the process? We have learned that all of those things are dangerous and safety only lies in the closet of shame. And the reason for that is that anything you say, can and will be used against you. It's sad but it's true. Although I have met incredibly supportive colleagues, bosses and mentors in my years as a banker, life inside a bank is spent mostly dodging bullets and deflecting poisoned arrows. Internally launched in an endless nonsensical battle for resources, airtime and supremacy that may turn into currency at bonus, promotion or redundancy time. You don't know when you are going to need it. And the old hands play a deft game. As a newbie all this is above your head. But the time comes when you start to rise and the surest sign of impeding success is that the missiles start pointing at you. A dubious honour and one that feels deeply personal at first. Then you learn.

You learn to hate neither the player nor the game. You learn that a good boss is a shield. You learn to become a shield for your people. You learn that trust is a different kind of currency inside a big bank, and a constantly appreciating one. And you learn about the unspoken truces and the battle-ready mountains of paper that surround the closet of shame. Just in case. You know that if you fail (and come on, you will, in ways big and small, you will because only those who don't try don't fail) there are two paths: the door, or the closet of shame for your misdeed. It's not a pardon. It's a polite 'we shall not speak of this again'. If you try for the third path of 'let's talk and learn and reflect' you will find arrows galore pointed at your head: because nobody fails alone and nobody wants to join you in your Quixotic quest for self-reflection.

So we learn.

We learn from our mistakes. We learn who to trust. We learn how to protect ourselves in order to live to fight another day. We learn how to dodge bullets and work around assumptions and sacred cows. We learn who we can count on and who is waiting to pounce before the closet of shame does its job, when things are still raw and it's fair game to use them against you. We learn all this, and it is useful. What we don't learn is how to estimate bloody better. How to support that project manager develop and not watch the same chaos unfold each time she's at the helm. How to have checks in place so that, if a junior working late into the night forgets to drag the month tab 12 clicks on his spreadsheet and sleepily only goes as far as 11, the whole division doesn't down tools for a month because nobody picked up on the error, and how embarrassing is that?

Before you suggest it, yes banks do retros.

And they are sad affairs and a dangerous placebo in cahoots with the closet of shame. Bank retros involve dancing around elephants in rooms and flagging things like 'we should talk more, email less', 'we should have involved Jane earlier', 'we should have had a coffee machine in the project room', and 'we should have pre-agreed holidays to align to the skills matrix so that Joel didn't go away on honeymoon when we most needed him'. All probably true. All probably beside the point that probably would have entailed a conversation about departmental politics delaying approvals, the fact that releases are timed by people who have not been told the 1980s are over, the fact that some tech choices were made that are no longer fit for purpose but who's going to tell the CTO that? The fact that we missed things. Were wrong about assumptions. But now we know. And what we know is uncomfortable because it involves changing a lot. And having hard conversations about people's styles and personalities and actual commitment. The things that can really make or break a project. The things we don't talk about because we know it is above the pay-check of the people in the room to fix and because it's no skin off our nose, right? We won't even be working as a team in this guise on the next piece of work so what's the point? Plus we have probably told our boss over a drink and now it's his problem.

Only he really doesn't feel that way. It is not a problem for him.

Not really.

He didn't lose sleep over it. He didn't feel its consequences on his skin like you did and nor will he suffer from re-living it next sprint. Your boss will protect you from yourself and not let you flag and fight this. He will let it go the way of the closet and look after your career.

LEARNING TO LEARN FROM OUR MISTAKES, ONE TEAM AT A TIME

How do you break the cycle? In a bank?

I am not sure you can to be honest. But I hope I am wrong. You can definitely widen and broaden and stretch the cycle. By protecting your teams, by retaining and sharing some of the knowledge without making a big thing about it, in a way that would trigger a witch hunt or a search for a scape goat. You can make it so that people don't have to learn all this from scratch, on their own, each time.

Knowledge is power. Only if you use it. So use it.

Don't file it away for the opportune moment, don't leverage it for political gain: just share it.

And outside a bank?

In our efforts to build and create technical solutions and culture wedges to help the banking industry from our hipster offices? How do we ensure this doesn't happen, because we are not immune. It is human nature to want to let mistakes be forgotten. It is human nature to try and protect yourself from potential blame. It is human nature to see something going wrong and try and put it at someone else's feet. It is human nature and it is entirely, totally and irredeemably damaging.

So how do you stop it? Seriously, DM me, call me, send a courier pigeon. I want to hear your solutions. Here are mine.

Unless another person has been hurt, upset or in any way emotionally involved, any mistake big or small is mine as much as the person's who made it.

I am the boss, right? My team. Their success is my success, no? Right. So are the mistakes. And on a fundamental level, they are. Errors of omission or commission, bad behaviour or genuine fuck-ups, they are my responsibility and my fault as much as the perpetrators'. For missing them, if nothing else. And mine is the responsibility to solve things.

Second. It doesn't matter who did it. Who broke it. Who didn't think about it. Whose idea this was. Who should have been keeping an eye on it. Unless it's malicious. Unless someone did something destructive or hurtful on purpose. Unless someone was hurt in the process, never ever ever ask who. Ask *what now*, *what next* and how we will prevent this from happening again. Ask how do we fix and how do we learn from this. Do not seek to blame. It won't help with the solution and it will lead your team by example in a way that just perpetuates all the habits we are trying to break. For this very reason, equally, do not permit blame. Even when people are potentially right. Even if they are conceivably notionally right. The minute your team start pointing fingers at each other and say he did or didn't, she could but hasn't, is your moment to act.

You are what you tolerate.

And if you tolerate that, your own closet of shame is not far behind.

In our team, when something goes wrong, we roll up our sleeves and say, 'this is a fine mess mate, how do I help?'. And when things are no longer on fire, we talk about how we can do better. Together. Because that is how we work and how we mess up and how we fix things. And maybe every problem is fresh and we can't learn all that much from our errors. So be it. We will at least have learned how to have each other's back. How to pull together. How to be a team. And that, is everything. Or would be, if we made it a principle and a mantra and a mission. But we don't, not at an industry-wide level. We pay lip service to talent, we pay lip service to humans and then treat them in all the ways I have described here and create an environment inhospitable to dialogue, learning and creativity. And then we wonder why innovation is a department and not a way of life inside banks.

The answer lies with people, habits and environments more than it does with tools, technologies and office furniture. And in the next chapter we will delve deeper on the question of talent by focusing on the talent we often exclude. This topic is usually branded 'inclusion' or 'diversity' and white men may feel 'ah here we go, this one is not for me'. Wrong. It is absolutely, *also* for you, both in the ways it may affect you even though you may not think it does, and in ways you can help affect change.

We are all about the actionable advice here.

So please read on.

CALL TO ACTION CHEAT SHEET

1. Tech change starts with people. It also dies at their feet. So start with people. Stay focused on the people.
2. You can't solve new problems with old solution kits, old tools or the behaviours that caused them. The change needs to start in the solving, it won't just appear when the solution is ready. The way you go about making change happen has to be part of the change.
3. Make time to think and protect your team's time to think. Complicated work cannot be done in 30' intervals.
4. Be careful what you measure: it defines what's important.
5. Resist the 'way we've always done things' if it makes no sense, if it is counter-productive, if it is not fit for purpose.
6. When you see bad behaviour: call it out. Do not join in. Show by word and deed that there is another way: that better is both possible and expedient.

4

Painting by Numbers: Diversity, Innovation and Why Lip Service Won't Move the Needle

SNEAK PREVIEW

If you are thinking 'she's a woman, of course she will come to gender before long', stop.

If you are thinking, this is the zeitgeist and everybody pays lip service to inclusion these days, stop.

If you are thinking, I am a man, this chapter is not for me, don't.

This chapter is exactly the opposite of all this.

Diversity of thought is how we get new ideas. How we stop doing more of the same. And yet 'diversity' and 'innovation' suffer the same insidious fate inside our organisations.

If you find some of this chapter uncomfortable ....

Good.

It means we are getting somewhere.

This is a chapter about diversity.

But not the way you normally think about it.

It is also a chapter about inclusion.

But not as a tick-box exercise, and not as a lament against white men.

And equally not as an act of charity from them to the rest of us.

This chapter will, yes, be a bit about women and a bit about class and a bit about race, it will mostly be about corporate arrogance and how it kills creativity and innovation by discouraging or antagonising difference. And this is a problem, as, by definition, innovation doesn't come from sameness.

DOI: 10.1201/9781003364436-4

That doesn't mean, of course, that innovation only comes from 'fresh' demographics. Your existing employees can and do have new and creative ideas. My dad can have creative ideas. And does, bless him.

It just means that you cannot create something new and different by *doing* and *being* the same.

And the focus of this chapter is on all the ways, big and small, that the industry perpetuates 'sameness' in word and deed.

> You cannot create something new and different by doing and being the same.

The angle through which we will explore this question will, indeed, be the banner of inclusion, but by picking up incidents, anecdotes and stories of *exclusion* the chapter is not simply an argument in favour of diversity. It is an argument in favour of the things that nurture innovation. They just happen to converge. The focus here will be on the net impacts some of our institutional choices, conscious and unconscious, and behaviours, intentional and not, have. The impacts of entrenched behaviours that keep vast tracts of the *population outside our offices* or *marginalised inside our halls*.

And the impact is waste. Awful waste of talent and opportunity. This chapter is about the behaviours that lead to this awful waste and what we can all do about it in ways big and small.

So, as this is me, let's start with a story.

THIS IS A STORY ABOUT MANSPLAINING

A few years ago, it happened to me for the first time.

Or maybe not for the first time at all, but rather for the first time *since* I had a word to describe it for what it was: someone (in this case a white, middle-class man) dismissing a point or conversation in a way that was patronising and condescending while insinuating that the person speaking (in this case a white immigrant female: me) has no credibility on the topic.

That definition was eye opening. Having words to describe things is powerful. And depressing.

The tell-tale sign of mansplaining is that you are dismissed, irrespective of whether you have credibility on a topic. The problem is, we only notice it when the person speaking has, indeed, credibility on the topic. We have all enjoyed the tweets of NASA scientists having their books mansplained to them because their long hair obscured their name tag and professor so and so couldn't be a girl, right? That's when we notice. But the point is, mansplaining happens irrespective of your credibility and it is equally insidious if it is done to a professor or an intern. In fact, it's worse with the intern. Because they are silenced, not challenged.

The key trait of mansplaining is the dismissal of the views of another person. It has nothing to do with the quality of those views. And this is important. Someone who is dead-wrong should still not be dismissed out of hand. Mansplaining an idiot doesn't get a reprieve.

And it has nothing to do with gender.

It has everything to do with the fact that someone decides to come to a conversation they don't enjoy from a position of power and choose to dismiss the conversation and the person instigating it as irrelevant because that seems preferable to actually having the conversation and easier than admitting they would rather not talk about this.

If you ever tried to bring a new technology, a counter point of view or a challenge of any sort to the body corporate, this will feel familiar even if you are a white middle-class white man yourself.

So maybe the term is inadequate.

But the problem it describes is true and it happened to me. And here's how it went down.

THE SCENE OF THE CRIME

I guess it was a matter of time.

In the span of my career (two decades and counting) in a male-dominated industry, I had thus far been talked over, had my point ignored until a man made it to general applause and been told my body, clad in its standard-issue corporate suit, is distracting by dint of its existence (more on that later), I have been propositioned by colleagues, bosses and clients.

If male readers gasp at this juncture, female readers are nodding.

I'm not special, this is our life.

And one day it happened, clear as day: 'mansplaining'.

It was baffling, infuriating and enlightening in equal measure.

Women have given 'the act of shutting others down in a way that is off-hand and so casual as to be invisible to most-everyone' a name, but 'mansplaining' doesn't just happen to women.

It was baffling because it was entirely unnecessary, infuriating because it was seemingly only obvious to me and enlightening because its pattern was so banal.

And that is exactly why it merits pointing out. Because people shutting others down in a way that is off-hand and so casual as to be invisible to most of the colleagues in the room hurts all of us. Because women may have given this behaviour a name, but 'mansplaining' doesn't just happen to women and it is a crime, my friends, it is a crime against the future we champion and it has the anatomy of a crime and that anatomy is how you identify it in the wild.

Observe:

If every crime requires motive and opportunity, here the underlying motive may vary (arrogance, insecurity, bad corporate habits already discussed or someone having a really bad day) but the trigger is always the same.

A conversation they don't want to have or a point they feel they need to win for whatever reason (and it could be something as banal as 'they are used to having the last word') and the profound belief that shutting it all down is their prerogative.

I will. Because I can.

So all it takes to trigger a mansplaining incident is a difference of opinion.

Or an opinion voiced by someone different.

That also works.

Someone who either looks different or thinks differently, or – god forbid: both – challenging the way *things are*. Or maybe they don't challenge, but question. Or simply voice an opinion at the wrong time and place, where the person who feels empowered to shut you down is having a bad day and now you are at his cross-hairs. And the reason I am flagging it here is *not* because I am a woman. Actually.

It is because, if you start rocking the boat the way I encouraged you to throughout the last chapter, and the way I will continue encouraging you to in the chapters to come, it will definitely happen to you no matter what your chromosome arrangements. So it's good to be prepared.

THIS COULD HAPPEN TO YOU. IN FACT. IT WILL

The incident I am referring to was a 'water cooler' type conversation about how (if) you can motivate employees who are disengaged, for whatever reason.

It could be lack of personal ambition. It could be feeling trapped in what Douglas Coupland would call a McJob,[1] the type of dead-end, menial job that nobody thinks of when they think of banks *and yet* the vast majority of folks inside the building do exactly that. Someone could be disengaged because they are treading water, because they are going through a bad patch in their personal life. Because of who they are as a person. At some point in your career, you will encounter them. Those people who are so disengaged at work that their indifference becomes destructive, to themselves as far as their performance goes, and to others as far as their attitude goes.

Coming across them doesn't make you a bad boss, by the way. It just makes you observant. But back to my story.

We weren't discussing specifics – just having an abstract conversation among colleagues about managing people who are not as driven or focused, as we are in a context where they abounded. We were casually discussing people whose personality is prickly and uncooperative. Who do not, seemingly, care to do well in the workplace.

The topic was serious but the chat was light-hearted and triggered by the fact that we both had one of those in our teams. Literally, he started it as well.

Plus. Nothing was riding on it. We were not meant to resolve anything. The conversation could have gone deep into what motivates different people and what triggers certain behaviours, whether people's attitudes can indeed change and whether some folks are just dancing to their own tune and that is that. We could have discussed whether one bad apple spoils the barrel or whether a culture can embrace and transform a person.

Equally, the conversation could have drifted to another topic with minimal effort. *Do you guys want to order in for lunch or shall we just go to the canteen?*

But before either of those things happened, mansplaining occurred.

It is important to stress that it happened during a conversation that was, just like our digital forays, open-ended, exploratory, premised

> Exploration rests on empowered vulnerability: that is, acceptance of the idea that I don't know everything there is to know about everything.

on the desire for exchange and learning. It was a moment of empowered vulnerability – accepting there may be things we haven't thought of, accepting *I don't know everything there is to know about everything*; testing and learning,

---

[1] That is a low-paid job with few prospects, a term coined by Douglas Coupland in his seminal novel 'Generation X'.

and inviting others to join me on the journey. That's the premise of how we work in this brave, new FinTech world.

Or is it?

Because the person who will sweep in to 'mansplain' will take your experimentation for lack of conviction, your eagerness to learn as a sign of lacking expertise. Your acceptance that you don't know all the answers as an admission of inadequacy. Your empowered vulnerability, your *choice* to admit there are things you're still working out is exactly where they will choose to strike, whether you're a woman or a digital advocate. Whether you are a brown face, a young face or a different voice.

Sound familiar? Then so will what happened next, in a layered crime of omission and commission.

He laughed.

He interrupted me. With. A. Laugh. And told me the problem was easy to fix if you were willing to tackle it decisively and focus on what mattered.

And here he is. Step one.

OMISSION

A cackle, and he dismisses the conversation; questioning my conviction and leadership abilities; not to mention my judgement and capacity to know what matters.

He then proceeded to explain something entirely unrelated (albeit vaguely similar) to what I was describing. The problem he chose to focus on, as well as the intention he presumed upon, were different, the solution was therefore irrelevant if you were trying to actually reflect on a real challenge. Here's the irony: my question had been around how to engage someone who currently doesn't care. His solution was, in his words, about making under-performing staff members 'someone else's problem'. Essentially his solution, offered with a laugh, was that if I had any leadership qualities, I would just pass the staff member to someone else and focus on more important things. Where do you even start with this?

Let's just say, for the record, that under-performing employees and disengaged employees are, of course, not the same thing and wouldn't be solved by the same blunt instrument, if solving was what you were after. But he wasn't. The facts of the story are that he was a terrible conversationalist, an uninterested manager and I should have just said 'you are so right man' and transferred the team member over to him (which I could actually have done for reasons I won't bother you with here). And yet, the facts of the story are not where the juice is. The interesting thing here is not in the specifics of the encounter but rather in the *mechanics* of dismissal.

Of course he is an idiot. That goes without saying. But the problem is: he is not the only one.

If this sounds familiar, then I am preaching to the choir. But if it doesn't, then please trust me when I say to you that women, youngsters, people of colour, people with working-class accents *and* innovators alike suffer in the hands of this specimen: the person who dismisses you entirely because you want to explore, claiming they already know the answer. Yet, it's only to an entirely different question.

Now ... as a crime of omission, that is bad enough. But it doesn't stop there, as it is *almost always* compounded by a crime of commission.

Stay with me.

COMMISSION

I am lots of things, but meek isn't one of them, so I calmly (but forcefully) explained the problem I was talking about was different, *and* that his solution was not a solution to any problem. His proposal displaces the challenge. It doesn't solve it. Now in most situations the 'alternative' offered with the laugh and shrug of 'this is so simple if only you silly sausage could see it' is not as starkly irrelevant as in my situation. Very often, you are offered an equally untested alternative. In every way, similar to what you were suggesting but also, materially, *not that.* Or a solution that worked for a completely different problem. And every time you try to pursue the conversation to the logical conclusion of how this is different, you will hit a dead-end.

This is bad. But it's about to get worse.

Because, very often, this is where audience participation is sought by the perpetrator, and the crime of commission occurs. Because our culprit turns to the colleagues or bystanders and invites them to share in the laugh or just nod along. It could be a meaningful glance and an unsubtle eye-roll. It could be a half turn to a senior member of the team and an exasperated 'move on, shall we?'. Or it could be a swift slide into victimhood, the mansplainer raising their hands, palms forward in surrender, saying 'easy now, calm down dear, I was only trying to help'.

Hint: sorry folks but here we are in the presence of an unreasonable female. Audience participation here is key.

A strategically timed use of the word 'we'. A joke, left hanging in the air, a smile invited and not refused over the implication that *our collective time is being wasted.* That *we* are indulging *you* here. But there are limits to our patience because *you* are being difficult. Defensive or aggressive depending on circumstance. But not a good sport.

And there you are: on the back foot.

What started as a constructive, immaterial and exploratory peer conversation became an apology of motives. 'I'm not dismissing you – just pointing out the lack of data,' or 'that's not at all what I said, you are putting words in my mouth' or even 'that's not at all what is happening here'. And while you are trying to go down a reasoned path of falsifiable testing along the lines of 'this may work. It may not. But in any case, the hypothesis is different. Your arguments are counterfactual. Plus, the ad hominem attack was really not necessary. *This* is really not necessary' you get mock outrage at how you are escalating things.

You are trying to have the conversation you started. Or at least the conversation your interlocutor sort of started instead. Only you can't hold onto either because the conversation seems to be about how you are not making sense or not being clear or not knowing what point you are trying to make or patronising dismissals of a similar ilk. On this momentous occasion I got: 'Oh, long words, relax.'

Now … I'm a woman, so I'm conscious that if I raise my voice and stop smiling *for a second*, I will be called hysterical, so I keep my voice even and measured at all times and *no matter what is happening*. Still, I'm told to calm down anyway and in the same voice executives told me APIs would never catch on all those years ago.

Silly me. Different room, same patronising dismissal.

But let's face it here.

APIs *did* catch on *and* our culprit knows exactly what he's doing.

Mansplainer or old school banking apologist, he knows that the odds are stacked ever in his favour. He has found himself in a conversation he doesn't want to be having and a conversation he doesn't want *you* to be having, for whatever reason.

Why would one assume something is simple before knowing what it was? … Because he is going for the kill and needed it to look like an accident. Because this is about winning, not communicating.

The attempt to belittle and dismiss didn't work, for I persisted, so he attacks. 'If my explanation isn't correct, it's because you didn't explain your case adequately', he says. Only I did. But even if I hadn't, why did he not ask me questions? Why did he choose to resort to assuming he understood and had already solved my issue? Why did he call it 'simple' before he knew what it was?

Because he was busy constructing an alibi, not having a conversation. Because he was going for the kill and needed it to look like an accident. Because this was about winning, not communicating.

COLLUSION

'This isn't rhetorical', I actually said, with a smile. Forced and insincere, I will confess. Still ... there.

But before I tell you what happened next ...

Do you realise how many women live through this each day? How many digital entrepreneurs? How many youngsters? How many folks who attempt having opinions while black?

How many people who look different or speak of things that jar against preferences and habits?

Do you realise how many unnecessary and unnecessarily fraught conversations are had every day because someone behind a real or imaginary desk will scoff and dismiss and belittle for no reason other than ... they can?

The answer is simply: Too. Bloody. Many.

And exactly because of this ... I persisted. I calmly did what I always do: I explained.

I tried to live by the whole 'if they go low, we go high' malarkey. I pointed out gaps, logical fallacies, counterfactual arguments and other long words. I also pointed out that *he didn't need to have this conversation with me*, and this bit is important.

He did not have to have this conversation; he was free to stop and talk about the weather. Or talk about nothing at all. He didn't need to talk to me.

But if he was going to have this entirely optional conversation, having *the same* conversation as me would be both courteous and logical. Talking *at me*, throwing irrelevant albeit tangential topics *at me* in the hope of either scaring me or catching me in an assumed inconsistency that would help justify an 'aha' was neither pleasant nor useful. It was also not even remotely novel, as experiences go. This is a thing that happens to us. All the freaking time.

This is familiar territory.

We come to the table with a hypothesis and an invitation to discuss. He could have said 'I don't want to talk about *this*.' He could have said he doesn't want to talk to *me*. He could have said he finds the topic dull. That's all fair and totally OK, yet he engaged, then proceeded to dismiss the exercise and the challenge; not to mention ... me to boot. Belittled the effort, the ideas and the bearer of both and proposed a solution that was irrelevant, facile and unhelpful. When challenged on the argument, he attacked the person. When told his solution doesn't address the problem, he said without shame: 'In that case, you didn't explain it adequately.' It is my fault you see, that his pre-existing thought doesn't fit the new problem. Why? Because he represents established wisdom that didn't need to explain itself any time before, and he likes it that way. More to the point, *because he can*.

And he can because we let him.

And this is where the crime of collusion comes in and why you should keep reading even if the point I am making is by now very clear and rather uncomfortable.

I invited him in a conversation, colleague-to-colleague. He chose to simplify and dismiss. I gave him the option to rectify (actually in those words). He chose a personal attack. Then I gave him the option to stop and talk about something else; retract and apologise; or actually salvage the conversation by actually having it. I told him that I found the argument far from constructive and the attitude baffling and unpleasant. The response? 'You're overreacting.' And a chuckle. The reaction of the others in the room? Silence. And when I walked away thinking this is not a good use of my time, what they segued to was ... a chat about the weather. I kid you not. I could hear it down the corridor.

And if you are thinking: yeah that's me, awkwardly standing by, willing this entirely unnecessary argument to end, I say ... you are part of the problem. In fact, you are the problem even more than he is. Because *this* is how the innocent bystanders lose their innocence, for they become accomplices to bad manners, lazy reasoning and poisonous relationships. And they're all as damaging as each other to your business as well as our society, because ... do you actually know what *you've just done* as an audience member in this – be it a case of mansplaining or a case of dismissing digital innovation or any permutation of the same bad behaviours?

And if you are thinking 'oh come on, none of this sounds so bad. Tiresome but frankly, why didn't you just drop it, what point were you trying to make, you are as much at fault as he is here'…. That's exactly what bullies the world over hope for.

If you are silent when injustice occurs you are guilty of collusion. Even if it is the tepid variety that just wants the discomfort to end without needing to take sides. Only … silence is very much tantamount to taking sides. And I hate to burst your neutrality bubble here. But it gets worse.

If you are silent when injustice occurs you are guilty of collusion. Even if it is the tepid variety that just wants the discomfort to end without needing to take sides. Silence is very much tantamount to taking sides.

DOUBLE JEOPARDY

Are you familiar with the term *double jeopardy*?

It means that the same person cannot be tried for the same crime twice, and since my mansplainer here committed the crime, was called out on it by yours truly in very clear terms and a jury of his peers found him innocent by their deafening silence, he was given licence to do it again; to dismiss and confound where analysis is needed, belittle and mock where a splash of imagination or just some active listening would have helped the situation as well as the person in front of him, but *even more significantly* taught him something about himself, his team and his business.

Just imagine being subjected to this jarring, unpleasant, frustrating and fruitless exercise.

Now imagine this happening again and again. Because again and again is what happens. And it is folly. It's a crime.

And silence is collusion.

It's how the perpetrator of these micro-aggressions learns it's OK to do it. Silence is why he can (and will) continue to do it. And if you think mansplaining only hurts women, you've been mansplained to/at one too many times. The belief that anyone knows best without asking any questions, the conviction that a personal attack and a cheap jibe can adequately substitute a reasoned argument, the willingness to sneer at another human being without anyone calling foul … all rest on the knowledge that the status quo will be protected by those around you.

So all you need to do is brand difference as weirdness and deflect any challenge to your comfort zone through ad hominem attacks or cheap jibes …

that's what drives women into silence. Which you may not care about, but it also drives creativity into silence.

Who wants to be mocked seven times before breakfast for just having an idea? Who wants to have their accent mocked, because it's easier than arguing against their idea, or answering their question? It's the same thing actually and, frankly, this behaviour being normalised kills innovation in your company, and that will affect profits first and then survival, so it would be wise to care.

This is not about women. This is about your bottom line. And the people affected are not snowflakes. They are just people. And they are being bullied in a web of constant micro-aggression. And you should care. Because it costs you and your business real money.

Mansplaining is corporate arrogance by a different name; the attitude of the comfortable male, pale and stale executive who sneers and dismisses women, foreigners, fledgling entrepreneurs, digital natives and youth in the same manner, in the office and beyond. Call it what you like for heuristic purposes, especially as I am sure senior women can be as dismissive and caustic as any man, if they are institutionalised. Whatever you call it, however, see it for the crime it is: it's killing exactly the sort of conversations your business needs to have, in order to flourish in a digitally native ecosystem. It's killing the sort of conversations society needs to have to become fairer, smarter and more connected. And not because it silences women. It's because it kills any conversation without a predetermined outcome. Because it teaches folks to come to a conversation ready for battle. Because it belittles people who don't fit a mould, for whatever reason. It is because they chose to be vulnerable and say that they don't know. It could equally be because of how they look, where they came from or what they believe in, how they work, what they think we should try instead of doing the same things in the same way day after day.

> Mansplaining is corporate arrogance by a different name; it is killing the sort of conversations society needs to be having. And not because it silences women but because it kills any conversation without a predetermined outcome.

If calling someone out on sloppy reasoning, patronising tones and bad conversation skills warrants being told one is 'overreacting', if seeing these behaviours as the single biggest obstacle to the innovation we need and crave is an over-reaction, then all I have to say is: buckle up. This chapter will be uncomfortable or frustrating. Or both. And I will plead that you persevere and read on. It is important that you know what is happening and why it actually affects and hurts you, even if it is not directed at you. Even if you are a comfortable and respected, middle-aged, middle-class white man who has never been treated like this any more than you have treated anyone like this and you wouldn't treat anyone like that because you are a good sport.

Please read on. You may find things worth thinking about in these pages, even if you disagree with them.

WALKING A MILE IN OUR SHOES

The principle here is that this habit, this muscle memory-level of an easy dismissal of any idea, can and is directed against folks who bring unfamiliar ideas to the table. So if you champion people who do exactly that, then you should know what their life is like. Because if you are aware of it, you will start noticing more. And if you notice it, you can help us stop it. And I hope that once you start noticing, you will realise just how common this is. How much what I described here shapes the experience of many of us working in this industry. And maybe each individual event doesn't warrant bringing the world to a screeching halt but, if you start noticing, you will realise it's constant, it's relentless, its ubiquitous. And then maybe you will see why it hurts us all so much.

A male colleague sat in on a call one of his female colleagues had not so long ago. He didn't declare his presence. He just sat in to observe. Why do you tolerate being spoken to like this? He asked her. Because it's everyone all the time, she answered.

It is real and present and bad. Even if it's never happened to you.

And we need you to be able to believe and also accept the significance of something that has never happened to you.

Women and people of colour often describe their tenure in financial services as 'surviving'.

> Women and people of colour often describe their tenure in financial services as 'surviving'. That doesn't bode well, does it?

That doesn't bode well, does it? But let me tell you that surviving this industry as someone who looks different (I am a woman after all), sounds different (I am an immigrant and although my English is fluent and effortless, I do have an accent that gets mocked very regularly) and acts different (I champion, embody and drive change. I can also be a tad relentless), I have had three choices. To exit and do something else; to shrink and shuffle along in the margins; or to be a tough cookie. I was expected to be one. And I had no choice but to be one. We've covered this already. And we have said it is profoundly problematic exactly because of what we are trying to achieve: change.

The need for transformation is not debated any more inside banks. It is a fact. We know we must. We acknowledge the need to transform, through programmes of work and large associated budgets; we advertise and celebrate our intention to create something new through innovation departments, events and press releases; and we declare our commitment to doing things differently in a changing world by investing in brightly coloured furniture and IDEO courses for our staff. But *all the while* we hold onto habits, structures and demographics like our life depends on them.

Because for some, I guess, it does.

So, even though every bank has at least one digital transformation department, budget and ambition, the same bank will hold on fast (consciously or not) to habits, systems and structures that are not only *not* useful for a digital organisation but actively get in the way of what we are trying to achieve, as we already discussed at some length in the previous chapter. That covers everything from pricing (an API call and a manually collated report cannot and should not cost the same and yet the old pricing models are both familiar and more lucrative than this new digital world, and resistance is real), to risk assessments (real-time alerts vs after-the-fact checklists) and everything in-between. But accepting that real-time risk awareness is a better idea doesn't translate to knowing how to tell a false alarm from an early warning sign of something momentous. And rather than taking the time to learn, the real-time solution is dismissed as immature and checklists reign supreme.

As the picture painted in the previous chapter demonstrates, banks *can* and *do* get in the way of their own transformation journeys, by perpetuating dysfunctional realities and bad habits with pervasive impacts. These are not technical problems and therefore technology won't solve them. They are human problems, and they need to be addressed at the organisational, structural and behavioural level. At the individual level (with your daily acts of resistance and leading by example) and at the collective level (which I will get to in a later chapter). Further, and as my opening story also demonstrates, we are dealing with acts of omission and commission: they are things the industry does … and things it doesn't do … and both the actions and the gaps, of course, play themselves out to the tune of 'if you always do what you always did you will always do what you always got'.

And although the industry has been talking about change being the new normal for almost 20 years, does it really believe it? Or rather does it appreciate how deep the new normal is going to go?

I am going to go with no.

Because even if they believe it, they probably hope otherwise. And they hope otherwise because the way things are is familiar. Comfortable. And in some cases, very very profitable. So change isn't just hard because of the complexity, and habits and structures and all the human foibles of unintentional resistance. It is also hard because some folks are asked to give up or at least share privileges they felt were theirs for good. I had shirked away from facing into that obvious fact for a very long time, saying well yes, it is human nature to try to hold onto the familiar. But in a recent conversation, Chair of the Innovate Finance Board and all-round superstar, Louise Smith flagged the undeniable fact that personal motivations are not incidental. Especially as the low-hanging fruit of transformation has already been reaped. The work that remains to be done is harder and resistance to it is cloaked under more careful language, language adapted and evolved to not sound like downright hostility, while folks are hanging on for dear life onto a set-up that doesn't just convey reassuring familiarity but also comes laden with power, status, material advantages and privilege.

And that is *why* all this matters.

People like us, the folks that drive and champion digital transformation, are not just bringing in new tooling, we are also, and by extension, helping accelerate a socio-economic shift that challenges and endangers the very things that motivate individuals who historically sought a career in banking in the first place: their status, their position and all that goes with it.

MOUTHING THE WORDS

Acting like we embrace change while holding onto the way things have always been for dear life is a very expensive and counter-productive way to be.

It is also the norm.

For instance, as we mentioned already, every bank has an innovation department. That is a very public way of demonstrating that the

Acting like we embrace change while holding onto the way things have always been for dear life is a very expensive and counter-productive way to be. It is also the norm.

bank is *au fait* with the need to learn, experiment and try things out before transforming. Is it mere lip service? Not for the people toiling inside the department.

And not entirely, even for the rest of the organisation. But.

Most innovation departments are 'to the side' of the main business and their experiments, even the successful ones, never see the light of day, as the benchmark that needs to be met keeps shifting, as do the urgent priorities that devour limited resources and headspace. Even though innovation and transformation are loudly espoused as cherished principles, they are rarely plugged into the main business, seldom looked upon to deliver the answers as to 'what should we do next', never asked to drive, always challenged for proof points more than any other department. And the charade continues as innovation is happening in pockets so small that they never truly reach the customers in a meaningful way.

As if the body corporate grudgingly accepted the need to change, but would rather not.

A client once said that programmes of work that seek to radically transform the bank are never released. There is always a hold up … or ten. There is always a delay. Some, however, he said with a mischievous smile, some manage to escape. Despite it all.

If that sounds counter-intuitive and mad, that's because it is. It is also very true.

On the one hand, handling transformation as a project or programme of work, while business as usual continues in parallel, makes some sense. You acknowledge the need to transform your business but can't down tools on the services you are currently offering. You still have a business to run, a business to save, the very business you seek to transform. You have customers who rely on you so, until you can replace today's service, you can't turn it off.

This means you are running in two gears, two parallel realities, trying to simplify the scope of the work that needs to be done, to de-risk it to the extent possible. While all the other stuff I've been describing in earlier chapters is happening anyway, making a hard job, harder. Meanwhile everyone is shying away from the simple fact that this balancing act is valiant but doomed to fail. The whole point of transformation is to stay in step with a world radically changed. So unless the transformation effort encompasses the very heart of the business, it won't work. If the whole point of transformation is to change, doing it 'on the side' won't work. That's problem one. Problem two is that the end game of this change is to ensure the continued survival of the business. By definition, that can't be to the side of the business, while folks over here carry on with the real work.

And yet. That is exactly what we do.

Doing things side of desk is *not* how you do them when they matter to you.

And that applies to *everything* done side of desk. Innovation and 'diversity and inclusion' both.

And the reason I am telling you this is not that the two are vaguely similar in shape and pattern but rather because they are cumulative. As us tough cookies find, it's usually a double assault.

Although the two initiatives are never connected, they are actually very much linked both in how they are approached and in their chances of success. They both seek to transform a business that won't give them headspace, having first told them they are so very important ... trying to invigorate the stale demographics of an industry that knows it shouldn't be all male, white and middle class anymore but 'we have diversity initiatives for that sort of thing so we can't hold back the main business while we let it do its work' ... just like a big bank will de-fund its APIs to pay for the legacy technology stack that is 'on fire', they will also happily recruit from all-white, all-male, all similarly educated long lists of candidates for a role because 'it is urgent to fill the vacancy' while vocally reminding everyone they are committed to their digital future and an equal and diverse workforce.

There is a bitter and non-coincidental parallel there.

Diversity becomes a department, a committee, an 'employee resource group' sitting somewhere to the side, usually in HR, sometimes sponsored, sometimes genuinely supported. But apart. And. You have the exact same outcome you do with innovation departments: the thing we all agree is key to our future is put to the side, while real life continues like it always has. And you sit in meetings that agree diversity metrics and spend a good hour trying to present the numbers in a way that looks better than the measly reality that it is.

If you are still wondering why I keep sliding from innovation to diversity and back again, you are not paying attention. They are mirror images of the same thing. Paying lip service to an idea that we know is good for business, and definitely good PR, but not being willing to fully commit to the work to get us there. And they are mirror images of each other in one more way: the things we do that perpetuate the Old Ways despite the language of support and the opportunity cost are starkly similar. And I have been twice over at the receiving end of all this. By dint of demographics and job description.

THIS IS NOT A PERPETRATOR-LESS CRIME

I won't lie.

This was not an easy chapter to write. Every word grates. Trying to describe the insidious effect of constant micro-aggressions the build up to a consistent macro image, as my friend and lloyds Banking Group Payments Industry and Development Director Sam Emery eloquently pointed out, recently[2], brings you constantly face to face with the knowledge that people will dismiss it as an over-reaction to isolated incidents. That's what happens in the workplace. That's what happens every day. And that is why it is important to write about it. But it doesn't make it feel any less like pulling teeth.

Plus I can't hide from the fact that there is rawness in what I am describing here. And vulnerability. And in the effort to try and make it objective and compelling, I leave a lot of how it feels out. But is that right?

Cos the truth is: I am angry.

I have spent way too long fighting against the very people that hired me to be the canary in the mine, the corporate's better demon standing guard against their baser instincts. Brought in to do something everyone agreed was important and then

I have spent way too long fighting against the very people that hired me to be the canary in the mine, the corporate's better demon standing guard against their baser instincts.

labelled a troublemaker for not leaving well alone. With the new ideas and the new ways of working and the daily, constant insistence of being consistent in the change we want to see. Fancy that.

The reality of dealing with the tough cookie on a daily basis is that the cookie is a pain in the ass. And things are pretty tough for the cookie too. So before we get any further let's talk about what it feels like to be the cookie that needs to be tough in an environment that says it wants to change but then challenges you to change it with no cooperation or assistance. Because when we talk about transformation and FinTech we don't just mean tech. We also mean the talent, the humans and the way they organise themselves. The habits, the conduct, what we tolerate, what we perpetuate and what we reward.

And this has been the arena of empty gestures more than any other.

And yes, I am angry.

Which is why, for many years, I didn't talk about behaviours at the personal level. And I did not talk about diversity in our industry. Because

---

[2] https://www.fintechfutures.com/2022/10/actions-not-words/ for a joint piece with Sam on exactly this topic

I didn't want to over-simplify and generalise like almost everyone around me. And also exactly because I was angry and my grandmother used to say that, sometimes, if you have nothing good to say, you should consider saying nothing at all. Grandma didn't mean 'be sweet'. She meant 'be constructive'. And for a very long time, I found it very hard to talk about the experience of being a woman *and* an immigrant *and* a change agent in this industry without getting angry. Fire and brimstone, angry. The inarticulate, despairing, why-are-we-even-having-this-conversation kind of angry.

Why?

I have been asked if I plan on having children before getting a promotion in a bank. I have been sexually propositioned by a former boss. I have been accosted by a client in a lift at a conference. I have been told my looks are distracting in senior meetings (no, it is not a compliment). I have been talked over. I have had my point dismissed only to hear a dude repeat the same point five minutes later to general applause. All of those things have happened again and again and and if I make repeated references to them in this chapter, it is because they are repeat offences and repeated incidents. And I see them happening to women all around me. To brown faces all around me. To people whose sexuality doesn't fit the mould or their background doesn't fit our expectations.

Again, and again, and again. They are not the whole story. But they are the part of the story that is personal, ugly and constant. And no Diversity and Inclusion initiatives touch on this side of the reality of being a little bit different in the workplace. Because it would entail moving away from the benign discussion of Diversity as a perpetrator-less crime. If you actually got into the gory detail of *what* actually goes on, you would need to address *who* does it before long. And D&I would go from being a nice employee initiative to a witch hunt and we don't want that, do we?

Only witches aren't real. Whereas inappropriate behaviour, racism, sexism and class discrimination in the workplace very much are.

Oh come on now, here we go.

I can just see some of you sitting back in mild exasperation.

But are you really telling me that nobody has ever mocked your cockney colleague's accent in a meeting? And those of you in the US, nobody, jokingly, told your Southern friend over drinks in NYC that their accent makes them sound stupid and it's always a pleasant surprise that they are not? Because I heard that more than once in the hallways of NYC offices over the years. Nobody asked your black colleague to fetch coffee? Was your Asian surgeon friend never called nurse and your Indian colleague asked to look into why Webex isn't working? Did your young, female colleague get asked to take minutes even though she is a contributor to this meeting? Did your black friend get called by the name of the only other black person they work with and when they said no I am not that person they were told 'oh you know you all look the same, ha'. Or did it all of this happen, because all these examples are real, and you just normalised it because it's not so bad, really?

Because it didn't happen to you.

No D&I panel talks about what you do after you went to HR to say your boss made some very inappropriate suggestions and HR responded with: oh honey, I am so sorry, but he's been here 20 years, has an impeccable record and it's your word against his. Do you really want to put yourself through this? If you want to, we will help you, but is this what is best for your career?

Nothing about these moments is unique.

And HR was giving the best 'damage limitation' advice in the circumstances. Because, let's face it, we are dealing with three things here: microaggressions, macro-narratives and all-weather idiots. And the reason I am angry is because this nonsense is constant and universal. It has happened to your girlfriend, your wife and your daughter. It is happening to your colleagues right now. It is small things. All the time. Small things some of the time. Occasionally pretty big things too. But mostly constant small things. Too small to raise sometimes. Too small for men or white people or straight people or people who are not at the receiving end of the thing, whatever it is, to notice most of the time. And really, it is not everyone. It is not always. And it is not the whole story. And it's probably safe to guess that the people who do this stuff to women aren't your favourite folks in the office anyway. They tend to also be dismissive to juniors, cavalier about power and generally entitled. Know the type? We all do.

They are idiots. Of course they are. The world has its fair share of them. And banking has more than its fair share because the fragmented attention of the individuals in a mildly aggressive environment is a breeding ground for the type that is likely to dismiss, put down and move on.

They are not the whole story. And you shouldn't let them become the full story ever. Not yours. Not anyone's. I will be damned if my story will be reduced to what some idiot decided to say or do. As I rise through the ranks – because you can put me down, but you can't bring me down, buster – as I rise through the ranks, I try not to hire idiots. And if any slip through the net (and some always do) I make sure they don't get to act out their idiocy on my watch: you change your tune or change your job. The story we live on my watch is not one of micro-aggressions. It is one of hard work, opportunities and only the tensions that emerge from people spending a lot of time cooped up together doing hard work, often under pressure. It's not always smooth sailing. But it is never diminishing. That needs to be the point of the story.

USE THAT IN A SENTENCE

The problem is, nobody will disagree with this.

Don't hire idiots seems so obvious and it could be my advice on how you can help.

Don't hire idiots.

But the problem is nobody ever sets out to hire idiots. Nobody really thinks they are hiring idiots. Plus nobody realises the impact of what they are doing when they let people who are normally not idiots get away with being momentarily idiotic in ways that may seem too small to address. They rightly think: this is not the whole story, would I be making more of a deal of it than it actually is, if I pick it up? Move on, the macro story wins even if the micro moment fails.

Or so they think.

So, they don't talk about gender, in the moment. They don't talk about race, in the moment. They don't talk about patronising remarks on accent, origin, appearance, in the moment. They don't talk about the junior employee laughed at as if they invented the technology they were tasked with researching and found naïve and silly, in the moment. The

> By the time corporates get to the panels or the D&I strategy review, their intent is pure but their aim is weak as we collectively fall down in the moments that don't get addressed. And that is the story we live in, even if it is not the story we tell.

moment, however, matters a lot. It's not the only thing that matters. But it *also* matters. And by the time they get to the panels or the D&I strategy review, their intent is pure but their aim is weak. And they miss the mark because we all collectively fall down in the moments that don't get addressed, don't get picked up, don't get corrected. And that is the story we live in, even if it is not the story we tell.

And before you go 'I am sure I have not seen racism or sexism at work', pause. Social media is rife with men telling women their lived experience is not representative of what they know to be true. White folks telling the world racism isn't a thing because they don't see it. The privileged diminishing what it feels like to have your accent, vowels, clothes or postcode diminished daily. The same dismissals play out in offices, zoom calls and stores the world over. And if you are still thinking 'I am sure I have not seen racism or sexism at work', think of this.

You sit in a meeting. It is the third meeting of its kind because one of the dudes in the meeting is passive-aggressively failing to bring the information needed to this discussion, so the meeting gets kicked down the road. This time is no different. Everyone is cranky but nobody says a thing. We will be back next week. As the entirely waste-of-time meeting wraps, one of the other men asks the only woman in the room (me) if she's read his email. I haven't yet, apologies, I've been travelling. And he loses it and gives her a lecture on accountability, having said *not a word* to the colleague who is holding everything back. But that's not sexist, right?

So here's more.

Woman says a thing. Let's pretend what the woman says is, 'we have a problem here. We want to achieve X and we are not going to have enough time to do it if we don't accelerate now', or 'this project could lead to a very substantial piece of work if we allow the client to guide us as to their ambitions beyond the current scope. We need to expand the team to include people who understand the bigger picture', or 'we have a process for this thing but we don't seem to be following it and the results show this, so we need to change the process or implement the process differently: we cannot just carry on doing the same things and expecting a different outcome'.

Let's pretend these conversations happened in workplaces. Sure, in all three scenarios a challenge or problem is flagged. In all scenarios, the problem is flagged *before* it is on fire. Before heroics are needed. Before scapegoats are required. When there is time to do something about the whole thing. That is already slightly counter-intuitive for the way banks work where things are usually left to catch fire before someone rushes in to save the day. Now let's stop pretending, because all three conversations happened. The woman was me. The situation each time was imminently salvageable and my tone was calm albeit forceful because that is who I am as a person.

Would you like to guess what the responses I received were?

On the first one it was, 'let's not do this here, I don't want to embarrass you in front of people'. On the second one a man started screaming at me to f**k off for thinking that 'I know best'. And on the third it was a chuckle about how Greek I can be sometimes. And if you are thinking how irrelevant and uncalled for and how *goddamn personal* the reactions were, you can join the club.

Meanwhile. No prizes for guessing I wasn't yelled out of town.

As it goes: nevertheless she persisted.

It wasn't pleasant. This is important.

The fact that we stand tall doesn't mean this doesn't hurt.

And it wasn't easy. Because the person who escalates immediately seeks to act as the victim of you not running scared.

And the fact that I shouldn't be accountable for containing or withstanding people's bad behaviour doesn't change the fact that it is what happens.

And the outcome?

In the first instance, we very much had the conversation in front of people who didn't call his behaviour out, really wished they weren't there for it. Why?

Because I was not the one who ended up embarrassed: I had done my work and I just needed him to do his. I had facts and figures and was not afraid to use them and he was shown to be the playground bully that we all secretly knew he was. But people still thought of me as difficult. I am not guessing. I know it because I got all the unfunny jokes afterwards. 'Oh better make sure I don't cross *you*.' And 'don't ever tell Leda you will embarrass her'. And 'oh you can be one scary bitch'.

And no comment about the manipulative behaviour addressed at me. Of the fact that someone chose to deflect through cheap jibes to hide the fact that they hadn't pulled their weight.

Only the fact that I resisted it.

Funny that.

Also. Never call your female colleagues a bitch. It's never a joke any of us laugh at.

In the second instance, I did not f**k off but the rest of the men around the table told me to chill and trust him. He did *not* get reprimanded by HR, he did *not* apologise, we did it his way and lost the business because, it turns out he didn't know best either and I had a point. The client told us 'you missed a trick there, you could have beefed up your team with some folks who see the bigger picture and landed a much bigger piece of work here'. And yet nobody even had the good grace to look embarrassed.

Funny that.

And no, before you ask, there is no triumph in 'I told you so'.

It tastes of ashes.

Finally, in the third instance, my Greekness had nothing to do with the fact that a process not followed is not a process, it's a piece of irrelevant art, not a tool and therefore you are blundering in the dark. When I pointed that out, I was told to relax.

Do you want to guess how many times I have had conversations like those in my 20 years in the industry or shall we stop this game and play another?

IT WILL HAPPEN AGAIN, BECAUSE YOU LET IT

This stuff happens. To women. To non-white folks. To non-binary folks. To working-class folks. To younger employees. Yes, even the white men. To people who sound like they may not belong, because of an accent that betrays a long journey, be it from another country or a part of town that doesn't normally produce office workers. People around you are getting shut down all the time. They are calling out a problem looming. They are calling out an issue approaching. They call out bad behaviour. And they get looked at like they are the problem. They are dismissed. Ignored. *Diminished*.

And if they say, 'hey, that's not cool, you can't talk to me like that', want to guess what happens?

They are looked upon like 'they started it'. Like they are being difficult and troublesome.

'I am sure you don't mean to be patronising, but you are so please reflect, reconsider and desist.'

You know how many times I have said that sentence in my career? You know how much time and effort it took to hone it to such a conciliatory, joking and yet succinct shape? You know how jarring it remains for the people who, having patronised me, were astounded they can't get away with it? That I am *precious* enough to make a point of their entitlement?

My former colleague Annie Mbako[3] once tweeted, 'they are allowed to be like that in the first place, and so they continue'. And frankly, all the words I type here are in excess of that phrase and redundant. And yet a succinct and valid point does not win the day, it seems. It gets drowned in the sheer volume of noise. So the pushback continues. I have been told to grow up, grow a pair, learn to take a joke, chill out, relax, behave myself, calm down (that old classic) and, my all-time favourite, I have been told not to be so dramatic. That's one of the hits, that is.

I'm afraid none of these tactics work, though. Displacement and victim-blaming is a strategy as old as the hills. As are ad hominem attacks for effect.

---

[3] @Annie_Efosi 14/12/2021, 16:40. Go look for the tweet if you want. And give Annie a follow. You won't regret it.

If I criticise a process and you respond by mocking my accent, it's not me missing the point, surely. And if I challenge your behaviour and you choose to mock my hormones for my boundaries, who is escalating this, exactly?

How about we try another route: if you behave badly and someone calls you out, *apologise.* This is a call to action right there. If someone says you hurt them, upset them, disrespected them or offended them. Apologise. Even if you don't mean it. It's good practice and may create some much-needed muscle memory.

Also, another call to action: Ad hominem attacks are not big and they are not clever. Telling people who challenge the content of your position to 'calm down' is belittling and laden with assumptions about their present mental and emotional state that are presumptuous, poten-tially erroneous and most definitely irrelevant. Has it ever occurred to you that if the experience of being called out for bad behaviour is jarring, this has more to do with the fact that you got away with it for way too long, rather than the 'other' being too 'other' for comfort? Ultimately, these are teachable moments even for those of us who were never challenged before.

> Has it ever occurred to you that if the experience of being called out for bad behaviour is jarring, this has more to do with the fact that you got away with it for way too long, rather than the 'other' being too 'other' for comfort?

It's ok. It's never too late to start learning. But learning is a choice. And in meeting rooms and offices, shops and bus stops the world over, 'othering' is taking place constantly and people don't take their teachable moments to their karma bank. Instead, they take a moment of discomfort and turn it into a missile. They start a fight they have no intention of finishing in the hope that the other side will cower. In the belief that they can start a fight that the other side won't finish for them.

So if you are reading all this and wondering how you can help then the answer is: be an ally. An ally that goes to war with us. Not one that agrees in principle and misses the moment. Because these battles are fought in the moment. So that is one thing you can do for us. Be there on our side, in the moment. Be it a racist remark, sexism or mockery of a new idea. Call it out. Make it *not* ok. Have the conversation, discuss the idea. Dismiss it by all means. But don't mock it. And don't mock the person who brought it to you.

And if you say 'I never would', good. But please stand up to those who do. As an ally. We need you.

STILL STANDING

'How bad can it really be though? You are still here, aren't you?'

That's the most common refrain from men and women alike when I speak about the micro-aggressions many of us experience at work by dint of looking different, thinking differently or both. When I talk of the process of 'othering' (defined by the Oxford English Dictionary as 'viewing or treating a person or group of people as intrinsically different from and alien to oneself') that takes place in every office I have ever worked in. So yes, I am still standing. And that is undeniably part of the story. But is that the standard we will hold ourselves to?

On one level, it is at least honest. We value tough cookies, so we make it hard for everyone, in order to separate the wheat from the chaff; so that we, as an industry, can see which cookies will crumble. The ones that don't, get to … what? Continue being beaten down?

Because there is no prize for withstanding this, and it never ends. The ones that don't crumble get to keep doing it. Keep enduring micro-aggressions and bad behaviours ad infinitum. Put like that, it doesn't sound like winning.

So let's talk about this.

Why is diversity in the workplace important?

Because it brings better results.

Forget happiness and creativity for a second. I am talking bottom line here. In every industry, in every geography, at all levels of a business, diversity of all kinds (class, gender, ethnicity, background, sexual, religious and dietary orientation, you name it) is good for business. A McKinsey report[4] showed that diverse teams (be it gender or race) outperform non-diverse teams both net-net and year on year: diversity being the gift that keeps on giving for both *sustained* and *substantial* growth. What's not to like about that? Other than 'jobs for the boys'.

We shouldn't be having this argument in the first place. For two reasons. First of all 'diversity' is a fallacy. Women are already roughly half of the population and in many cases slightly more than that. Many groups classed as minorities are set to reach 'majority' status in multi-ethnic societies this side of 2050 and the 2020 US census showed that almost 50% of generation Z is 'non-white'. So by advocating for inclusion, you are not doing

---

[4] https://www.mckinsey.com/featured-insights/diversity-and-inclusion/diversity-wins-how-inclusion-matters

anyone a favour here. Or rather you are. Because if the demographics are what they are and research proves diverse companies have higher cashflow per employee, higher revenue and steadier financial returns, then retaining existing demographics is doing a small minority (white, middle-class men) a massive favour.

One more time, louder for the people at the back: diversity is not a concession.

It is a demographic *fact* outside your office and would be good for business inside your office, if you let it. The evidence is compelling. And yet even the researchers confirming these numbers seem surprised[5] because habit is strong.

> Diversity is not a concession.
> It is a demographic fact outside your office and good for business inside your office.

So although numbers point in one way, our language points in another and diversity is *talked of* in terms of a concession. Men *gave* women the vote. White communities *allowed* de-segregation. Male, pale and stale boards launched diversity and inclusion initiatives. And gave young women the pleasure of being patronised in an implicit accusation that if they weren't young, pretty and female they wouldn't be here.

I was recently approached for a board position with the following killer chat-up line: they want a woman and it helps that you are *ethnic*, but you should tone down the digital stuff a bit. They want it, but they don't understand it and it may intimidate them that an ethnic woman knows more than them. Get your little violins tuned, this is a good'un.

It never occurred to the person approaching me that any of this was a problem. That he wasn't 'just helping'.

God forbid that I have a set of key competencies beyond my ability to help them meet their diversity statistics. It didn't occur to him I may not *want* to be part of a board that thinks like this. That I may have no intention of toning anything down because, if I tone down the thing I do, what am I doing here anyway? I guess if you want a diverse appointment (check) that is advised to not appear too different, we have reached peak hypocrisy.

---

5 https://www.piie.com/publications/working-papers/gender-diversity-profitable-evidence-global-survey

DIVERSITY IS A FACT. NOT A FAVOUR

So here we are, having to explain that diversity of thought helps creative problem solving. Diversity of lived experiences accelerates creativity and improves results. It seems logical that we would be all in favour and yet we have to explain that diversity is good for your business every day of our lives. So here it goes again: this is not a concession to anybody. It's fuel for growth and innovation. If the numbers didn't stack up, don't you think the experiment would have been reversed pretty damn quick?

Diversity is also good for the soul.

Not because women can't be idiots. Sadly we can.

Diverse hires don't insulate you from all-weather idiots. They come in all shapes and colours. You still need to filter those out actively and deliberately and at all times. But overall, diversity helps limit those micro moments that insidiously change your macro narrative and you don't even know they have. Diversity in your meetings and your corridors means that certain behaviours are less likely to happen and more likely to be picked up and challenged if they do. And that is a lateral benefit of sorts. Because it makes everything a little bit better, a little bit easier for everyone to just be in the workplace and do their best work.

And happier people are more creative. Happier people work harder. Happier people bring their whole self to work and that will make you more money, delight your customers and fortify your culture. It will do you nothing but good. So let's get there by dealing with the big stuff and the small stuff with equal urgency. Let's

Listen to these stories, so you know what you are looking for. And when you see it happening, nip it in the bud. Then normalise what you just did. Talk about the act of being an ally. Of not needing things to be truly awful in order to take a stand.

get there by doing and stopping and starting. Ultimately, telling these stories isn't what matters. Stopping them is.

And stopping them is urgent. And not one for your Diversity Champions. This one is *your* job. No matter who you are. Because this is everyone's job. So add this to your repertoire of small acts of resistance in the name of the change we champion: listen to these stories. Not just my ones. The ones your friends live through each day, so you know what it is you are looking for. And when you see it happening, stop it. Nip it in the bud. Then normalise what you just did. Talk about the act of being an ally. Of not needing things to be truly awful in order to take a stand. Make it normal that we don't tolerate passively aggressive, micro-aggressive, patronising and dismissive behaviours around here. This is something you *can* do. This is something we can all do. And I am talking to myself as much as I am talking to anyone else. Because, as I said at the top of the chapter, for many years, I refused to talk about gender. Partly because I wasn't sure I would be able to contain the fiery rage that envelops me when I hear men telling me that 'in their experience, I am homing in on exceptions'. That 'the women they know, don't feel this way'. That 'speaking about it perpetuates divisions of old'. The rage that threatens to consume me when I am told my lived experience is irrelevant or circumstantial, that the aggressions and transgressions we are subjected to each day are incidental and irrelevant. When the onus for dealing with bad behaviour is on me and not its perpetrator.

But that is not the only reason.

The other reason was that I didn't want to be reduced to my gender. I didn't want to be the woman who talks about being a woman. I have so much to say about the complex art of digital transformation, about financial services and technology and regulation. I know things. I know banks inside out. I can run very complex businesses successfully. I can fund-raise and manage complex delivery and do 10 things at once. I can build and manage high-performing, cross-functional teams. I am bloody good at this. Why should being a woman be what I talk about? Why should it even be relevant?

But, of course, the answer is: because it is. And the implications of that are twofold. It is relevant because it is real, and it affects us all and the longer we let it, the longer it will carry on being the case. And it is relevant because it gets in the way of the transformation we try to drive. Everything we champion, everything that is essential for a truly digital economy to thrive, forces us to look at things that are different to the era of fortress balance sheets and mainframes. The way we always did things is fundamentally and axiomatically not the way we need to do things next. Diversity isn't a photo op. It's a survival mechanism for the business and the industry. So it is relevant because it is existential. And it is not the full story any more than building an API gateway solves your digital woes. But it is a part of the process. We cannot get good at this without understanding that tech is *part* of how we will change. And the humans are *how* we will get to change.

And the way we think about our humans has to change, or this will be a very expensive way of chasing our collective corporate tail.

IT IS TIME TO MAKE INTENTIONAL, CONSISTENT CHOICES

The thing about diversity is choice.

I have been working in finance for 20 years and I have been 'other' for exactly as long.

When I first arrived, I felt that I needed to catch up with my peers who had been climbing up the greasy pole over the past 4 years while I was buried in the PhD wilderness of comparative constitutional amendments and hunting down nationalist monuments and iconography in rural Turkey. (I didn't have to look very hard, to be fair, they are everywhere, but, hey, any excuse for a road trip.[6])

Then, I was keenly aware of my foreignness. Sometimes, people pretended they didn't understand my English. Hilariously, my accent seemed to become incomprehensible only when I challenged a finding or reminded them that they were behind on work that we were all depending on.

On more benign days, it was a novelty act. Guys, Leda doesn't just have a funny name. She is 'first generation', as a colleague loved to say. And every personality trait that was not as they expected or preferred was deemed to be a national characteristic. But no.

Me not laughing at your racist jokes isn't a Greek thing. It's a me thing.

And me not shying away from an argument that you started isn't a Greek thing. It's a me thing.

And me not being a sweet-tempered wall flower is not a Greek thing at all. It's a me thing.

But truth be told, it took a few months to notice this constant displacement of my nationality being blamed for all the ways in which I was not abiding by standards of femininity. You are brash, loud, feisty they said. How Greek.

But eventually I registered my other 'otherness' and it hit me like a speeding train. I stood up to go grab lunch, go to the photocopier, go to my boss' office … I don't even remember. But I stood up and looked across the floor of desks and saw … men. Just men. Only men. Nothing but men. And I turned to my colleague and said to him, 'all I see is dudes' and he laughed and said, 'you are talking to the only brown face in the room'. And so I was. That was

---

[6] If you want to go down a rabbit hole of reading about semiotics, legitimacy and the tension between secularism and the rise of political Islam in post-Kemalist Turkey, my thesis is available on the LSE website: http://etheses.lse.ac.uk/423/ and you can download it and knock yourself out wondering how did I get from that to this.

20 years ago but Shanaka's voice rang loud and clear in my head when, in the summer of 2021, I read an article called 'The only one in the room' recounting the experience of being a black executive in financial services in the US. *Plus ça change.*

My mum used to tell me this poem when I was a kid. And I will paraphrase it because I am refusing to look it up, the memory of her voice is so ingrained in my head I want to remember it authentically if not accurately. And it went like this: 'First they came for the Jews and I did not speak up, for I am not a Jew. Then they came for the communists, and I did not speak up, because I am not a communist. And so it goes. Until they came for me. And there was nobody left to speak up for me.'[7]

The first time I was involved in a diversity meeting, I realise now, I was not expected to speak. I still opened my mouth ... twice. The first time I was put in a small box. As a woman, my view on women's issues was ... you know. Personal. And we all know objectivity is important. The second time I spoke, I was put on the naughty step. Because I am white. So what do I know about race? Said the other white people in the room.

Can't win, I thought in exasperation.

Then it hit me: I wasn't meant to.

The meeting went on to be dominated by a man who explained that we needed positive discrimination (even though every woman and brown face in the room bristled and objected) because of ... wait for it ... rape. The argument was nonsensical and led nowhere. But unlike every example I have described above, *he* wasn't shut down. He wasn't dismissed or mocked. He was listened to. He had the floor. Nothing was proposed and nothing happened and he walked away without anyone in that room laughing at him the way that would have been the case if the shoe was on the other foot. And I am not saying we should have mocked him. Civility is key. I chalk this up as a very perverse victory. I just would like the same courtesy extended across the board. Because the lack of that courtesy and the constant jarring double standards have a lot to answer for when it comes to the exodus of difference in our industry. Because diverse talent isn't just not getting hired. It is also not getting retained.

---

[7] https://www.hmd.org.uk/resource/first-they-came-by-pastor-martin-niemoller/ for the full poem. I was close enough.

TALKING LIONS

In the year of our Lord 2021, Bloomberg ran with the story that out of 1,500 Goldman Sachs executives in the US, fewer than 50 were black. The gender pay gap was alive and well the world over and, in London, I was still the only woman in most rooms I walked into for work. So the only thing that changed over the last few years was our corporate dress code (hurrah for jeans and converse) and, for me, my relative seniority in each organisation. In real terms, the change is not so much what I do with my voice but how easy I am to dismiss and silence. The small box and the naughty step don't apply to me anymore. It's not nothing. But it's not enough.

And the industry has moved on a bit, don't get me wrong. We have all finally come to accept representation matters. Seeing people who look like you doing things, going places, matters. But somehow, we took that to be licence to paint by numbers, tick the box and hope that interracial couples in mortgage adverts on TV are a ballast against institutional racism, and women being cast as senior cops in Line of Duty makes up for the under-representation of women in leadership positions in real life.

A study in ethnic diversity in UK children's books published in 2020[8] (CLPE Reflecting Realities Report 2020) found that the previous year – we are not going into the depths of publishing history here, we are talking 2019 – in the UK, a diverse society recently proudly announced there is no institutional racism here, 57% of characters were white, 5% any potential skin pigment covered under the banner of BAME and 38% animals: a talking lion being a more likely occurrence than a brown face at the heart of a children's book story.

In my 20 years in the industry I have seen diversity stay resolutely a tick-boxing exercise and representation become a PR weapon in the pursuit of doing as little as possible for the maximum impact. I have personally directly worked for or with exactly as many talking lions as black executives in my time in the industry (yes that's right, that's a cool, round zero) and the only place where I walked into a room full of decision-makers who happened to be women was Oslo. Everywhere else has a diversity problem and you know how they deal with it? With diversity targets. But you know how those targets are set? They are not population averages. They are industry averages. So if you are 1% above industry average you can legitimately say you are

---

[8] See https://clpe.org.uk/research/clpe-reflecting-realities-survey-ethnic-representation-within-uk-childrens-literature for some of the excellent work CLPE are doing.

exceeding your peers and leading from the front. And you can set yourself a mission of say year on year 10% improvement so you can keep doing 'better'. And it all sounds great. But in real terms it boils down to a handful of folks. And it skilfully avoids measuring your churn, when it comes to diverse hires.

We can all make the numbers dance if that's what we are trying to do, but I wish we didn't, because the way we do diversity targets in the industry is the story-book equivalent of having 5% non-white, non-animal minor characters in each of your publications and you are golden.

Let that sink in for a moment.

Why do companies do this? Are they bad people? Are they all sinister white men? Or are they HR professionals who don't want to take on a task they don't know how to successfully complete and why risk underperforming on a personal level by taking on a target that will become a millstone around your neck in an industry that does no better anyway? Is it because people don't feel accountable for an industry-wide problem? Whatever it is, don't talk to me about representation as if it is enough. Because it becomes its own death sentence if what was meant to be precedent is nothing more than a highly visible exception.

> Don't talk to me about representation as if it is enough. Because it becomes its own death sentence if what was meant to be precedent is nothing more than a highly visible exception.

Now I am not saying it doesn't matter. It matters hugely. But what it achieves is getting us on the road of change. Representation matters because it ignites the art of the possible, because it can and should be to inspire deeper change. Not replace it. So representation matters *exactly* because it is meant to be the start of something bigger.

Ruth Bader Ginsburg was famously asked how many women is enough women on the Supreme Court bench and she said: nine. That's all of them. And you know what my first reaction was when I read that quote?

I gasped.

Were we even *allowed* to say that? Were we allowed to hope for that?

Something happened in my head the day I read that. Something major shifted in my own perception. Before I move onto speaking about the mechanics of how we hire and the danger of self-perpetuating demographics, let's allow the fact that even to me, an outspoken, glass-ceiling-bashing ambitious woman, the mental barrier that said 'the world as is, is my starting point' was well and truly in place. The world of all-male boardrooms, all-male-judge benches, analogue experiences and bank branches. See what I did there? I connected diversity to innovation again.

Because although I have no trouble imagining a world of no bank branches and although I am both capable and confident in my own abilities, imagining a world where the Supreme Court of the US could be all-female felt like a bridge too far. Even though women are a little more than 50% of the population.

Let that sink in, if you ever question whether *what we know* colours how we think of the world in ways that go beyond the immediate effects we think it may have. The very world that we are trying to change.

Do you see why you can't even divorce diversity and innovation?

CHANGING ALL THE THINGS

The shift we claim to represent, the digital avalanche we are flagging, comes fully loaded with different ways of doing *everything*: different ways of imagining service, delivery and monetisation. Design, functionality, distribution, pricing. What we champion required the imagination to *not* digitise the yellow pages but to create an interface that allows you to book a plumber, purchase theatre tickets or make a hotel reservation for you and Clive, your pet iguana, without the in-between steps that used to be essential to achieve that.

This hinges on the ability to imagine a world different to the one we are in. This ability is key to doing the job at hand.

The ability to imagine things being different is key to doing the job.

Let that sink in.

Let that sink in as we struggle to get our own self-perpetuating demographics to admit that there is anything strange about the make-up of our offices or anything surprising about the predictability of decisions made by the same group of folks. The truism of 'if you always do what you always did, you will always get what you always got' extends to you if you always do what you always did with the folks you always did it with, you will get same old, and may not even know it.

But back to the Supreme Court.

If it is possible to have nine men on the bench, it should be *possible* by a process of absolute meritocratic selection to have nine women. In fact, it should be easier, as there are a few more women than men in the world. Digest that for a second because we are not moving on. That's the whole story and the take-away I need you to remember as an ally, as a practitioner, as a member of the tribe of folks who will change the world through consistent integrity.

The world's smallest civil resistance movement: you.

This mental image is powerful because that is the benchmark of success, in our diverse societies.

Until you can potentially and entirely accidentally – not by design, positive discrimination, quotas or affirmative action but a pure meritocratic selection through a competitive process and a diverse talent pipeline – end up with a team that is all non-white, non-binary, *non-predictable* individuals, then you have work to do. *We* have work to do. Until it is possible and it doesn't have to be engineered. Until you can find them and they can find you and it is possible for a room full of decision-makers to be all non-white non-male without it being a conscious act of defiance then we are nowhere near done. And this is not a problem for the diverse candidates to solve. It's a problem for the industry to solve.

> Until it is possible for a room of decision-makers to be all non-white, non-male without it being a conscious act of defiance then we are not done. And this is not a problem for the diverse candidates to solve.

Now, exactly as a bank can't wish its mainframe out of existence and leapfrog to a Minority Report-type infrastructure (all the fancy tech, none of the fascism, ideally), our demographic skews being what they are, we have work to do and that work starts, as ever, from where we actually are, not where we say we are or where we wish we had gotten to by now. Before our talent pipelines and our experience selection pools are fully loaded with diverse talent, we have work to do. Frustrating as it is, you can but start from where you are. Be it the terrible choices your IT predecessors made that have locked you into a COBOL estate decades after it made any sense or the legacies of sociological realities that meant women stayed by the stove, non-white populations in white-majority countries did menial manual labour and working-class people stayed largely in their place. I want to smash it all and propel us into the future as much as you do. Ok maybe a little more because I lived out my life at the wrong end of this equation. But I promise you moving on will be good for all of us. It won't disadvantage anyone. Losing privilege isn't the same as disadvantage, you see. But the road ahead is long and it isn't getting any shorter while we obfuscate.

The reality of both digital transformation and true equality is that we need to start from where we are. Even if this is not where you would start from, wanting to go where we are going.

THE THING ABOUT MERITOCRACY

The parallels between our analogue estates and our monochrome management structures can be taken too far. They are similar in that they constrain us with received wisdom anchored in something that worked well for a time, for some measures of success and for some people. And they are evidently and self-avowedly at a loss when it comes to coping with the world we are now living in, be it the avalanche of new technology, what it takes to build it or the equality implicit in new ways of working. They represent the past we need to depart from, the legacy we need to tackle and, frankly, a future we need to avoid. A reality we inhabit and need to depart from. And that means, as above, starting from where we are. To go to where we are heading to.

So digital transformation and equality and inclusion have similarities in that they entail hard work and consistent choices. They are also similar in that they both require a robust acknowledgement of *where we are*. The hard truths of our legacies, habits and work still undone. The parallels start straining perhaps when you enter the discussions of power dynamics around entrenched systems of power. But fundamentally, the same urges that make a traditional board reluctant to risk their quarterly returns by spending time on a new technology, quarter on quarter, until years later they look back and see a different picture emerging, these are the very same urges that make short-term change unlikely even among those who imagine themselves among the good guys.

Of course we want diversity. But. We need to make a quick hire. All the candidates were white and male and what can you do? We will do better next time. Or the time after that. Meanwhile let's measure diversity across our *entire* team because all the EAs, receptionists and most of HR are female and that makes the numbers look a little bit better and we are all one team, right?

Wrong actually and someone joked semi-seriously a few years back that, by hiring a male EA, I was destroying our diversity stats.

Actually, I have been in multiple situations where I was the one fighting for the white heterosexual man to get the job ahead of the female candidate because *he was better* and the hiring manager was reluctant to hire him because they wanted their stats to look better.

I don't know who needs to hear this but STOP.

> There is no space for your mainframes in the future. But there is plenty of space for those who originally built them and their sons. Just not them alone.

Do not, I repeat, DO NOT do this. That is another way you can help us and this matters. Two wrongs never make a right. A diverse world is not a world where white men don't make it to the top. It's *not* a world where a mediocre candidate with certain protected characteristics gets picked ahead of a stellar white man. A diverse world is a world where the white men *are not the only ones* that make it to the top. And that's the difference between the digital transformation and diversity analogy. There is no space for your mainframes into the future. But there is plenty of space for those who originally built them and their sons. Just not them alone.

And, before you even utter the words: if you think that opening the door to competition makes exclusion somehow inevitable, it only means one thing: that you see that the dice are loaded and the cards marked in your favour. I totally get you wouldn't want to be at the receiving end of that. It ain't pretty. Frankly, I am done making the business case for diversity or pandering to the 'yes, but' brigade. You can pack up your little violins, we are no longer engaging in that conversation because I have finally wizened up to the fact that you are not listening to our answers. Your concerns are not objections to be addressed, they are obstacles meant to distract and slow us down. And it's working. It's working way too well and has done for way too long.

I shouldn't need to explain that I have nothing against white men any more than I should have to say that the best people should always get the job. The implied assumption that the only way a white man would be dethroned entails a compromise on meritocracy has defined our conversations for way too long.

The thing about diversity is that representation matters, of course it does. But it doesn't matter as much as access. In fact representation is meant to inspire access. Otherwise you are doing it wrong. So if your business thinks of success as hitting industry averages, you are part of the problem. Choices are being actively made and you are either making them or letting them be made by others while staying silent. And silence is collusion so please stop staying silent. And if the argument you are presented with is 'yes but it is hard' then welcome to our world.

As you can see from these pages, it happens and will happen again and again. Conversations and debates people don't really want to have. Tactics mostly geared at deterring or delaying you. If you can see through it, resist. Do not be deterred. This is both possible and beneficial. So what if it is hard? We can do hard things. And the hard thing we would need to do here is unpick old mistakes and entrenched privilege. As hard jobs go, this should be cathartic.

We live in highly diverse societies. We work in highly non-diverse industries. The only way you get to this is by an active choice to only let some people in. The only way you stay this way is through an active choice to *not* to better. And for the avoidance of doubt: setting yourself industry average targets is part of that choice. And the thing about choice is that it is active and intentional. And you can stop. Now. Were you to choose to. So that's my ask. Notice. Reflect. And make choices.

YOUR CALL TO ACTION

1. Make it a priority to notice what your colleagues and friends experience in the workplace. Not everyone's lived reality is just like yours.
2. There are no innocent bystanders … When you notice bad behaviour and do nothing, your silence is collusion and the surest way to ensure that whatever you are witnessing will happen again.
3. If you behave badly and are caught out, even if you didn't intend to cause hurt or offence … if you are told that you have … apologise.
4. Don't dismiss the moments: they matter. Be an ally in the moments that matter, not just the grand narratives.
5. Try not to hire idiots.

5

Fierce Grace: What Drives Us On, Despite Our Bad Habits and Demographic Constraints

SNEAK PREVIEW

In our industry, we have been saying that 'change is the new normal' for years and yet it seems to only now be sinking in: what it actually means is twofold. It means that there will ever and forever be more for us to learn … and it means that doing 'something' isn't the ballgame. Innovation isn't its own reward. We need to do a lot of very specific things, some of them very hard, to survive in this new landscape and find ways of being successful and competitive.

The choices of where we focus our energy, how we do the hard things well and how we navigate the constraints of our current condition are rendered ever more complex by the bad habits we have discussed at some length.

So, how do you do it? Despite it all?

By forming new habits and resisting the old.

If the challenges start with people, that is also how they are resolved. So let's turn to how you find, organise and deploy the right people for the task ahead.

Diversity is *not* the key organising idea of this book.

But the way we approach diversity, in this industry, is symptomatic of a wider set of behaviours towards both talent (i.e. humans) and new ideas (yes, diversity). So we need to face our self-imposed constraints before we can meaningfully discuss how we can better attract and retain talent that is critical to the change we need to drive.

At the end of the day, innovation is the key to surviving in a changing environment where 'what got you here, won't get you there' and innovation is achieved through talented individuals coming together in high-performing

DOI: 10.1201/9781003364436-5

teams that collaborate and support each other.

> Innovation is achieved through talented individuals coming together in high-performing teams that collaborate and support each other.

That is what we turn to next.

We just couldn't get to it without painting a picture of the context in which we are trying to build those teams. The bad habits and failed promises, constraining demographics and the behaviours that perpetuate them.

Talent is a necessary but not sufficient condition in the quest for profound and lasting transformation. Getting this right is a key ingredient of innovation.

Getting it right is also fairer.

Which is a key ingredient of integrity and trust. Which in turn fuels collaboration, commitment and creativity. A virtuous circle if I ever saw one. And not a moment too soon. Because the reason we need innovation in the first place is that the party, as we knew it, is over.

The way we used to make money as an industry is changing. The way we used to live has changed. Dramatic? I don't think so.

THE BIGGEST CLICHÉ OF OUR TIME IS ALSO TRUE: CHANGE IS THE NEW NORMAL

Change is a constant of the human condition and technology has been a key component of that change throughout human history. From the advent of the steam engine and the Industrial Revolution, labour-saving devices and the advent of the internet, tech always played its part in a social web of overlapping contexts. The advent of new technology also consistently unlocked new sets of possibilities that created opportunities that, in turn, opened new horizons but also simultaneously brought categories of jobs and entire industries to an end. And it did that again and again and again, directly by rendering the job itself redundant or, indirectly, by causing profound social change that made the job untenable. Technology has transformed the landscape of what people do for a living in agriculture and manufacturing, and most definitely in the services industry. The advent of technology and socioeconomic change always go hand in hand and fuel each other in ways that are often hard to disentangle.

And the world keeps changing. And industries and jobs are created in the wake of this change but equally and significantly many categories of employment disappear too.

Nobody employs scullery maids anymore and thatchers are rare specialist craftsmen in quaint corners of England. Farriers are no longer on the main street and commerce relies much less on 'representatives' with every passing year.

So it is hardly surprising that the advent of technology changes how we work and how we make money in our industry. We were hardly going to be exempt. And this is hardly the first time this is happening. To the economy or the financial services industry. And yet this time the tech change is a little bit different.

Firstly, because, historically and as far as banking was concerned, new technology brought with it little downside and a lot of opportunity to make new money, more money, money faster. This time, digital transformation was a little bit more of a mixed bag as it opened up the competitive landscape and started challenging the way services were packaged and priced, paving the road for greater transparency and leaner profits.

Secondly, and again, historically, banking as an industry had the power, tools and intent to try and resist or at least moderate the impact of external change. And that's exactly how the industry approached the digital era, for a while at least: genuinely trying it on with the idea that a report that took weeks and a few people to collate could, nay should, cost the same as an API feed. And that digital services could be designed and managed in the same command-and-control manner for approvals, risk analytics and people management as our traditional way of doing things.

> The digital era is here, uninvited perhaps but triumphant. Being changed by it isn't a choice. It's an inevitability.

Thankfully for us all, that did not work, but it was not for want of trying. And I will give banks full marks for effort when it comes to resisting wholesale change. But sadly it doesn't work that way. The digital era is here, uninvited perhaps but triumphant. Being changed by it isn't a choice. It's an inevitability. And inside banks, pricing is not the only thing changing. The entire economic model a digital economy plays to is different: the fundamental rules of what the service is and who the consumer is and what the rules are in an era of hyper-connectivity where the bank is part of a web of services, be it through open banking of a Banking as a Service model, the rules are different, the interdependence is different and the profit-sharing is different.

Why am I telling you all this?

WE ARE NOT TALKING ABOUT NEW TOOLS. WE ARE TALKING ABOUT NEW ECONOMIC MODELS

This is not a book about platform economics (if you really want to read what I have to say on that topic, you are welcome to petition my publisher and I will get writing), for now trust me when I say that the economics are different and that matters.

That difference is very much fuelled by the advent of digital connectivity but is not reduced to it.

In plain English this means that 'digital' is not an app. In fact, you can get yourself an app and build the required API and still fall short of 'doing digital' which only comes from participating fully in the digital economy, without trying to make concepts of value, profit and exchange fit into old-world mental models.

What does that mean?

It means many things.

Firstly it means interdependence. Uber didn't build its own version of Google Maps nor did it build its own payment rails. The entire business model rests on other businesses being part of the process, the success and the resilience. If you understand that as a construct then you probably understand why in the summer of 2021 the world's financial services providers all held their breath during a global Akamai outage. Or you appreciate the significance of your onboarding provider of choice having 'issues' the day you launch a new savings product and new customers can't sign up. It's not your fault. But it is your problem. And the solution is not to build everything yourself. You don't have that kind of time or that kind of money.

Because another thing that is part and parcel of the new digital economies is a heavily differentiated, subtler and lower price point. This digital thing costs less. The consumer expects it to cost less and your competitors expect it to cost less. And if you try and do everything yourself it won't cost less and it won't be as good as it would be if specialists built each part of it. It will also not cost less if you try to do the new things alongside or on top of your old technology and business. That will add cost and you will find yourself trying to square an economic circle.

And it will cost more in opportunity cost as building everything yourself will take a long time, time you don't have.

And that's before you've started looking at operating costs.

Because the digital era gives you options. So imagine you are a pension provider. You have a choice to distribute your products via brokers called Gary and Sam or you have the option to work on top of a variety of platforms, in partnership with aggregators and alongside a variety of solutions for money management and saving. The choice comes with infrastructure implications. Your business looks different, has different needs, a different org structure and different operating costs.

Need I go on?

When I say the economics are different I mean in their entirety. And although the detail of how the digital era ushers in a new economic model warrants its own book, it is important to not forget it as, for the purposes of this book, a lot of what we spend our time looking at is all the ways in which banks tried to shoe-horn the new capabilities into their old economic model, retaining old price points, trying to do everything themselves but not lose their competitive edge and run parallel or incomplete, overlapping and non-differentiated operating models.

Why did they do such a crazy thing?

Because they thought they could get away with it.

RESISTANCE IS FUTILE

The idea at first was that resistance to the pace of change would slow things down and abstinence from the conversation would mute certain topics altogether. My sister does this when she gets up from the family table to fetch something from the kitchen: don't you lot dare say anything interesting while I'm gone from the room.

Needless to say, the strategy worked neither for my sister nor for the banks.

First of all, digital capabilities were not the exclusive and proprietary domain of financial services. They were transforming the economy as a whole. This is important and we don't talk about it enough. My 70-year-old mother in Athens shops online, reads news on her smartphone and calls me on Viber. She doesn't use online banking but my 77-year-old dad does.

Neither has used an encyclopaedia or recipe book in a while, will book theatre tickets online and have a Netflix account.

So what?

So a lot.

The transformation of the economy is profound. Both because my mother is not a digital native, she is most definitely not an early adopter and she is in no way the obvious or primary user persona such services were originally targeted at ... but now they are ubiquitous enough in both geography and demographic reach that she uses them without hesitation in a country that still mostly uses cash. But also, less personally but as significantly, because each of those services fundamentally disrupts the economic models of the industry it replaces or 'evolves', and the services it displaces. In everything from Hollywood to broadsheets and the high street to telco, 'digital' is not just about how you interface with the product. It is about a new product that you consume in different ways and that operates in a different context and with different economic parameters at work. That's pretty much everything.

So believing that delaying the adoption of API-first connectivity in banking would actually dictate the pace of change sounds ... insane?

I guess. From this side of the last 15 years, thinking the banks could stem the tide of change seems arrogant and slightly unhinged. And yet. From the far shore of change, 15 years ago, that is exactly what they thought. They thought we could dictate the pace if not the direction of change. They thought they could control this in its specifics if not its shape.

Needless to say ... That didn't quite work.

The economy, commerce, news, art all moved rapidly in the same direction.

'Digital' was not yet another channel. It represented what philosopher Thomas Kuhn calls a 'paradigm shift'. Industrialisation, world wars, 9/11 all presented such shifts. The term was originally intended for use in concepts of experimental science,[1] but it has been enthusiastically adopted by sociologists and political scientists as it provided a way to denote the moment after profound change has occurred in a fundamental set of perceptions. What is normal shifts, after a paradigm shift. It is radical, pervasive and irreversible – albeit non-permanent.

So forgive me if I laugh when I hear of job titles inside banks including 'head of digital channels', 'head of digital architecture' and 'head of data' alongside each other but separate and not even reporting to the same people.

[1] The Structure of Scientific Revolutions (1962).

CHOICES, CHOICES

It soon became rather obvious that resistance was futile in terms of holding the world back.

Getting on with the programme or staying put at whatever cost that choice ended up exacting, emerged as the only choices to be made. But getting with the programme was easier said than done. For it entailed technology investment, wrapping our heads around the new economic models mentioned above and trying to make those new models work in unknown and shifting market conditions, only to stub our toe against our existing ways of working and bad habits that stood in the way of success in a way that was insidious and profound. Which explains why I started with spending so much time talking about those bad habits so early on in the book. It also highlights the obvious but salient fact that what needs to be done is not a simple piece of work.

This is everything. All at once.

It's hard and its scary.

Change in tech, organisation structural, economic imperatives and culture all at once … is a tall order. That's a lot, right there. And when you stop and think about the fact that what you have to do in each of those categories depends on what you are trying to achieve, what you've done before, what you are doing in the other parallel work streams and a whole host of other constraints, it really is even more than a lot. That's not even a proper sentence, but you catch my drift.

And it doesn't come with a playbook. You have to do all this without guardrails, blueprints, established wisdom, benchmarks or guarantees.

So you can't blame the folks who were winning at the game we used to play for hoping they could carry on playing it.

Only that was not an option. Change was inevitable and it had to be wholesale. But there was so much to do that everyone was a little overwhelmed and a little slow and the industry is nowhere near where it needs to be. Even a decade and a half in. And that is as important in itself as it is significant in the context of the wider economy. That has not stood still.

The connecting thread to everything that makes this change difficult and everything I advocate in this book (and in this life) is that choices need to be made, across the board. A lot of choices. And yes some of those are about tech, but it's the best tech to support our changing business models. So actually the harder choices are around that business model itself and the organisational structures and behaviours to support it. And frankly the real challenge, once we've accepted this, is that the decision-makers don't know enough about what is needed and what is critical, from a standing start. Because it's all new. Hence the hesitation.

Hence, also, the significance of getting the right people to look into options and choices, when choices are so critical to your future survival. So how do you make sure you have the right people, given everything we have discussed so far? And how do you make sure you keep them, if you have them? And how do you support them but also sort of get out of their way? A lot of the last couple of chapters have been about how we need to get out of our own way which is no small feat. But, as if that wasn't complex enough, getting out of our way isn't actually adequate. It's only one step on a much longer journey.

And before you roll your eyes and say 'disruption is the new normal' I need to warn you I am kind of up to here with the wanton use of the word disruption.

Seriously.

It's been 20 years since I saw the phrase on an IBM deck lying open on my boss's desk. It felt daring to my young eyes back then. I know now how those decks work and how far the power of a phrase is diluted if it's invoked again and again, and nothing happens.

So here we are, two decades on.

The great and the good of our industry privately still go around saying to each other things are changing but we've got this, right? Things are changing but not too much, right? Things are changing but we will be ok, right? And no, there is no secret cabal. They don't say it in so many words. But they think it and hope it is true. You see that in the way they discuss budgets. In the way they sequence protects and sign-off expansion plans and investments. Because they know that the wait-and-see approach of the last few years didn't work. And they may not know exactly what choice is the right next step, but they know more of the same ain't it.

So let's face into this.

We are living through decades of unprecedented technological progress, the tempo and breadth of which is staggering compared to any other sustained period of change in human history when seen in capability terms and not pure socio-economic vectors.

And rather than unleashing its transformative potential for our organisations, for our communities, for ourselves, those of us in FS, spend our lives looking at the change, taking a guess at the least scary potential outcome, declaring it inevitable and then settling in to wait till the storm of getting there passes. What do I mean? I mean we have spent 15 years doing stand-alone innovation projects. An API here, a Watson pilot there, a blockchain experiment yonder. In a lab. While the bulk of the business continues as it always had. As late as 2022 I have been invited to regulator-sponsored round-tables on key trends and broke everyone's heart when I said 'all of it. And all of the bits that came before that you are yet to engage with. That too.'

Let's face it: that's what financial services have done for most of the past decade. But so have many other industries. Look at the ocean, pick a wave that doesn't scare you and call it 'innovation strategy'. Some budget gets allocated, licence to play is granted and – and this is the important part – the rest of the business does the things grown-ups do to make money. I remember one of the most senior sales folks in a bank I worked at many years ago telling me 'some of us have to do real work sweetheart' and he had no interest in what our API gateway was for.

If only life and business worked that way … and the point I am making is that not only does life not work this way but finally we are also realising that.

So at least now there is a sense of acceptance. And the next question you get time and again is 'where do I begin?'.

WHEN 'THE VERY BEGINNING' IS NO LONGER 'A VERY GOOD PLACE TO START'

Yes that's a Sound of Music reference. I like to mix it up. I am large, I contain multitudes. Yes that's a Walt Whitman quote. See what I did there?

But back to choices.

How many times a day do we hear that phrase? I should have started 15 years ago and didn't, so where do I start now? I can't go back, there is no time. And I can't just go forward, I don't have the right pieces of the puzzle in place to even know which way 'forward' is. So what do I do, if I have no time to go back and no way to go forward?

If you have ever asked me in real life, by the way, you know my answer is always the same: in the middle. Start in the middle. Because the middle is messy and where everything happens so might as well get right to the point. Also. The middle is where you are. So might as well start from where you are.

Not the middle of the digital revolution, for the avoidance of doubt, not at all. You can't catapult yourself there. Waiting and hoping someone else would work out a short-cut didn't work. So not that middle. But *your* middle. The bit where something has happened, though not enough, and a lot needs to happen. Fast.

But the middle is messy and telling what's important apart from what isn't, in that mess, is not easy. And that's where choices come in. Because the whole point of waiting was in the hope that choices would get easier if we waited for other folks to make some mistakes first, for some things to play out. If we could wait long enough ... then we would see ... and that didn't work. So choices now have to be made in even more constrained circumstances than when we thought we'd wait and see rather than make choices in such uncertainty.

Oh the irony.

The challenge with looking at the choices ahead of us in all their staggering interdependence and complexity is that it feels appropriate to start at the beginning. Only the beginning is not available to us. That ship has sailed.

That place of a pristine blank page and zero on the counter. Gone.

Also, if we try to start from an imaginary day zero (which, incidentally is where most strategy decks start and why they are no use to you despite the 'reassuringly expensive' price tag) you load yourself up with unnecessary assumptions that, maybe, should have been important but ended up not being even remotely relevant, hindsight being 20/20. But even that isn't helpful because the important bit is not what wasn't significant but how your perception shifted in the process. So you can't buy that knowledge in a strategy deck. You have to do the doing.

So that you can work out for yourself what makes things loom large before we get started that will then fizzle out faster than fast.

Starting at the beginning is overwhelming and not hugely helpful.

So what then? Start from the end and work backwards? That doesn't work either. Because if you think about every successful journey you or your fellow industry leaders have completed, if you look back from the finish line, you cannot learn anything about how you got there. You can see where you got to and all the gambles that worked, as if they were inevitable. And that makes for a great photo op but isn't helpful for the next venture and adventure.

If you try to work backwards from an imagined end-state, you will seek a linear path, you will make assumptions based on what worked for you in the past. You will seek a bit of predetermination and you will struggle to account for uncertainty, confusion and lucky breaks when they come.

And I assure you, they will come.

That's why banks never talk about any of that, by the way. Because they plan from a blank page forward, or backwards from an imagined end-state. Never in the reality of the middle. As if success were predetermined if you are focused and clear. But given what we are dealing with here, fluidity is the name of the game and the story we need to hear and the reality for which we need to plan. That's where things get tough and execution falters: the moment when the next thing is not clear and nothing feels certain or inevitable.

HAPPY ENDINGS ARE NOT INEVITABLE

Truth be told we have not done each other many favours here.

From Hollywood love stories to FinTech Legends, we tell stories of businesses, careers and lives as if the happy ending was foretold and axiomatic and all it took to get there was a journey of grit and determination in a swift and impassioned montage. You can do *anything* if you believe in yourself and work hard. Errrr. No.

We teach people to persist and persevere as if determination was the only thing standing between you and being America's Next Top Model. I don't know who these people are. These people for whom such things may be true, if they exist. These people who perpetuate these myths, as if true, oblivious or indifferent to the damage they cause.

Most businesses fail. Do you want me to repeat that? Most. Businesses. Fail. Statistically speaking.

And I am sure they believe and work hard in their vast majority.

Most entrepreneurs do not become unicorn founders. Most plans change.

And most people won't ever become America's Next Top Model because they are not tall enough, good looking enough, American enough (or at all) or didn't even know it was a thing they could go for. And that last part is important. If you don't know something is possible, you may not start trying for it on time. And that really has an impact on your chances of success.

> You are not guaranteed a seat at any table. You may not make it into the future. The future will happen. That is a given. But it may happen to you rather than for you and we don't think of that possibility long enough to be scared into action.

So not everyone gets there (wherever that may be) in the end and this is important.

You are *not* guaranteed a seat at any table. You, at an individual and business level, may not make it into the future. The future will happen. That is a given. But it may happen to you rather than for you and we don't think of that possibility long enough to be scared and that is terrible, because it would help to have a reality check when urgency is of the essence. Because you may work hard and still not make it. And this really matters especially in light of all the bad habits we already discussed and all the weird and wonderful ways in which we get in our own way.

So what I am trying to say, I guess, is get your skates on.

If a happy ever after is not guaranteed, and it is not, *choices* are more important than ever. Oh and hard work. Hollywood is right about the determination part. You can't do much without determination and hard work. It's not enough, but it is essential. Grit and determination are needed *because* things never work out as planned or expected. You will get blind-sided, you will make mistakes, profoundly unfair things will happen and the earth will not stand still … and you need to pick yourself back up, take stock, do some accelerated learning and start again. So yes. Grit. Determination. Hard work. Absolutely key. But also the ability to pivot and take stock and learn from the things that may actually be your fault. Because not everything that happens to you is external. You will make mistakes and miscalculations on this journey.

To be able to know when to dig in and when to pivot and take stock, you need a North Star.

You need to be going somewhere, somewhere specific, otherwise why bother?

And, before you sigh with relief, this is very different to a predetermined end-state. A sense of vision is very different to a blueprint you can follow to an inevitable photo finish. And that's where choices start coming in, as your North Star will help drive a lot of the choices you need to make, from tech to conduct and everything in-between.

But you have to pick a North Star first and that in itself entails a nuanced and complex set of moves.

At this point, I need to confess that I am deeply suspicious when I hear people describing their current situation as their younger selves' Valhalla. And equally suspicious when I hear organisations describing their future Valhalla with great precision and confidence in its specifics and their role in it. A North Star isn't a guarantee. It's not an inevitable photo finish by another name.

It's a dream. A burning fire, not a roadmap. A set of beliefs and convictions and ambition. Not a tale of linear inevitability. Now you may already know all this, but to actually speak to your teams and the industry in terms that don't indicate robust confidence in the (fiction) that the world will turn out just so, goes against the grain of how we do things in the industry. And in fact, this language of confident precision, that the future will behave itself, has actually had a rather deleterious impact on the industry on many levels. And I don't just mean the young entrepreneurs who don't take advice because, in the stories, the nay-sayers are the bad guys and pivots are Road to Damascus moments and somehow the two look profoundly different from the far shore of a story. Less so in the mire. Yes I mean exactly that: How do you know when it's time to double down or time to pivot? Other than instinct and good advice and reflection … in the moment … and hindsight. Always 20/20.

And yes I mean that opportunities are missed in an industry that has forgotten how to tell determination and obstinacy apart.

THIS IS GOING TO HURT

The damage I speak of refers to the businesses that have decisions to make but find themselves unable to make them. They also have cash to burn and burn it they do. Because they have set their sights on how the story *needs* to end, have positioned themselves on the road, facing towards the Emerald City and the rest shall come, is the attitude. That is not just naïve, it is dangerous. Life waits on no man and time pauses for nobody. And yet I have spent the entirety of my career seeing organisations set their hearts on a future, declaring it inevitable, deciding what risks they are *not* prepared to take in order to get there (as if that was a choice) and then sort of wait life out.

This reminds me of a conversation I had many years ago, in a different life altogether that ended with a young student telling me he will pray for my soul. I had a teaching scholarship for my PhD which meant many hours spent in classrooms with bright-eyed young things teaching them the rudiments of political science. The offer of prayer was preceded by a question along the lines of 'so do you really not believe that the democratic, territorially-bound nation-state is the culmination of human civilisation and the inevitable outcome of inexorable human progress, the happy ending of modern politics?'.

Words to that effect were spoken to me over 20 years ago, outside an LSE classroom. I had just finished teaching a year's worth of classes on the evolution of modern state forms. The whole course was about how what we consider good and inevitable today, inside our nation states with their representative democracies and moral high ground, is just a step on a road of shapes and ways of organising public life that felt as inevitable (if not as good) to those living inside them in the moment as any other. 'Glad you've been paying attention' was my sentiment if not my exact words. Do you really not believe progress is inevitable? He doubled down. Nothing is inevitable other than death and gravity, I said to him. Everything else is sociologically constructed. It is built. It can be broken.

'I will pray for you, miss,' said my student who didn't much like the idea of life without a happy ending.

And walked off.

I laughed then. But I have thought of him often as I sit in meeting rooms with executives who have decided what future they would like to be a part of, bought themselves the right hat and now are waiting for things to play themselves out to the inevitable curtain call. And they believe, just as my student did, in Progress. In things moving in one direction – with no wrong turns, dead-ends, reversals and roundabouts. They believe in life moving towards things that are Better – ignoring that Better is contextual, situation-specific and looks very different for the Haves and Have Nots. And above all, they seem to believe that those who have a seat at the table today will stay there, those who hold a hand of cards today will be in the game no matter how that hand is played. That the hand may change but the game will not. So they do what they can to strengthen that hand. Blind to the world changing in ways wild and unpredictable. *Wilfully* blind to the radically shifting change of the game itself, the players and what winning may look like.

Picture this …. The bank grudgingly accepts the future will look different. Innovation is key. It stands to reason as the change they have to respond to entails learning how to do a lot of things differently and with different tools to boot. Technology will have to be used differently. So the bank gets itself a lab and a couple of partnerships with accelerators. It funds conferences and pilots with funky start-ups. Especially after they tried to create some KPIs for the team and it was easier to say how many pilots you will do vs how many ideas you will have or how many problems you will solve or how you will drive things forward, since the business doesn't yet know which way is up.

So this is a start, right?

And an epiphany may come.

Meanwhile, the same bank has a payments' gateway that leaves some of its subsidiaries exposed and others swimming in unused liquidity because of the foibles of time differences and misaligned working weeks (true story, by the way). And when the innovation folks say 'we can use technology to fix that' they are told that is real stuff, cross jurisdictional and Big Boy Work so no, not yet. Or a bank (still a true story, different bank) has no identity management infrastructure so when a customer comes of age, moves house or gets divorced, the system needs to re-onboard them as a new customer and when the digital kids say 'now that's a meaningful problem I can solve for you', they are pointed towards facial recognition software innovations for staff access to the building. Or (same bank this time, still a true story) the bank that has by this point an innovation team in *each* P&L and really knows how to do sprint planning and all the cool stuff also has a loan management system that requires an 8-week project of harsh deadlines and long days to change an interest rate because, you got it, the innovation team is not allowed to work on this kind of problem.

Picture this: a hypothetical bank could, on the same day, decide to de-fund the effort to replace a piece of archaeology, such as a COBOL-based loan management system and, that same bank, on the same day will issue a press release celebrating an award for its amazing hackathon programmes or the go-live of an ice cream vending machine with facial recognition running on its very own Kubernetes cluster. And I will confess to making myself sick on ice cream once, trying to see how genuine your smile needed to be before you got your magnum. What I learned is: not very, it was all in the tilt of the lips, and three magnums is the limit. The fourth definitely makes you feel queasy.

But back to that hypothetical set of priorities. Why would they do that? They probably would tell you the two decisions were not connected, it wasn't a case of either or, this was all down to different priorities and budgets and levels of decision-making. But that's no answer. It's obfuscation.

Why *would* they do something like that?

Because. Because of regulatory pressures needing funds be spent elsewhere, because of COVID being the excuse for a whole multitude of sins, because of a change in leadership, because it was a Tuesday. But mostly because replacing the bits of archaeology dotted around the banks *matters*. You get the ice cream machine right and everyone says hurrah. You don't get it right and who the hell cares. But you get the loan redemption dates wrong and *everyone* cares. All the more reason to do it and do it right, I hear you say. Well yes. But it's hard. And choices have to be made including the very choice to stay the course when it's hard and the *next* choice is not clear. That is where all the bad habits and monochrome leadership we have discussed conspire against us because muscle memory pulls you back to the predictable and familiar. There was a reason why we started there.

THE PROBLEM WITH THE FUTURE IS THAT THE PRESENT WAS HERE FIRST

Picture this: you are inside one of those banks we have been discussing.

Say the business made a decision. One of those blank page/specific future type decisions. And what they decided was, take your pick, they decided cloud was the future and wanted in on the action. Or smart contracts were the future and the bank would not be left behind. Or they decided that the future is digital and they need to improve their mobile channels. They have made a choice now, right? I should be getting off their backs with my 'choices matter' nag-fest. They made a commitment, they have picked the thing they believe is key to the future. And they are now doing 'stuff' around this 'thing'. Projects and white papers, consulting engagements and conference appearances.

But back at the farm what they have done is twofold:

First they decided they can't do everything and therefore they shouldn't have to. Then and only then, they made a set of choices about what to do next. So by design or default they have decided to *not* act on a whole host of things by virtue of what they decided to focus on. They *then* added whatever it is they did choose to focus on, to an otherwise unchanged entity, selling the same services in largely the same way with the new capabilities added to the roster (same old only now there is another line item – 'also available in black').

There is no doubt some change is taking place. The company has decided the future is different. Cloud-native. Distributed. Immutable. Whatever. The company can see it's coming and has decided it needs to do a bit more than just experiment. By virtue of its business model or market position, its ticket to the races requires a bit more than a bit of experimentation. So it does a bit more. Adds some capabilities to the mix. Some investment is made. It talks the talk. It even runs a LinkedIn campaign on NFTs or whatever else feels zeitgeisty enough. Decisions are being made. That's what I have been going on about all along, right? The business does not feel unprepared.

But neither is it committed.

Because the firm may be confident it knows how the story ends, but the problem with the future is it isn't here yet. And the present is. Here. Fully loaded with its own problems and foibles. With its own opportunities and profitability structures and pressures and storms in teacups that,

The problem with the future is it isn't here yet. And the present is. Here. Fully loaded with its own problems and foibles, opportunities, profitability structures, pressures and storms in teacups that may feel like the end of the world as they unfold.

as they unfold, you have no way of knowing if they are indeed a storm in a teacup or the end of the world. Until they end, one way or another. And to sacrifice the present for the future seems foolish, especially when the future looms inevitable. Do you see the problem with all this?

I hope you do. But most decision-makers don't.

Having picked their chosen future, the idea that it is not *The Future* is no longer entertained. So they battle the challenges of the present, making moves towards this inevitable future but without the urgency of uncertainty and pathos of firefighting. That is the exclusive reserve of the present, strangely.

Meanwhile the company adds a bit of technical garnish to its current set-up, adding a bit of the Thing that is needed for this very specific future that is now believed to be inevitable. A bit of funky kit. A few keywords. Some new talent. A new division or two. And then the company looks around the room. Maybe a few partnerships are the way forward? Not too risky. Not too bold. Not too daring. Or at least not too 'alone and out there'. And please go for things that won't take up too much headspace. We have a business to run.

Besides, why would we take risks and gamble a profitable and stable present, when the future is inevitable? And not only that, but we have procured the Thing, right? We have the talisman, the piece of the puzzle that was missing. Be it an API gateway, a team of Data Scientists, a DeFi lab. Whatever it is.

So. Now we wait. For the inevitable future to happen. For the happy ending to come. Smug. All-knowing. And oh so very wrong. Not just because we think we know how the story ends and we will find that we are not quite right when it's too late. Not just because, by thinking we know how the story ends, we miss out on everything we could have done and should have learned on the journey. But because, by thinking we know how the story ends, we miss out on the opportunity to be anything more than a passenger, we squander the chance of driving to a different end, we gamble away our one and only go at writing our own story, exactly when the ending is unknowable and there is everything to play for.

THE ARCANE ART OF CONSISTENT DECISION-MAKING, CONSISTENTLY

So. When I speak of choices, I don't mean 'some choices need to be made'. I mean consistent, intentional, active leadership is required for a sustained period of time to take the business you are in into a future that is not set or specific but is undeniably different in every major way: economics and profitability, talent and structures, products, services and the technology that delivers them. That's pretty much *all* of it. Given that you probably should be sourcing your stationary from more local and sustainable partners, I am going to guess that you can't even take your current set of pencils into the future. So the decisions you need to make start with the big heroic stuff of 'what will we be' and 'what will we do', they lead into the less heroic but equally important 'what will we *not* do' and 'what can we *not* be even if we wanted to' and then, just as you are feeling exhausted and start thinking 'are we done here', you realise you need to continue making daily decisions of all shapes and sizes to ensure entropy doesn't set it, existing bad habits don't derail your new intent and an organisation that was successful for a long time doing something stays the course towards something else.

Consistent choices consistently made over a sustained period of time. That's what we need. Auto pilot is not an option. If you are wondering why, go back to Chapter 1.

For the rest of us, back to choices: if we want to stay in this business, we need to accept that it is an altogether different business. So we need to understand and align with what the business is *becoming*. Not just the technology that enables the change but the economic structures the technology creates.

In practical terms, we need to start providing new services (ranging from banking as a service to embedded payments and from micro-insurance to FX volatility insurance); we need to wrap our heads around new ways of delivering against those new ways of making money (so that our unit economics come out in the wash and we don't lose all profitability). With that come decisions about what to build, what to buy and where to partner; and new ways of adding value. And that doesn't *just* mean new ways of making money. It genuinely means new ways of being useful in the context of a new economy, cost structures, new competitors and what clients may be willing to buy from you. To do all that, a lot of what we do and a lot of how we do it needs to change. Dramatically. Organisationally, operationally, fiscally and technologically.

And the people who do it need to change. So now we are getting to the 'what can you do about it' bit.

As a leader you need to accept that to do all this we need new skills. New ways of working. Previously under-valued traits such as imagination, creativity and innovation. These are not multiple ways of describing what I mean by the way. It's an 'and' list. We need new skills: from design to pricing and DevOps to data science, we need new skills. We need new ways of working that are appropriate to those skills and the task we have to fulfil. Some of it about learning how to run scrum rituals and use design-led and research-led product development and some of it is simply 'stop throwing people under the bus to cover up things you forgot to do or don't understand, that old chestnut doesn't cut it any more'.

And we need imagination and creativity for innovation in a digital-first world, as rendering what we used to have in a new channel is not enough. Creativity is required to reflect on what people need and useful ways of delivering it. Sometimes it is as simple as the Monzo feature that tells you a bill is about to hit and you don't have enough funds vs your old bank telling you 'oops you are overdrawn'. Sometimes it is a feature that allows you to trade on a security as you are reading the market news on your phone, the widget picking up what you are reading about and giving you the option to engage. Or, for the less affluent, the option to Buy Now Pay Later, à la Klarna or Afterpay. And for the avoidance of doubt boys and girls: BNPL is a loan, not free money. Unregulated, but a loan nonetheless. It can accrue interest (late fees. Whatever. Potato, potahtoh)... It will affect your credit rating. It will impact your life if you use it recklessly.

I'm glad we had this little chat.

So, back to my original point: you need the imagination to think of the feature, the technical acumen to build it, the ways of working to marry the two without creating a banking Frankenstein, unrecognisable from the original intent and the agility to do all this fast, or what's the point? Each of those is a way of rendering your service that is useful and in line with the way your consumers live.

That is innovation at work: new ways of servicing your customer in line with their needs and preferences.

You will notice that despite being a former chief innovation officer myself, nowhere do I say that you need an innovation department. Because you don't. What you need is an innovation mindset. What's the difference? Most innovation departments are *things apart*. They embody a recognition that learning and new ways of working are required and a simultaneous absolute refusal to let those new behaviours affect, infect or infuse the rest of the organisation until such a time as is deemed appropriate. Should that time ever come. Those departments have occasionally done stellar work either on their own or experimenting with start-ups. They have often built something useful (a big UK bank's first innovation department launch was an app for ordering coffee in the canteen, cute, innocuous and not entirely relevant to the business) or built something weird and wonderful (I have played with drones in Singapore and smart fridges in London and Oslo and a very cute 'identity asset trigger' in Madrid that turned different music on and off depending on who entered the room. All in bank innovation departments). My team and I created the carbon footprint calculator for pension funds and asset managers as well as a 'listening service' that would aggregate news regarding portfolio companies that we discussed earlier, useful for comms and PR teams. Useful. But it wouldn't drive or break the business and that is the point.

An innovation mindset is the idea of collateralising a goat to offer liquidity in real terms to rural communities in Africa.[2] It is solving a problem that we have indeed solved before but solving it in a way that is brand new, creatively applying what is *now* possible to an *old* problem: people needing cash. Bridging loans and collateral-backed lending of all sorts are not new. Seeing a communally owned goat as collateral is new. The way the problem was solved was new. It was made possible by technology then newly available. It is creative and fresh and it blew my mind when I first heard of it.

Why couldn't we think of something like this?

NOT ALL INNOVATION IS GOOD FOR YOU

Why can't banks come up with the amazing ideas?

The answer isn't exactly 'because they are full of bankers' but it is 'because they are full of behaviours and demographic biases and bureaucracy designed to perpetuate stability' and that is the opposite of change.

---

[2] This is a real thing done by the team at www.stellar.org

Why didn't a bank think of collateralising a goat, seriously?

Part of the answer is you don't necessarily have the right talent for that level of left-field thinking. You don't hire them usually and, if you do, you rarely empower them. Hold onto that thought, we will come back to it later. The rest of the answer is that the stellar solution (the collateralised goat) didn't start with the mission of preserving the bank. Just solving the problem. Because you will notice, if you look through the case studies, the problem was solved *without* a bank being required at all, on this particular occasion. And although I am not a believer that banks are doomed, I am a believer that if the thinking is 'how do we change as little as possible to retain as much of what we now have as possible' then creativity is stifled and if the starting point of every innovation is 'how do we preserve our upper hand' then they will be by definition limited.

Before you shout me down: I know this is business. I know banks have shareholders who expect returns. I know. So let me clarify. You should always seek to leverage your competitive edge, use any and all advantage you may have (unfair or otherwise) to do better and continue surviving and thriving. I am a big believer in that. Trying to maintain the upper hand is not quite the same and it has long been the unspoken mission here. And it is not working. Let me give you an example. About 15 years ago, a small blockchain-based start-up walked into the offices of a company that holds 80% of the tri-party repo market, globally. A bit of geekery is required here to make my point. If you already know what tri-party repo is, skip the next paragraph. If not read on because it helps to understand the 'catch'.

The tri-party repo market is created by securities dealers finding short-term funding for substantial portions of assets through repurchase agreements, or repos. Essentially: Party A sells an asset to Party B with the promise of repurchasing it at a pre-specified later date and price. It's like a collateralised loan but governed by bankruptcy laws so it's more beneficial to cash investors. In this situation, an agent, the third party (usually a clearing bank), acts as trusted intermediary holding the assets and managing all the admin for the duration of the transaction (payments, collateral management, etc.).

Now the little start-up in question came into the office with unjustifiable swagger.

They had a good point to make. Their technology could use smart contracts to entirely eliminate the need of the third party for both the admin work and the custodial work as immutable ledgers could hold the answers as to who needed to do what when, how long for and for how much. They had solved the problem in a way that reduced its overall cost footprint. By eliminating the people providing those services for substantial fees and replacing them with a tech-based utility. It could have revolutionised the industry, by where is the incentive for the industry itself to pay for this? Which is what the ask was.

Christmas and turkeys come to mind.

Give me one reason why anyone would do that to themselves?

Which of course creates a very tense environment for innovation departments as they need to learn widely but experiment in stagnant waters.

Disrupting your own business is terrible business.

That is why Goldman Sacks launched Marcus and JP Morgan Chase launched Chase UK. And that is why in late 2022 Goldman Sacks is, reportedly, shrinking the Marcus footprint, with no real impact on the main business.

They chose to innovate and leverage new technologies and new business models in someone else's backyard: be it a new vertical (mass affluent for GS) or geography (outside the US for Chase). New tech at the service of new business. Music to my ears. But sadly still rare.

Most banks still try to balance their innovation departments in the very narrow space between not disrupting the existing business and not serving a bold new business vision like the examples above. That's a losing bet and yet that hasn't stopped many a bank from playing that game so the departments, staffed usually with eager, hard-working and creative sorts, once they have been brought into existence, find themselves constrained by budget and compliance, by the art of the possible and the creativity of their teams, of course. But mostly by the bank's own reticence. The things it didn't have the appetite for. The things it didn't want to believe in. The things that weren't 'how we normally do things around here'. As if that wasn't the point all along.

And this is worth pausing on for a bit as we have been doing this innovation malarkey wrong for the best part of 20 years and this is coming from someone who set up and headed up more than one innovation department, in more than one bank, in more than one continent, always with the best possible intentions. Even when I sat in an innovation function, even when I was busy building a lab and department, setting up the process and 'capability', and had my organisation's full and vocal support in doing so, I would actually caution partners and vendors (start-ups and challengers, designers and researchers) against talking to Innovation as a function. I mean, sure, we will open doors for you. And that's not nothing. But neither major decisions nor substantial budgets sit with the innovation folks. They can be your friends, and they can influence the people up top and help them think through things, but they cannot be your champions. They can be your allies, but they cannot be your sponsors. And since I have crossed over to the tech side, providing truly innovative capabilities to banks, our 'stakeholders', the clients we pitch to and sell to and work with are never the innovation department even though the banks still have those.

And there is a slight method to that madness.

You see, ironically, even though every innovation function was set up to deal with the world out there and the rapid evolution of knowledge and technology, that big scary place of breakneck change and mercurial impressions, the actual job of the innovation department was always mostly internal. We were paid to look outwards, engage and learn, sure. But the main function was to explain. We were also paid to represent, sure. There were conferences and media pieces and hackathons and our organisation was seen to be in attendance. But mostly our representation duties were outside-in: for every panel showing off our bank's latest digital riches, there were a thousand internal meetings, each a battle, representing the world back to the bank's own decision-makers and custodians. Progress. Change. Tech. Hope. For every time we represented the bank's 'cool factor' to the world, we represented the world to the bank 10 times over. And to a much cooler and suspicious response, let me tell you. Not all those sessions were equally friendly or inspiring.

A PLAGUE OF INNOVATION TEAMS AND HOW TO SALVAGE WHAT MATTERS

As innovation professionals, we were paid to find a way into a contentious future that would cost and hurt as little as possible. Which is not a terrible mission. Only we were then held responsible for the cost and the hurt of each and every option, as if both the changing world and the banks' appetite to make changes in order to still thrive in it were our petulant fault and doing. You may be thinking 'oh this sounds familiar to those doing transformation work' and it is in ways. But having done both, the key difference is that transformation starts when the company has admitted to itself something is well and truly broken and not fit for purpose. The transformation representatives may come laden with unwanted gifts of complexity, cost and new habits, but their existence is accepted as inevitable. Innovation is all that but without the starting point that something is no longer viable. The starting point is that some things will eventually become nonviable and although we all agree we don't want to get to that, the urgency around when we start, how far we go and what we commit is lacking. And that matters because the vast majority of banks are still replicating the innovation centre model, despite the high-cost–low-reward net result it has yielded for some of the front-runners.

Let's be honest here.

Doing 'innovation' as a thing apart has its moments but it's overall a thankless task. And yet people do it.

Trust me. I was for a long time one of those people and a lot of my peers still do it.

And those who do it well, actually find a way. Despite it all. And I want to take a moment here to talk about these people. Not the individuals, although there is a book in that for sure. But the type of person and the type of attitude we hired for inside those departments, to get things done. It is important to know what you are looking for as these folks didn't always sit in innovation, and in fact, increasingly they don't. But they are the same folks. Small teams with diverse skills and insane focus. Teams hell-bent on getting things done, making things better. And across those teams, there are traits in common. And those traits are worth jotting down and actively hunting down when you are looking to build a team yourself. Here's your call to action. Take note.

'It takes virtue and daring to be free' (obscure Greek poetry quote, check[3]). So what you are looking for is guys and gals that have the guts to come in, day after day, and do the thing you as the organisation at large mock for being a waste of time. Diminish for being learning time, playtime or 'just marketing'. As if your innovation team has the power to decide to coast, even if they wanted to. As if how they spend their days inside the body corporate isn't pre-ordained and predetermined, controlled and accounted for through bosses, committees and quarterly KPIs. Not to mention their own burning desire to do good work and deliver against the mission you theoretically hired them for. But why let logic stand in the way of a good story?

These folks come in to work, day after day to do what you tasked them with and be met with your mocking, dismissive remarks. And the doubts. And the snarky commentary. And the unrealistic expectations. They come in with half-explored ideas and big dreams. And they know they will take a beating. Over risk factors and revenue projections, over implementation

---

[3] 'Let those who feel the heavy brazen hand of fear, bear slavery; freedom needs virtue and daring.' Andreas Kalvos, 'Lyrika, ode fourth, To Samos' (1826).

schedules and acceptance criteria for the thing that doesn't yet exist. They come in. Because they remember what you said when you offered them the job. And because you may no longer believe, but they do. They believe in better, in new, in 'viable yet profitable'. They believe in the very thing you hired them for. And they have the guts to come in and try to remind you, day in day out.

> Gumption is not enough. Standing there, like erstwhile guardians of Hope, is not enough. Your team needs to build the hope. Give it shape. Give it wings. They need to imagine a future. Do you have any bloody idea what that takes?

But gumption is not enough. Standing there, like erstwhile guardians of Hope, is not enough. They need to build the hope. Give it shape. Give it wings. They need to imagine a future. Do you have any bloody idea what that takes?

Do you know what we are talking about here?

We are talking about the ability to move away from the mental constraints of what is known, received and familiar, and imagine a way of organising life and human activity that achieves the same, or better ends, via different means. That achieves new ends not previously possible. Do you know what intellectual might it takes to break away from what you know, and imagine something that doesn't yet exist? Whether they achieve it through their artistic streak, gaming, a solid liberal arts or experimental science education, a love for theatre, volunteer work or travel, they are doing *something* outside your four stolid corporate walls that keeps opening their mind that allows them to, in turn, open yours. And you still mock. And exactly because you mock, courage and imagination are not enough. Their ability to withstand and create is not enough. Because you, the wider company, the management, the peers in accounting or the industry average of 'this will never catch on' brigades, still mock and challenge, not what they say, but their right to say it. Their sanity. Their perception. Their abilities to deduce and interpret. All the things they do well. All the things you hired them for.

So to stand a chance of landing a message every now and again. Of getting you to understand the why as well as the what. Of getting you to commit time, attention, effort ... they need some serious fire-power. Beyond that of their sponsor and patron. They need to have big guns of their own. Be it knowledge, credibility, your respect from the job they had before, your grudging acknowledgement of results delivered, the ability to generate something you want and trade it for something you need but would rather not think about. And before you say 'whatever, our innovation team has achieved a lot over the last few years. Actual, tangible results. Meaningful impact. Traction. So you can't be right.' My answer is *exactly*. They have achieved a lot thanks to guts, imagination and unbridled fire-power. Imagine how much they would achieve if they also had your help.

THE 'INNOVATION' TRAP

Now you are probably thinking 'phew this is not us, our innovation department just launched an initiative to install these super cool compressors that compost paper towels in the washrooms (true story, by the way), they have budget and support and are doing cool things'. To that I would say nice try, but no.

Innovation department budgets have indeed grown in the last decade and a half but their remit hasn't meaningfully shifted, so the battle for innovation has moved to the main bank, unchanged. And most of that battle plays itself out in the tension between knowing you need to change, accepting you need to change, hiring people whose mandate it is to help you change and feeling daunted by the uncertainty of that change vs the certainty of making money in the old way 'for a little while longer'.

From an innovation professional's perspective, the frustration of trying to do the job you were hired for while battling against the very people who charged you with the mission, remains. A team building a new platform and constantly being tripped up by compliance who forgot to ask for something or didn't understand something and feel empowered to pull the emergency chord again and again is in exactly the same position as the innovation director was 10 years ago when compliance didn't trust GitHub or APIs (true stories, all).

Or maybe their position is a slightly worse one.

Because an innovation department I know decided to create a bank account that plays a tune for every debit and credit that hits the account and they actually got budget for an up and coming band to work with them to develop those sounds and the overall proposition solving exactly *zero* problems and annoying absolutely every user they tested it with after it had been developed to a rather advanced stage. Meanwhile I also know of teams building BaaS solutions that will make their bank *new* money and they are being asked to do a whole host of work to make up for something compliance forgot.

Something internal. Something Olde Worlde and aligned to how things are set up not the problem we are trying to solve. Organisational structure rather than an actual need. And although this isn't required by a regulator, it is not actually needed in any real sense, you can't go ahead without it. It has to be done. And you will have to find the time and money 'somewhere'.

If that doesn't sound familiar I fear you are more likely to not be paying attention than you are to work in a magical land where these behaviours don't occur. And if you don't think it matters, you are part of the tough cookie problem we discussed before.

When I resigned one of my innovation jobs (toss a coin, there were only two) one of my very senior stakeholders came to see me to tell me I was letting him down. It was a personal disappointment, he was not speaking on behalf of the bank. *He* was disappointed in *me*. That's never a nice thing to hear. And if you grew up like me, you don't take well to being called a quitter: people who only can afford one go at things never quit. We may fail but we don't quit. We literally can't afford to. So his disappointment cut me deep. But what had I done that was such a let-down? It turns out that my ability to fight an uphill battle and not give up, and still get things done, and still smile, no matter how hard the organisation made it for me was what made him see me as a kindred spirit. It was what earned me his respect. It was what he thought would keep me there forever.

The fact that I can work like this doesn't mean that I should, I said. the fact that I can take it doesn't mean you should throw it at me. He didn't get it. And that saddens me.

But I don't regret the choice. I only regret that what changed for me is not changing fast enough for the industry. What are you on about, you may be thinking, you have gone live with so many brand new initiatives, brand new technologies in a dozen banks by now. What are you on about, what you are describing doesn't chime with the outcomes? But that is the point. What I am on about is the ratio of effort to outcome. For every major milestone you see, the iceberg effect of what *could* have been had the bank gotten out of its own way is mind boggling. And yet here we are, actually succeeding exactly because of the people who won't give up. And I am about to repeat myself here and re-quote something for the second time but it's worth repeating. Because it was uttered by one of those people who won't give up, after we had just gone live with something major for us, for their bank, for their market and we were exhilarated but also nowhere near done as the thing was live but the things we still had to do to satisfy the bank's own insecurities were plentiful. So we were live but we were not entirely done, a strange feeling as you can't quite experience relief or jubilation, there is almost always more that can go wrong internally than externally. And he said 'nothing is ever released in a major bank. But some things escape'. With a wry smile and a wink. The man knows. He has the scars and the wins.

So if you are blessed with a team who have the guts and brain fire-power to explore different intellectual possibilities, the focus and determination to test options and present you with viable proposals for things never done before, and you still value their tenacity more than the world they bring you on a plate, then, after all these years, you no longer deserve their fierce grace nor the future they are exploring for you. And this, too, is your call to action because these folks are not wedded to you or your organisation. Lift your head from BAU and your endless meetings and senior review boards for a second. Look back and around you and take stock. If you have a team like the one I described, or individuals like that dotted around, surrounded by folks who keep tripping them up, go over right now and hug them. Metaphorically, if you are not a hugger or the team is distributed.

This doesn't need to get weird.

But you ought to show them you realise now what you may have previously missed about exactly what it is that they do for you and the organisation and how. So go hug them. And then huddle around a whiteboard and hear how you can make their life better so that they

> If your team has the ability to explore different intellectual possibilities for things never done before and yet you value their tenacity more than their work, you no longer deserve the future they build for you.

can save yours. And if, in reading this, not a thing sounded familiar, go out and hire people who can take you boldly forth into the unknown: hire them for their intellectual prowess and old-world credibility; hire them for their creativity and insane work ethic; hire them for their fierce grace. Then get out of their way and let them work. Time is not endless here and enough of it has been wasted.

This is not an uplifting section ending. It is a call to action. Find these people. Hire them. Listen to them. Again and again. As you are probably beginning to realise, consistency is the name of the game as the work we are trying to do is complex and it will take a long time. So doing something once or doing it and leaving it to its own devices is tantamount to not doing it at all.

What we do 'in the middle of it all' matters most.

MAINTAINING URGENCY IN THE MIDDLE OF THINGS

Let's face it, time running out is not a real worry in banks.

It's perverse, really, because time is running out for everyone, axiomatically.

Plus banks spend their time worrying. They hire people whose full-time job is to worry. Affectionately known as the business prevention departments, CARL (Compliance, Audit, Risk and Legal) are paid to think about everything that can go wrong. And I mean *everything*. One of the banks I worked in had a lady with white gloves who walked around all day running her finger over surfaces, testing the quality of the dusting. And this wasn't for our well-being or to ensure our offices looked good for client visits, but rather to avoid a potential health and safety-related lawsuit. I know because I asked her.

There are policies about wearing your badge with your photo and name turned into your chest when you leave the building to avoid potential exposure to blackmail or identity theft and protocols about what can happen when. There are cascading approvals requirements, sometimes perverse, as I once had to personally activate our CEO's badge to come into the innovation centre. It didn't automatically happen without my say-so. Oh the power. I equally needed my boss' boss to sign-off on a $150 headset. (Given my role at the time, that meant I had to go to the President of the firm for petty cash. Not ridiculous at all.)

Managing risk is a key function in a bank. Not a side show. And checklists and frameworks are a foundational piece of how banks perceive risk management. And of course all of that makes sense or at least did at some point, for a certain set of circumstances, including specific regulatory requirements.

The intent is largely clear but it's formulaic. And the big risks, the scary risks, the risks that are hard to model, are left to dance around the boardroom like the proverbial elephant in a pink tutu. And the biggest risk of them all currently dancing forlornly around the boardroom is the risk of running out of time before some real commitments are made.

What does that elephant look like?

It looks like the digital economy maturing rapidly and the niche you currently occupy being filled by others, who moved in step with the world. It looks like a regulatory fine because you moved to the letter of the regulation but not the spirit of the regulator for a digital economy. It may look like you leaving doing anything at all so long, that the sheer amount of stuff you now need to do is too daunting for anyone to even contemplate getting started.

And when is all this likely to happen?

That's the whole point. We don't know. If we did know, it wouldn't be a risk, it would just be a project plan. But we don't know so it is very much a risk as it may happen sooner than we hope. And yet running out of time is never a worry, not a stated one at least, for banks. And this particular kind of oblivion manifests itself in and affects how technology strategy is shaped, how market landscapes are scanned but also, more viscerally, how time is spent inside the organisation.

HALF WAY HALL OR A VERY PERSONAL STORY ABOUT 'MIDDLES'

Take planning for instance.

Planning is a total waste of time, but it absolutely has to be done. Thus spoke my first-ever boss. And he waited for me to ask why, which I, of course, obligingly did. You don't get to be an A-star student without asking the questions and pleasing your teachers, I can tell you that for free. It has to be done, he said. Because it forces you to think, prepare, assess. But it's a waste of time because, let's face it, *no plan survives first contact with the enemy*. Figuring out what you need to do, how and when at the beginning of a journey or piece of work is essentially a call to make the most decisions at the time when you have the least information. Right at the beginning. When you don't know what you don't know. You don't know what will go wrong. You don't know how things will behave, pan out, which assumptions are right and which are wrong. It's next to impossible to get it right.

Remember the weird floating feeling you got as a teenager when people asked you what you wanted to be when you grew up? Some of us knew the answer with conviction, or at least thought we did (I was convinced I would either be an astronaut or a primary school teacher. Turns out I am too claustrophobic for the former and too impatient by half for the latter. Which goes to show).

> No plan survives first contact with the enemy. Figuring out what you need to do, how and when at the beginning of a journey or piece of work is essentially a call to make the most decisions at the time when you have the least information.

Some of us are still working it out. None of us knew exactly how to get there.

And just to book-end it all nicely, the same haziness applies to experience. Looking back is great for anecdotes and war stories but, really, it is one path, one story, one set of serendipitous, momentous and mundane events that could have gone many other ways, but didn't. The place where the decisive turns are taken in the middle, when accident, choice and serendipity mingle. The middle is all that matters but we don't talk about it because it's messy and unreadable. The middle of both life and projects is messy but more on that later. First let's talk about life.

My life, for a second: story alert.

I don't know if Halfway Halls are *a thing* more widely or whether it's just something the communists thought up. (I went to King's College, Cambridge, in the 1990s. Everyone called us the Reds and we wore the badge with pride. There was a hammer and sickle on the ceiling of our college bar and sit-in protests against bourgeois vegetables. We were our very own caricature and loved it.) My college had quirks many of which I didn't appreciate till many years after graduation and, with hindsight, the best tradition of them all was Halfway Hall. A formal dinner paid for by the college – best food we had had in months and free wine flowing – exactly halfway through your time in college. And all of us had a moment of wonder, without fail. Oh God, it's gone by so fast. Where does time go? How can we be halfway already? And before we knew it, that sense of bittersweet nostalgia quickly gave its place to white hot panic: man … finals are closer than we realised. And back into the books our heads went.

My Half Way Hall was a quarter of a century ago (plus some months in change). Twenty-five years from the time of writing, assuming good health and continuous employment, I will still be a good decade and a bit from retirement so this is not some grave mid-life crisis thing. It's just a 'you don't need a momentous date to take stock' thing. Eat cake even if it's not your birthday. Raise a glass even if it's not a celebration. And when you have enough miles on the clock but even more road ahead, have your Half Way Hall, force yourself to think: so far so good but what next? With no crazy momentum or firefighting. A conscious moment of choice, a personal or organisational Halfway Hall.

It is not figurative. Do it now if you must. It's a call to action and an important one.

Look back before you look ahead, before you decide on the next thing you need to do.

What do you see? Seriously. Shall I go first?

When I started my career we had superusers, remember those? People in the business who would learn a new system so they can help their colleagues with adoption in the months after roll-out. Yes, youngsters. I said months. And that's after the years we spent building the bloody things using the voodoo known as business requirements documents (BRDs, may you never need to know them). Now we work with user behaviours as well as business deliverables. Now we have designers in the room. Now we don't plan everything on day one. We have come a long way. When I started work, smartphones did not exist. My first-ever job (a summer internship to be fair) was on dial-up and some of us didn't even get given computers in the office and most computers weren't hooked up onto the internet. Now the world is mobile-first, cloud-native and built for personalisation at scale.

We have come a long way. Have we got a long way to go still? Sure.

Have we left some of the hardest questions unanswered still, as an industry? Yes.

Have we *also* come a long way, all things being equal? Also yes. And it is not nothing. We have learned a lot. Built a lot. Changed a lot. We hear bank CEOs speaking knowledgeably about their tech estate and showing an appreciation of the impact it has on their value drivers. We see executives facing up to the hard decisions. Sure, sometimes they lose heart. Sometimes they are half-hearted. Sometimes they get it plain wrong. Humans. It happens.

And it will never stop happening.

But circumstances have presented us with an opportunity for reflection: although COVID is not over at the time of writing, 3 years in, with war in Ukraine raging, conflict in Asia looming and a global cost of living crisis only getting started, this is as good a time as any to serve as our industry's Halfway Hall, albeit in a less celebratory manner.

Now, you say? We are kinda busy now. We are expecting a global recession, we are exhausted from a pandemic that lasted way longer than anyone had anticipated, energy supplies are challenged and prices are booming and you want a moment of reflection *now*?

Yes. Yes I do.

Now is all we ever have and there are enough unique events to make us pause, breathe and reflect before we continue. Now because it matters even more than ever. Now, also, because now is all we have.

Now is the time to get rid of some bad habits … you know … like your mate Lee who would spend the night in the JCR (Junior Combination Room, where the undergraduates hang out) playing pool alone after the bar was shut and everyone was in bed because he somehow felt getting into Cambridge was the prize and getting out would just happen on its own.

It didn't, by the way. Lee flunked out and left without a degree.

It didn't happen for Lee and neither will it happen for the banks by osmosis, let Lee be a warning to us all. It's not a perfect analogy but you know what I mean: you are not guaranteed a happy ending because you are in a position of relative

> Stay playful but stop playing.
> COVID taught us the hard way that time is not as plentiful as we had hoped and the work we have done to-date is ok but we are not ready for the finals.

strength now. So, enough with the horizon scanning and the incubators and the showcases. Enough with experiments you don't mean to use and capabilities you don't need. Funky as the drones may be, that time, energy, talent and money could really be used on something that will move the needle, help your communities, help your business. Unless you are considering switching from banking to aeronautics, stay playful but stop playing. This is our Halfway Hall people, brought forward because COVID taught us the hard way that time is not as plentiful as we had hoped and the work we have done to-date is ok but we are not ready for the finals. Far from it. And now there is a war to add to the burgeoning global supply chain crisis.

So it's time to focus. If nothing else, think how fast the last few years have flown by.

LOOKING BACK, TO LOOK AHEAD

2007, a year seminal for bringing us both the iPhone and the financial crisis, is at the time of publication 16 years past. And that's a long time, boys and girls. Looking ahead to the next 16, don't tell me what you expect to see because the truth is you have no idea, if the rate of change of the past 16 years continues and it shall. So don't tell me what your predictions are. Tell me what your commitments will be. Tell me what you will do. Tell me which of your learnings you will apply. Tell me which mistakes you will not repeat. Tell me what lessons from our journey so far you will cherish. Tell me what you will actively and intentionally learn next. Tell me what fires of rebellion you will start in this world, altered as much by the pandemic as it was by the advent of digital technologies, albeit faster and with no upside unless you are in the PCR test kit manufacturing business. What will you do now that you know more of what you need than you knew when we started this journey, now that you know much more than your younger self but still have a lot of mileage left in you? What will you do?

Yes, another call to action: a call to reflect and commit to intentional action. Shall I go first?

Learning is not about what you know. It is about how you go about learning. The last 20 years have turned me from a bona fide technophobe to a card-carrying nerd. Not because of what I learned but because I learned how to learn about tech in order to find the magic. I got to love the learning journey and thankfully there is always more where that came from.

Incidentally, there is a man called Mike. He is the magical Mike Gardner who ran the BNY Mellon Silicon Valley engineering school of witchcraft and wizardry when I was also working for the Bank and despite his all-time awesomeness and my greenness at the time, he always had time for me and treated me like a colleague, not a novice, all the while giving me a master class in leadership. He always had advice to help and bolster my career and when I asked him how to best interview engineers for the team I was building he said the one thing that matters. He said 'look for teachability'. Mike taught me that.

I got more though.

Culture is not soft. Pause and digest that for a bit before you say 'I know that'. Because having heard the sentence before is not the same as knowing what to do differently to make it true. So let me help with what putting this to action looks like by saying right out of the gate that I don't care to hear what your values are. I don't want to meet your culture champion and I most definitely do not need a copy of your manifesto, values mascot or 'calibrated performance matrix' mapped against said values. Although I will take a piece of complimentary fruit, thank you very much, but while doing so I will also tell you that everybody's got those. The fruit. And the values. And the matrix. And they are largely all the same. And if you have a culture champion I feel sorry for them and the un-winnable battle you put them in that no amount of board games and office massages will turn the tide on. Because ... and I am spitballing here ... I bet I can't guess what your values are by observing the behaviours of your teams. Because I am guessing your values are what you think of yourself on a really good day rather than the lines you wouldn't cross on your absolute worst day. And that's why you can write them on branded cards, graffiti them on the wall and emblazon your website with them, they won't be any more real than any other string of words.

> Your values are not what you think of yourself on a really good day.
> They are the lines you wouldn't cross on your absolute worst day.

Your culture is in your contracts and the way you run your recruitment process. Your culture is in the praise you don't share, the collaboration you didn't encourage and the secrets you keep. Your culture also is in the promises you made to your team and then didn't keep. The bad news you belittled or covered up and didn't trust your team enough to share with them. The bad behaviours you tolerated. *Particularly* the bad behaviours you tolerated, turning a blind eye, finding a circumstantial reason why it could be excused 'this once', or being genuinely incapable to telling what constitutes bad behaviour and what is just robust conversation, the difference between collegiate leadership and bad management. I can share a field guide on how to tell behaviours apart in the wild some other time, for now trust me that there is a world of difference and your culture lives and dies in that gap.

Your culture is also manifest every time you or your management *didn't* put their hand up to admit an error or oversight. Every time the narrative was more valuable to you than the realities of what working here feels like. Every time how 'the thing looks' was more important to you than how the thing affects the people in your care. Every time you treated your team as expendable. Every time you hid behind the corporate and pleaded powerlessness. Every team you treated another team in the organisation as the enemy. Every time you said no before hearing the question. And every bloody time you or your team realised you had missed something and, rather than asking for help, you went into a charade of mock outrage and faux surprise, shouting loud right out of the gate before anyone gets a word in edgeways and blaming all and sundry for things that are meant to hide the thing you missed, didn't understand or didn't do very well in the first place. That's your culture. The fact that that happens, and you let it.

I've got one more for you while we are at it because all good things come in 3s.

Impactful work is binary and that is easy to miss, especially in an organisation with misguided behaviours like the examples listed above. It took me a long time to admit to myself that hard work delivering results *can be* but *is not necessarily* the same as work that has an impact.

What do I mean by that?

I mean that everything we have described in the past couple of chapters generates 'projects'. That keep people very busy. Succeeding at those projects, meeting the milestones and producing the outputs counts as success inside the organisation. But does it have an impact? Does it change things, does it achieve the actual aim of the endeavour? Often not. So you can do really well especially inside a big organisation but all you have really done is moved paper around and your career along. And that is impact of sorts and there is nothing – and I genuinely mean nothing – wrong with it. But that part is not binary. You can do impactful work *and* move your career along and it is important to distinguish between what each of those things looks like and consists of. Especially if we are treating this moment as our theoretical Halfway Hall, then it won't hurt to reflect what impact means, *to you.* And whether the organisation you are working in sees the world the same way. There is no right or wrong. But there is right and wrong *for you* and this is the time to reflect on what you want to spend time doing and whether you are in the right place to do it. And yes, there are many right places and many wrong ones. And places that start right and stop being right and places that don't feel right at first but change – with you, because of you, around you. Whatever it is, it is not static. But when you know you know, and all you need to do is remember how fast the last decade flew past.

So: reflect. And make choices, even, and that is important, when you are not actively presented with them.

The reality is, only a few things matter. And they are not the same for all of us. For me it's integrity, purpose and people. What are yours? Take a moment to give a genuine answer, not just an answer that sounds nice. Give the answer that I would arrive at myself if I observed you at work. If I watched what drives your behaviours, what you don't tolerate, not what you say your values are but what your conduct says you value, what your principles are. And whatever they are, don't compromise on them. Make the next decade about them. Make everything you have learned so far an accelerant and an amplifier around the things that matter. Because, really, the clue is in the name: we need to focus on what matters *because* it matters. Those of you who have seen me present live, know I always wrap with the same single question. Today is no exception. Today we took pause to marvel at how fast time has passed. How much we have learned and how much we've done but also how much we still have to do and how fast the time ahead will pass. Today we took pause because we know so much more than when we started and still have time to do things differently.

So. *What will you do next?*

DOING THE HARD THINGS WELL: THE MESSY MIDDLE MANIFESTO

Now we've gotten all hot and heavy with the meaning of life, we can bring it down a notch and talk about what that looks like in our everyday working life. On a bog-standard rainy Tuesday in November, when you are a couple of years into a job and a good few months into a project. Nothing major has gone wrong on this day and no milestone was reached. It's an average day. No highs, no lows.

Nothing adrenaline-filled or exciting. It's the middle of stuff.

Gone is the heady enthusiasm of the blank page and the early days when a lot was unknown and everything was possible. And you are nowhere near the finish line, you are nowhere near done and nowhere near ready for a victory lap. There is a lot to do still and just as much that can go wrong. And everyone is a little tired and more than a little cranky because the organisation around you is doing all the things we have been discussing and lamenting so far. That's the most critical time for a piece of work (be it a corporate project or a start-up product build), it's the hardest part.

And it's hard because it's messy and unpredictable.

You know what you are trying to achieve but there is no blueprint for what you are trying to do and you are tired and you have so much more to do. It's the middle of things. And it's where ideas and teams and products prove their mettle so let's talk about the deeply unglamorous 'middle' of projects, endeavours and programmes of work, be it a start-up, a collaboration or a bank project. Let's talk about the middle where things go to die. Because people lose heart, focus, sponsorship or their way, frankly.

The middle. Not quite dramatic but supremely significant because the middle is when your enthusiasm may fizzle, when your management isn't necessarily paying much attention any more, when money may get short ... and it's so easy to forget how long we all knew this would take ... because yes we said this would take 2 years but when you see it on paper it doesn't feel long. When you live it day in, day out, that's a lot of days. And when it *feels* longer than it looked on paper, it becomes so easy to challenge the adequacy of the proof points we had agreed upon on the same day we discussed how long this would take. It becomes so easy to give up and not even realise that is what you are doing.

Many years ago, when I was a young and starry-eyed bank technology professional, we launched a thing. It was an alternative loan financing vehicle. It was not ground-breaking. But it was new to us, it was fresh or as fresh as these things can get in institutional banking and it moved us as a business in the right direction. It was a team effort: two chaps from the business (who came up with the idea); me and my team with the innovation 'access all areas' pass to go through the company bureaucracy, P&L moats and all the rest; and an enterprising senior client exec who brought her clients to the table. And they bought it. And I don't just mean they bought our pitch. I mean they signed on the dotted line and paid us, so we built it. And it worked. And then it started making money. This didn't take a week, truth be told, these things don't. But, by the end of year 1 we were ringing the register which was bloody good if you ask me. The work didn't pay for itself yet but it gave every indication that it would wash its own face very soon and be sustainably profitable in the long run. Plus we got the creativity brownie points. The clients liked the fact that we had an idea, we pitched the value and just built it.

That's how innovative businesses operate, right? Right. But then the bank pulled it. Pulled the plug, pulled the rug from under our feet, switched off at the mains. Why? Why would you do that?

Because it straddled two divisions and the heads of those two divisions couldn't agree on how to split the costs and profits and the number wasn't big enough yet for either of them to care too much and fall out over it, and it was just faster to be done with it. So they killed it. More than halfway through. When it had successfully reached every proof point – technical and financial – and it just needed to build up steam and pace. When it just needed to be left alone with no extra love or investment.

They killed right in the middle of it all when everything was going well because it wasn't done yet.

It wasn't meant to be done yet but try explaining that to senior executives who didn't even have a meeting on this, they discussed it on a flight to somewhere and agreed to not fight over this and still be friends. They killed it even though the rules we had agreed at the beginning said 'this is what good needs to look like'. So they broke those rules. Because their attention waned.

For this and many other reasons, the middle is dangerous. The middle is hard. The middle is where you may lose heart or lose your way or lose your sponsors. And for all these reasons the middle is important. And for the avoidance of doubt, what follows is a bit of a love letter. To the Messy Middle. And those who know it for what it is, and stay with it anyway. And if you have no idea who these people are in your organisation please read my love letter, then read it again. Because you need to add to your call to action list the task of finding the people who understand the Messy Middle and are not afraid of it.

So who are they?

NAVIGATING THE MESSY MIDDLE: HIRING FOR ADVERSITY

Who are the people who will help you navigate and survive the danger land that is the Messy Middle?

Well, first of all, they are the builders. Those who have toiled and sweated, feared and at times despaired, who challenged and questioned and pivoted but never gave up because it got too hard. Those who had the vision and made it to the finish line without jumping to the next shiny thing or passing the thing, whatever it is, to the guy next to them. Those who stuck with the team and the work through the Messy Middle that looms inconspicuous and yet treacherous between the pristine start and the photo finish.

> Look for the builders who toiled, and at times despaired, challenged, questioned, pivoted but never gave up because it got too hard.
> Those who had the vision and made it to the finish line without jumping to the next shiny thing.

They know.

They know the middle is messy. One of my guys, a brilliant, intelligent human being, once said: 'Well this is it, the middle, we are here. Anyone who has ever built anything knows this. And anyone who hasn't, doesn't.' Quite.

The Messy Middle is messy, what else is there to say? Life is lumpy, to quote Robert Fulgrum,[4] and the middle is the lumpiest bit. It's where the beginning of it all seems naïve and so far behind us already, and the end line still looms implausibly distant. And you stick it out. Because you believe. Not just in your vision anymore. Not just in the reason why you started this, whatever your 'this' is. But in the team. In the people you are doing it with and for. They are more real than any vision ever was when you are in the Messy Middle. The team. The partners. The clients. The people you toil with and for and the people who will keep testing and measuring and adjusting and asking whether we are still true to the mission. Be it a product or a revolution. The Messy Middle is hard for everyone. And equally baffling in its mundane terrors, irrespective of what you are trying to achieve. The builders know that moment when the process of building itself separates the wheat from the chaff. That's another way of knowing when you have reached the Messy Middle. When it gets hard. And it gets real. Want to know a dirty secret of the trade?

The builders love this bit the best. Because they know that the fair-weather traveller will check out roundabout now. A few things explode. A few folks implode. The builders know this is their time. This is when the team comes together, sleeves get rolled up and things come to life in ways that may not be the stuff of fairy tales because they are better. They are real life.

---

[4] I believe the full quote is 'life is inconvenient, life is lumpy'.

So find your builders. Hire them. Empower and shield them. They will shore up the disasters of the Messy Middle.

THEN, GO FIND YOUR STORY TELLERS

They are just as important. Because real life is amazing. But you may not even notice it happening in the chaos of keeping the Messy Middle going. So there is power in the telling. When you are in the messy, noisy, chaotic middle, there are those who can still say, 'can we take a moment?'. Because they see the story writing itself, before it is over – because, hey, a story with a beginning and an end is easy to tell and the Messy Middle gets glossed over in a montage or a gesture of vague reference to labour and toil between the glorious idea and inevitable success. As if. As if some of humanity's mightiest visions didn't die silent deaths in the quagmire of the Messy Middle and its toils.

So the impact of turning the Messy Middle into a storyline? Picking out parts of the day to day, with all its frustrations, and highlighting their significance? That is not nothing and it can help keep people focused. It can help people see the Messy Middle for what it is: the middle of the road and part of the journey, not a problem, not a failure, not a dead-end. Just a part that was always going to be hard and here it is and here we are and so it is: hard.

The story telling is important here. The ability to say: 'Hold up guys, this thing you just did? That is your own special version of heroism and magic' or the ability to point out a steady, repeatable, reliable string of events and say 'this is what we said good looked like and here it is, it's not all of what we need but it is part of what we said we need so all is going well'. Or 'the way you handled that mundane human crisis that feels so immense to those involved and so banal to everyone else? The way you handled that avalanche of work and frayed nerves? The way you have handled yourself and your team over the past few months? Maintaining cadence and velocity and laughs all round while we are scaling, delivering, seemingly not ever sleeping? Thank you for your humanity and grace', says the story teller. Thank you for embodying the reasons why we do all of this, day in and day out, thank you for living up to our values and our *reasons why* in the way you go about your work. In the way you speak to your colleagues. In everything you do. And *don't* do.

The story teller finds the narrative thread in the Messy Middle, where nothing dramatic happens. Where all the drama happens. Where nothing final happens. Where all that matters happens. The story teller takes the most mundane, messiest part of creation and says to the stressed and over-worked: 'I see you. I see *what* you do and *how* you do it come together in the most glorious arc, connecting why we started to where we are going in the most elegant trajectory of integrity, consistency and humanity. Not to mention kick-ass tech.' The story teller says to those toiling: I see you. And all you do. And it is glorious.

YOUR LAST GROUP, ONCE YOU FOUND THE BUILDERS AND THE STORY TELLERS, IS THE PLUMBERS

They are the most invisible and the most important and I will confess I love the builders and the story tellers but I love the plumbers the most.

'Talk to me about file transfers.'

I am not even joking. If you are a techie, particularly in FinServ, find yourself a team that loves the unsexy stuff. The middle of the stack. The people who look at the under-served, the over-charged, the excluded and marginalised and think 'infrastructure' before they even think 'social justice'. They think about accessible loans, affordable mortgages and non-predatory pensions as a problem to be solved in the guts of the financial system, not just at the proposition level. They are the people that think about democratising financial services and then go on to talk to you about containerisation and you may think you lost them but wait ... there is method to their madness.

They are thinking about scalable, robust infrastructure at a fraction of the cost. They are solving the problem where it's least visible and that's who you want in your team when things are tough. You want the people who care deeply about inclusion but they don't think of it at the community level. Not the product level. Oh no no no. They think of it at the plumbing level. At the level where the costs are incurred, where the systems break down, where scale becomes a challenge of cost or security and the choice can only go one way. They think of this at the level where the excuses are made.

These are the people who don't look for the pretty and sexy answers to big problems but actually go looking for the sticky, messy, deep and real causes of problems. The people who dig deep into themselves and into the world we handed down to them, they look at their local politics, the state of mental health care in their community or, in our case, banking infrastructure and say 'this won't do'. Nobody will write poetry about them. But they are the true heroes of the Messy Middle, where everything that ever mattered takes place. Where everything that makes a difference happens. Where life, change and creation happen. Where products are built. Where dreams meet their match and come kicking, screaming, dented and bruised into existence. It's where life happens: in the Messy Middle. And when you are in the middle of the journey, in the middle of the road and the middle of the stack and you look around you and see a team, who have each other's back, who know why they are here, whose sleeves are rolled up and every hiccup and problem and drama and occasional explosion is part of the Messy Middle they know and love, and they close ranks and pick each other up and remind each other why we are here and that we always knew the Messy Middle was, well, messy. And we knew because we love the unsexy stuff. The stuff that is important, even if it is not flamboyant. The stuff that is the Messy Middle in more ways than one. And this is the call to action: if this is new to you, now you know. So go look hard at your team and reflect on whether you have those guys and gals and just didn't appreciate them for what they are, or you don't have them and that's why this journey is that bit harder for your organisation.

Either way, go get yourself a team like this and appreciate them for what they are or you will never get through the Messy Middle. If this is not new to you, if you read this smiling and nodding and chuckling to yourself, then this is for you. My team. My tribe. The dreamers. The builders. My beloved plumbers. Who make change happen where it matters the most: where it is hard and invisible. And tell each other's story. And love the unsexy stuff that makes people's lives better. Everything that matters happens because of you and people like you who stick it through the Messy Middle. Where everything that matters happens. Where everything that *happens* matters. Because and thanks to you and these people you amassed.

SO WHERE DOES THAT LEAVE US?

This work is hard. And we have to do it.

As in: the work of digitising financial services for a fully digital economy is non-optional. The digital economy is here. The regulator is tapping their watch. The work needs to be done and the scale and scope of it is, as we said, staggering.

Does it have to be *us* who do this work?

Absolutely not. *Someone* does. It doesn't have to be us, but we are sitting in the seat of those who should be doing it so it's time to get stuck in or get the hell out. Plus some of us would quite like to be the ones who see this work through.

So. Do this we must. And do it better than we have to-date. And to do all that we need, as I keep saying, the right team. And that may look a little different than you would expect, or like. And that part is non-negotiable. Past errors will block your way to the future.

But 'different' doesn't look like a complete and total departure from everything familiar. There is a lot in the way we do things that is worth keeping. I know I have spent a lot of ink flagging all the things that bankers do wrong, all the short-sighted ways in which we get in our own way. But I am not a banker-basher, contrary to the occasional evidence. I flag what is broken because I want to see it made whole and I flag what is sub-optimal exactly because it is not everything. If it was everything, repair would not be possible. But it is. Hence my appeal. But I can understand it may come across as critical, so it is time I came out in defence of bankers.

I was recently asked, half in jest I think, to write a piece on the factors that suspend natural selection in the case of bankers. A little harsh. But funny. Two winning ingredients for a narrative arc. And yet. Is it true? It gave me pause. And that is a good thing. Anything that makes you think is a good thing. This is where I got to, in my thinking.

Traditional banking is an entitled business, there is no denying that. It's been going strong long enough for folks (particularly those who built their careers here) to forget it's not a given. To forget it's not a birth right. It's not immutable. It's not a forever kind of thing. It was a product of its environment: business need and technological possibility wed in a wrapper of opportunism and value-creation. And for reasons that I won't get into here, that set-up worked well enough for long enough. So long, that generations of bankers grew up, prospered and retired in largely the same landscape. And they bequeathed it to the next generation who expected the same thing. Anon anon. Until the iPhone arrived and changed everything. Just because of some new technological capabilities and new behaviours, now we tell them they are wrong. That what they took for granted is not theirs to keep.

And they are, indeed, wrong. But you can't blame them for hoping we are the ones who are wrong. For trying to hold onto a good thing. To a known thing. For trying to find ways to perpetuate the world as they know it. For believing, even, that the way things have been for so long is proven, tried and tested, reliable. Better. And all the while the world races on. Technology emerges. Habits form. Businesses transform. Expectations evolve. And yet our bankers are, largely, unchanged. A case, you might think, of arrested development. And as you see them in pin-striped suits and bling watches, armoured in fat pay-checks and obscure three-letter acronyms, it's hard to feel sorry for them. And yet.

WHEN EVOLUTION CAN'T KEEP UP, INTERVENTION IS INEVITABLE

I am going to argue that despite all these pages dedicated to bankers behaving badly, it is entirely and wholly not their fault. Bear with me. They entered a profession, much like apprentices of old. And learned what was taught, they consumed and assimilated what knowledge was offered. And as things changed, new regulations, new tech, new products came in, they learned new stuff. Theirs is not a static lore, it is just bound by itself and its self-perpetuating structures. It would be a blatant lie to suggest banking hasn't changed in 150 years. It has. The challenge is that, up until now, the industry evolved and structures, people and habits shuffled along with it.

Now it has to transform.

Faster than natural selection can do its thing. Faster than most organisms can adapt. Faster than the average banker can learn and unlearn while also doing the thing they've been doing all along, the thing we still need them to do, until the new thing is ready. It's not sheer entitlement that holds them back. It's the speed of change, the multitude of stimuli and inputs, the sheer volume of things one could learn and the hard choices of what to actually choose to learn while also doing the job and picking the kids up from school.

Sure, they grumbled and resisted and tried to side-step. Wouldn't you?

But in reality they are at a loss. They don't have a choice. It's all happening too fast. They can't evolve as there is not enough time for that. They can't learn fast enough, not in totality anyway. The odd person finds their niche, sure, but overall, as an industry? The habitat is changing too fast for natural selection. It is not suspended effort, it's not arrested development. It's just overwhelmed humanity. The change required won't happen on its own. Hoping it isn't so won't make it so. Waiting and seeing won't produce a silver bullet and the analogies of ostriches with their head in the sand, rabbits in headlights and headless chickens abound but don't move us forward.

The alternative to hoping it will all sort itself out, as you guessed, is not stasis. It's an intervention.

THE KING IS DEAD, LONG LIVE THE KING

About a decade ago, one of my colleagues (yes, you Matt) said to me 'not being funny here, if what you say about emergent tech is true, and I am not saying it's not, but if it is we will have to fire … like … 98% of our workforce through redundancy or irrelevancy. We will have to hire altogether different people in terms of skills and attitudes'. I paraphrase. I didn't catch the exact phrase then as I didn't expect to be writing a book about this a decade later. But I remember the sentiment strongly because I went: Ha.

It was funny in an exaggerated but 'sort of true' way. Only he wasn't joking in the slightest. And as it turns out, he may have been right. Banking is changing. It is inevitable. The regulator prescribes it. The challengers precipitate it. It's *do or die* for the incumbents and if it's one thing bankers get, it is how to survive as a business. So it's do rather than die, thank you very much.

Banking is changing and it is not all bad, really, some of that change frankly is also desirable from where I stand. It is good for people and communities. It is democratising. It is enabling. It is turning us into an industry of promise and opportunity to do good as well as doing well. That change is coming slowly and painfully. Or rather swiftly and painfully. Depending on where you sit, both the speed and pain are relative. But the change isn't. That we can agree on. It's happening. Those of us who welcome this change and work towards it, know it. Those of you who resist it and wish it wasn't so, also know it. We are now all talking about it quite openly. What we are *not* actually talking about, because there is no sugar-coating it, is that in this change, not everyone is a winner. Not on the business level for sure but, more painfully, not on the employee level. And you may not feel sorry for the entitled bond trader who may end up out of a job or at least out of a bonus at the end of this. But what about all the teams that do bond issuance, and coupon payments and redemption reconciliations and remunerated with salaries not too different from a shop assistant or factory floor supervisor?

Not all who work in banks are rich. They are not all entitled. They are not all opportunistic capitalists. And neither are they skill-aligned with the emergent era of digital banking. And maybe you don't think of them as bankers, and maybe they don't think of themselves as bankers either. Just folks who work in a bank, for a bank, in the same building as Gordon Gecko types but most definitely not like them. But the newsflash is they are the lifeblood of the industry.

The arrogant trader is outnumbered. And actually the one most likely to land on his feet in this transformation, overall. I am not suggesting you should or should not feel sorry for said trader. Not just because nobody likes him (although, that too perhaps) but because he is not the main story. Or she, sure. But traders are overwhelmingly male and with good reason rooted firmly in demographics already discussed.[5] But they are not the main story.

This industry is packed with a silent army of skilled folks who are not at the helm. They are not making decisions. They are not even necessarily seeing the fast-approaching pivot on the horizon. They don't know how to help themselves, what to learn, where to look, how to future-proof their livelihood. And they are not fat cats.

So, when you think of bankers being rendered redundant and a new banker emerging, just remember these folks. And use the time we have left before everything changes to make them part of the story. The king is dead. A new kind of banker is emerging. Less arrogant. Less entitled. More ethical and informed, tech savvy and less greedy. Less likely to wear cufflinks other than for his anniversary dinner. And even then, maybe not. Long live the new king.

Let's just make sure that in the chaos and hullabaloo of change from old alpha to new alpha, from old world, to new world, we take the silent armies with us. We re-train them. We teach. We up-skill. We put our digital empathy to the test. Because they are not the stereotypical bankers we all love to hate. But they are the folks that make the banks run today. And it is up to us whether we take them into the future and give them a future.

In fact, if your place of work gives you a collective noun, those are the true bankers. Who make the ship sail steady. Who do the work. Who keep things ticking over.

The banker you are thinking of is a small minority and these guys don't even cross paths with him.

So when you shrug your shoulders and say you don't care about the fate of bankers let me say hang on a second. The silent majority of the industry is

---

[5] For a biologically predicated analysis on why women may make better traders and, more accurately, a brilliant account of biology, risk-taking and the habits of banking, see the excellent book by John Coates, *The Hour Between Dog and Wolf: Risk Taking, Gut Feelings and the Biology of Boom and Bust*.

who I implore you to care about, defend and not leave behind. Or we are no better than the guys we love to hate.

FRIENDS IN LOW PLACES

I am not quite done yet, with my point about the invisible bankers. The reason I want to think of them and protect them isn't just because I am a nice, empathetic human. It is also because you need them. Your life, in fact, depends on them. Because if you want something done in a bank, particularly during the Messy Middle already discussed, the C-suite and the traders won't do you much good. You are going to need friends in low places. Stay with me here.

I have had my fair share of leadership training over the years and, I will admit, that the first time I heard the phrase 'sponsorship is an active condition' my little mind was blown. This is it, I thought. This is what I have been lacking all this time, I thought. Sure, I had a senior sponsor, we all know nothing happens in a big bank without them. But they were not active in any real sense. They were not present other than at the receiving end of updates and escalation channels; they were not engaged other than to assure us that they were. They had kicked off the programme, signed off the job descriptions, shook the new hires by the hand. Sometimes even gave us a budget. Not always. But sometimes. They occasionally checked in. Then moved on. There was a comms schedule according to which we would keep them updated and, for the rest, their people would be 'on point' day to day and they were apart, a red phone, a point of no return, an escalation point.

No.

An Escalation Point. Capitals. A bridge-burning, colleague-alienating, use-it-and-you-burnt-it card that nobody in their right mind plays. If only they were engaged, thought Young Me. They would know. They would fix. They would shorten some of our pointless, endless run-arounds that leave us exhausted and battle-worn, standing exactly where we had started after avoidable fights and unproductive confrontations seemingly designed to see whether we have what it takes to be allowed to live another day. A test of fitness rather than a way to progress.

If the sponsors were engaged, I wouldn't get stuck in the Swamp again and again, thought Young Me. Have you heard of the Swamp? Even if you haven't heard it called that, you definitely have encountered it in every bank or large organisation. And let me tell you, the day I heard one of the most senior people in our bank describe middle management as the Swamp, where things get stuck, where things sink, where things die miserable, slow, damp deaths, my little mind was truly blown for a second time. Firstly, because I discovered you are actually allowed to say what you think in a big bank (a lesson I didn't need to have repeated) and because I had, until then, lived in the vain hope that the reason we were all locked in this endless, fruitless battle with middle management was because the senior sponsors in their lofty High Places on the upper floors didn't know. They couldn't see.

They were naïve, distracted, doing more important things elsewhere. Whatever ... but they didn't *know* how we struggled through unnecessary minefields of the organisation's own making each day. And that's why they let it happen. Because it was too low level for them to be aware of not because they couldn't be bothered; because our work was too low intensity for them to register or too low latency for them to notice but not because they didn't actually care enough.

And then one day there she was, my boss' boss, saying oh we know. We know. It's awful, isn't it? The Swamp: pervasive enough for everything to get tangled, slowed, weakened and more than often killed in its sticky, a priori resistance. And here is the senior sponsor of many a bedraggled initiative, the shining benefactor of many a programme mired in internal feuds and entirely unnecessary battles saying: oh I know.

Middle management, she said with a bitter laugh, squeezed from the top (that's you lady, said nobody), challenged from the bottom (that was me then). Hungry for resources. Beaten back one too many times. Often not ambitious enough, more often than not, not good enough, to get out of that miserable place and, before you know it, they are part of a Swamp. A Swamp you have to cross to get anything done. The Swamp where everything will get stuck because that is sort of all it is there to do. Slow things down to make sure nothing untoward happens. Where pointless battles will be fought. Where the direction of senior sponsors will matter little, and the heartfelt efforts of young whippersnappers will matter even less.

I don't know that I have come across a sadder thing in all my time in banking. Sadder than the Swamp itself. The admission of its existence and inevitability. The acceptance that people will be stuck in it, become it, and all your best ideas will have to deal with it for no reason other than ... it's there and enough people seem to think it's here to stay so it does. And here she was. The senior sponsor ... being all honest and accessible ... saying this thing we all, sort of, thought … and isn't she one of the people now? Such authentic leadership, such honesty.

I will confess I didn't think then 'why are you not fixing it, if you can see it?'. At the time all I felt was disappointment. Today, all those years on, with a leadership mantle on my own shoulders, I think… if you can see it, you should fix it. Now, when not letting things like that happen is part of my mission, self-imposed or otherwise.

I will confess at the time I thought of myself, not the greater good.

I sat back in my seat with one thought. Hold up. I am less than middle management. Recently promoted at the time and at no small personal cost in terms of labour and effort. And here is the top brass saying good luck not getting stuck among the invisible disaffected masses of mediocre folks who never wanted more or never could achieve more and now they shuffle along the bank's corridors day in and day out, executing tasks and saying 'no' a lot. Because let's face it, middle management doesn't come with much power and the little you have, you exercise when things get desperate. And the Swamp is almost always desperate.

I had one thought that day: I can't stay.

SAVING GRACES

I thought to myself: I have to cross this Swamp fast and come the other side whatever that is and whatever it takes. I have never been so hungry for promotion in my life. I became consumed with the single thought of not being in the Swamp, not becoming *of* the Swamp. I became even more determined than normal – and let me tell you, that takes some doing.

And I did it. I was out of the Swamp double quick. I got the promotion. I got the title. I got the Keys to the Kingdom. I got to speak to the senior sponsors casually. No Escalation Drama. I could sound them out, get their thoughts, push and cajole. I was not quite one of them but I was one of their people. Or near enough.

And, you guessed it, the penny finally dropped.

Their absence was never an absence of awareness or interest. Fancy that. Their absence wasn't even in aid of a higher cause, they didn't absent themselves because they were engrossed in infinitely more important work. They stayed aloof because they didn't know what else to do. They let the Swamp do its thing because they didn't know how to stop it. They genuinely wanted the thing you were tasked with to succeed, although they often didn't believe it could because *they* couldn't see a path through the Swamp. Through the habits, through the process, through the bloody Swamp, from the way things are to the way things could be. And neither did they see a way to drain it or saw themselves as accountable to change the organisation they inherited. Not even to make it better. Not in the grey areas. That's why you were on your own. Fancy that.

And yet. You were never alone, were you?

For any of us who have navigated a big organisation to successful outcomes against impossible odds, for any of us who survived crossing the Swamp, there was always a long line of people, a group of humans of varying job titles and unwavering resolve, who helped. In ways big and small. By finding you equipment when the powers that be wouldn't sign off on budget (Ross, I am looking at you). By cutting code or encrypting and scrambling client data over the weekend to give the team a hand. By breaking a little rule here, bending a bigger rule there. By bumping you up in the release plan. By finding the right reference for the right form and getting a set of sign-offs unstuck after weeks in limbo. People who quietly did the thing that needed doing. Knowing that their own Middle Manager Swamp Lord of a boss would tell them off and make their ascent into the Swamp a little bit harder.

And knowing that the senior sponsors may never hear of their help. And if they did, they wouldn't understand or appreciate how important it is that the audiovisual guy found you a way to demo when the corporate wifi rules changed overnight and you had clients in the room and nothing was working; or the junior QA wrote test scripts in their free time to get you past their boss's intransigence, understanding that their resistance was part power-trip and part total confusion when faced with the new and unknown. The financial controller who unpicked the tangle of rules not designed for what you are trying to do, for you to get the approvals you needed, the HR admin who helped you stand firm by principles the company didn't agree with but didn't always need to know about.

So yes I have gotten a lot done in banks that didn't always expect me to succeed. In banks that occasionally did their level best to stop me, in order to make a point about Swamp

Every day of every year, someone in a basement or back room, with no grand title and no support from the top, quietly helps others find their way to the next step. They were and will forever be our saving graces: friends in low places.

Inevitabilities consciously or unconsciously. In banks that desperately wanted me to succeed but didn't know how to get out of my way.

Every job. Every project. Every day of every year, someone in an obscure desk, usually in a basement or back room, with no grand title and no great support from the top, quietly helped me find my way to the next step. They were and will forever be my saving graces, my friends in low places.[6] And maybe they wouldn't have driven the strategy all the way without me, but I would have not gotten past GO without them so, two decades in, I say: sure. You *need* a Sponsor in a High Place, but better if you *are* one. And sure, you will have to deal with the Swamp, but better if you don't think it inevitable and maybe give the people in it a path to being something else?

But whatever comes and goes in the management floors, if you want to get things done, if you want to get things moving, if you want to get around the bad habits and survive the Messy Middle, you need friends among the doers. Many, many floors down from the executive floors and largely invisible from those lofty heights.

We spend years telling people nothing happens without friends in high places. I beg to differ. Things may not start without friends in high places. Things may not get celebrated as successes without friends in high places. But you want things done, you want things moving, you want the impasse broken, the computer that says *no* circumvented and the Swamp crossed with silent dexterity? Then you need friends in low places. Who will save your life and think nothing of it. Who will do their thing with a smile and a wink. And they'll say, you go girl (or lad, or ninja, they don't mind which). And they won't want recognition. They never want recognition, that's how you know who they are. They have seen through the Swamp and don't care to become it or cross it with the fiery fury people like me are consumed by, and they are given no other option. So they stay put. They do. They solve. They save the day. Every day. And they stay on their invisible shores. They save the bank in small and quiet ways every day. And the Swamp stays murky. And the senior sponsors stay baffled as to how some of the magic happens.

So let it be a secret no more.

If you want something done in a bank you need friends in low places. And if you are a good friend, you don't expose the rules they broke and shield them from their bosses' ire. But if you are a true friend, you take on this madness as the next battle you fight. You will need all your friends and wits

---

[6] Friends in Low Places is a song by Garth Brooks in case a tune is niggling at the back of your head. But a much darker take than my own saving graces.

about you for this one, mind. Because of all the battles you have fought, this will be the longest, the hardest and the most meaningful. And that is ok, 'cos here is the one question nobody asked you yet: all the folks who were your saving grace along the way, what would it take for you to be theirs? And the answer is not obvious. What can you do for them, in a world where one size doesn't fit all, your fire doesn't consume all and yet all need *them*: those doers, those saviours, those quiet problem solvers, your precious saving graces and friends in low places?

It is not a theoretical question. It is part of this chapter's homework. If you are trying to find the talent you need to keep and nurture inside your organisation, because of their skills and attitudes, because they can help you get out of your own way, you need to learn to recognise these people. And you need to learn to understand how to reward and motivate them without assuming that they will be dazzled and swayed by money, status or power. Those banking staples. They may and they may not, and working that out is part of the homework.

YOU CAN'T ALWAYS GET WHAT YOU WANT

I've warmed to my theme now, there's no stopping me. I may have made my point but the point needs to be hammered home exactly because it is unpopular.

We all agree that we want to transform banking. And we all agree that the banks get in their own way. That means that the people in the banks get in the way of the work we want and need to do. What we don't all agree on is that some bankers are invaluable, like my friends in low places.

That's where I find myself often disagreeing with the bankers themselves. The friends in low places are never as popular as they deserve, inside the bank. And they should be.

But these are not the only invaluable bankers.

The truth is, and it is an unpopular truth, only this time the disagreement comes from the start-up world, the digital challengers and the cool kids that consider 'banker' a dirty word. But here is my unpopular opinion nonetheless. The friends in low places are not the only invaluable bankers. In fact, you can't really do the work of transforming the bank, without the bankers themselves. And although nobody wants to hear that ... what's one more unpopular opinion when it comes to this book?

So I am staying with it and I encourage you to do too. Because this is another bit of homework in your 'how do I get the right team for this' quest.

Admit it.

When we are talking 'digital', 'transformation' and 'fintechy stuff', there is a reluctance in hiring bankers. Even among bankers. Even for roles inside the banks themselves. The banks running meaningful transformation work don't actually want bankers running the work. Start-ups trying to sell to banks don't want bankers touching their product or their commercials and most definitely don't want to advertise that they have a team of bankers. I even have a t-shirt, courtesy of a challenger bank in the UK, that says 'don't be a banker' playing on the sound of the commonly-used British word for exactly what you are thinking.

And it doesn't stop there.

Start-ups don't want to hire bankers. Banks are reluctant to recycle bankers. Consulting firms selling strategy to banks don't really want bankers either.

We are all terrified of the paper-pushing inertia that may come with them. And the bad habits I have

> The reason we still hire bankers is that, when you get it right, these are the best FinTech hires you can ever make. The problem is, the odds of getting it right are stacked ever in your disfavour.

spent so long describing. We still do it. The hiring part. We still hire bankers, of course we do. But we don't like it any more than we like ourselves for doing it. And yet we do still do it because sometimes they are a safe pair of hands, a risk-averse hire that may be criticised for not being bold or inspired but it will never be dismissed as being irresponsible. But there is another reason and that one matters much more especially as my theme here is around being intentional about your actions.

The reason we still hire bankers is that, when you get it right, these are the best FinTech hires you can ever make. The problem is, the odds of getting it right are stacked ever in your disfavour. The chances of hiring the wrong banker are high, the stakes of doing so even

> You need to understand what we are changing things *away from* to make sure nothing is dropped or broken and end up in a future state that is in some ways worse than the place we are in today.

higher and the universality of the experience of getting it wrong means that dissing bankers becomes almost an instinctive position across the industry.

Nobody wants to hire bankers. But we all need to. And not just because there are so many of them in the industry. But because the good ones are so darn useful. When you are hiring for key transformation roles inside the bank, you are a little bit damned if you do and a big bit damned if you do not, because the bank wants fresh blood, ideas, a 'view from nowhere' surge of energy ... but ... And this *but* is important ... The bank has more self-awareness than we give it credit for. The bank *knows* that it is a weird beast, it knows that it gets in its own way and it doesn't have time to waste while the newcomer marvels or despairs. 'You do ... what?' is an inevitable reaction to how a lot of global banking practice hangs together. The bank values tough cookies not because it likes them necessarily but because it knows what the realities of survival are like.

So you hire someone with zero banking experience and you will spend weeks and months dealing with their exasperated confusion. And look. They are right. A lot of what we do is dysfunctional. That's why we are trying to change it. And *not* being constrained by The Way We've Always Done Things is really important in driving change but ... and this *but* is also important ... you sort of need to understand *what we are changing things away from* to make sure nothing is dropped or broken and end up in a future state that is in some ways worse than the place we are in today.

The endless pleading cries of 'why' that the non-banker will pepper you with as they try to familiarise themselves with their new habitat *do* have answers. But who has time for lessons in fiscal history, technological evolution and human nature when the world is on fire and there is more work to be done than we have time for? So the bank knows. They know they need to balance fresh ideas and the ability to ask 'why' with a solid baseline of relevant knowledge (in both banking and tech or reg or whatever it is that person is doing). The bank knows some things can't just be picked up as you go along. Or at least not fast enough to be effective. So the bank will hire more bankers than not. Not because they are scared to venture forth and get non-bankers, as influencers like to jibe. But because they value their own time and they put a premium on insight. They know you can't always wing it.

They also know another thing and I cannot stress this enough. They, themselves, will get in their own way. They don't mean to. But they will. And they know that they will so they need to work to that fact while they are mobilising the work to change everything, that ability to get in their own way included. So banks hire bankers to drive transformation initiatives because they know what the problem we are solving looks like but also and equally importantly they hire bankers because they know that they need them to get around the bank's bad habits and inertia. And that's probably the most important skill and, in that, not all bankers are created equal. And this is another take-away for your 'how do I find and keep the team I need for this type of work' so take note.

NOT ALL BANKERS ARE CREATED EQUAL

Not all bankers can drive work forward and the bank knows that only too well: the ones who are part of the problem have been perpetuating all the challenges we have discussed thus far. They know. We know. So the bank hires accordingly and start-ups would do well to learn this thing that the bank already knows and that is simply that not all bankers are created equal. Now it is not an over-statement to say that start-ups are wary of bankers. We see CVs of folks coming out of big banks and seeking to pursue new opportunities in our dynamic, lithe organisations and invariably we ask each other: their skills and experience are absolutely right, but will they be all Big Banky? We know what we mean. Some of us escaped big banks so we know *exactly* what we mean.

We mean will they be able and – equally significantly – willing to actually do things or will they just move paper around, attend meetings, say words such as 'alignment' and 'capability matrix', and just hope that either some-one else will do the work or nobody will notice? The thing is, these guys are indistinguishable from actual working humans to the naked eye. The start-up doesn't want them any more than the bank does and is much less able to carry them and their big salary and their team with their inexplicable titles and reams of PowerPoint that look oh so similar week on week. What the start-up isn't as good as the bank at doing is knowing which is which. It's a bit like mushroom picking (which I know nothing about) or diving for sea urchin (which I know a lot about): only some are good for eating. You need to know which, or you will waste a lot of time and possibly end up with severe food poisoning. A metaphor that works on so many levels.

There are three types of bankers, as any banker will tell you. The ones who do what they are told. No more, no less. And most definitely no different. It is not theirs to reason why. Often they know the work will end up on a scrap heap. They know nobody will look at it. Heartbreakingly, they often know whatever it is they are working on, won't work. More often than not, they don't know what the thing they are working on is actually for. And don't care.

And before you think, 'poor interns' ... stop. Some of these guys have a C in front of their title and a big office. Some of them get paid more than entire families. They are a species endemic to big organisations and they serve a purpose. They are good soldiers. They won't take initiative, but they will do the thing that they were told needs doing. They won't question it. They were neither hired nor trained to question and it's not their fault if the things they are told need doing don't actually need doing. And when you come in, sideways, and tell them something they inherited from above is no longer needed, they will ignore, resist or fight you. Because they have a mission and that's what good soldiers do. Whether their task has purpose or not, they are there to do it, not reflect on it. And they have built a career on exactly that skillset and they can't fathom what challenging the purpose of the work would achieve, where would it end. So they continue. They are not bad, you understand. But they can't thrive outside the banking ecosystem: they can't work without the structure, direction and momentum that the overall machinery creates. The start-up would be an awfully confusing environment for them. And they would be supremely dangerous for the start-up because one thing these guys *can* do is work without asking why. No start-up survives long if its people don't ask why and constantly align what they spend effort, time and runway on to purpose, mission and the collective journey. Let's be blunt here: people who don't ask why either shorten their own life expectancy inside the start-up, or more dramatically they shorten the start-up's life expectancy, by burning up time and runway doing work that has no purpose.

Then there is the sub-species we described above: on paper, similar to the worker ants who do the doing without asking questions. They look busy. They rush around. They play the corporate game and climb the ladder. They have meetings and send emails late at night and produce email attachments of varying lucidity. But they work hard. They are everywhere. And they are going places. Similar to those who do the thing and don't ask questions, in some ways, respecting the rules of the game. Oh, but they are different. These ones talk a good game. They spend a lot of time and energy on the talking up part of the game. They make a point of talking about the significance of starting with why, moving the needle and putting their arms around any manner of problem. Then they hand the needle that needs moving and the problem that needs hugging to the doers who won't ask, 'what on Earth is this for?'.

They will just do.

Meanwhile, our specimen will go onto another meeting where they will stay on exactly the right side of vagueness: things too theoretical to be objectionable, too high-level to be wrong. They are visionaries, you see. And they are dangerous. Because they drink their own Kool-Aid and, before long, they want to come work in the start-up, they think they chafe against the big bank guard rails, they rebel against the very things that make the mirage of their effectiveness hold. And often, oh so often, they fly high enough on their own hype to interview well and then land inside a start-up and try to ply the same trade and do the same tricks. And a few weeks into the hire you are looking at a badly written two-page memo and think, 'what have we done'?

So, of course we are wary of hiring bankers. Even the bankers are wary of hiring bankers. I should know. I am one and always wince when I see a block of solid banking experience on a CV.

But.

There is a third category of banker and when the market learns how to rec-ognise them, they will be paid their weight in gold, because frankly they are already worth it. These guys and gals come in all shapes and with all titles. They come in all ages. They are not your digital native UXers only. What makes them unique and valuable is not their possession of specific skillsets for the digital economy. They may have those skills and they may not. They may sit in compliance. They may sit in HR, finance or IT (not the digital part, but the hardware and cables and 'I need a new mouse' part). They may be young or they may be close to retirement. They don't fit a mould. And that's the point.

They are the people who get things done, they do the things, but emphati-cally *not* all the things. They do the things that need doing; side-stepping the things that don't actually need doing even if a million empty suits say something is top priority until it isn't and consign it to the closet of shame. They ask *why* without burning bridges. They go against the grain. They get things done. Through the noise. Through the inertia. They don't drink the Kool-Aid. Not their own. Not the bank's. Not anyone else's. They don't fall for the empty suits but neither do they let them fell them.

These are the people who get things done despite it all. Despite the bank getting in its own way. They are the reason that every bank is still stand-ing with some efforts of varying credibility to move in the right direction, despite the debris of pointless endeavour. They are the friends in low places, the builders and plumbers and story tellers. Sometimes they are the rebels, other times they are the leaders. Occasionally they are both and often they are neither, instead they are the quiet craftsmen. They come in many shapes and that is the point. They come in many shapes and they are why the banks are still standing: they know how the whole thing works, they know what needs to change and what's not worth the effort, they know when to stand tall and when to let people talk themselves out. That is how you will know them and that is why you need them. Because these are the folks who transform the banks they work in and the banking system they operate in despite everyone else's best efforts.

Those are the bankers you need: the ones who understand the thing you are trying to change (so they can change it) and get how to get change to stick inside a big organisation and they know how to avoid the noise and not get drawn to bright lights. These are the people the bank needs. These are the bankers the start-up needs. They are not easy to find, I will grant you that. But you need them. So don't diss bankers. Just find the right ones. And hire them immediately.

YOUR CALL TO ACTION

1. The economy is digital. If your business isn't, you don't get to pick 'which bits' you will engage with. You have to do all the things, the game has changed.
2. Innovation is not a department. It's a mindset that needs to permeate the whole business.
3. The work ahead is complicated and will take a long time. Be mindful of the middle: it's hard and it's where most people lose heart, lose their way and quit.
4. Look back, take stock and always treat 'now' as the best time to act.
5. Actively hire for people of integrity and courage. The time when we looked for the right skillsets is over. The complexity of the work ahead means you teach aptitudes and hire for attitudes.

6

So (Now) What?

SNEAK PREVIEW

If anything has been made clear during the preceding pages, it is that the work ahead of us is complicated and we somehow manage to get in our own way, making it even harder. But what if I told you that banking, at its very heart, is simple? Complexity is just in the delivery and that is where we need to remove it, by rethinking how we do the things we do, in a digital world. That is where we will unlock efficiencies but also a new-found purpose, as we can chart a clear path to doing our jobs in a way that is fairer and more inclusive.

There is a lot of work ahead of us. Leadership will be required. Intentional leadership and collaboration across the industry.

There is a job to be done. It will be done by bankers like us.

The message so far is, hopefully, clear: the work ahead is complex, necessary and inevitable. Surviving into the new economy isn't.

Those who do survive will have transitioned to the digital economy fully. But doing the work doesn't guarantee survival. So intentional action is necessary as going through the motions is not enough here.

The call to action so far is, I hope, equally clear: humans matter.

Understand that and start acting accordingly from the smallest habits to the biggest decisions; from how you choose and treat your trench buddies to how you engage with the world writ large and from how you participate in your community to your own teachability and willingness to include others in activity and opportunity. Focusing on the people, both within your organisation and outside it, where the humans you are building solutions for live, will take you a long way. There is nothing quite like solving real problems *for* real people and *with* real people.

All this will take you a long way.

But will it take you far enough?

DOI: 10.1201/9781003364436-6

And, more to the point, is it *specific* enough for both bankers and the non-banking business folk who may have found some useful tips or much-needed self-identification in these pages?

And the sad answer is: no.

Don't get me wrong.

I hope that reading these pages you exclaimed often 'I am not alone' and frequently 'hey I can do that'. There is a lot each of us can do to change this industry. But individual action will only take us so far and that's why I want to now turn to the logical connections between the things we have talked about in this book.

If that feels like I'm about to state the obvious, so be it.

In fact, let's start with that.

ADMITTING THAT 'THIS IS HARD' IS A SUPERPOWER

In the spring of 2021, I wrote a piece called 'the need for predictable poetry' in which I described myself as 'Captain Obvious'. Andrew Vorster immediately made me a 'Captain Obvious' t-shirt that I wear with great pride often including, occasionally, on my Twitter profile picture. So allow me to don my Captain Obvious cape here for a second and not only state the obvious in this chapter (although also that) but start by encouraging you to do the same. Your first call to action in this final chapter is 'call it out'.

We've talked about the power of putting words out into the world already.

The power of calling out micro-aggressions and bad behaviour and being vocal in our allyship. We talked about the power of story telling in bringing the link between vision, mission and our day-to-day work to life and light. Is it important to say the words even if we think everyone already knows. Even if the thing we are about to say is obvious.

Humans need to have the obvious stated. To hear 'I love you' even when it's not in doubt. To hear 'oh this is wonderful' even though you know it to be true. To hear 'that was weird' and know you were not alone in thinking it. You cannot underestimate the significance and value and need to hear that what we are experiencing does not isolate us. That we are not alone in seeing madness all

> Humans need to have the obvious stated.
> You cannot underestimate the significance and value and need to hear that what we are experiencing does not isolate us.

around us. Especially at work, when things are hard and complicated and folks aren't always behaving in a stellar manner.

So here it goes.

Captain Obvious reporting for duty: I have been in this industry, accidentally and yet fervently, two decades. In this time, a lot has changed. And a lot has remained stubbornly the same. Not static. Just the same. The language we use to describe and size our ambition has changed, but the feeling we seek to evoke has not. Dynamism, innovation, creativity, daring and optimism. Strategic vision, bold commitment. It's heady stuff. It doesn't matter if we work in an industry of ledgers and bips.[1] It doesn't matter if we work in a world of money, margin and heavy regulation. The humans in our industry need their William Wallace moment. They need to hear there is something bigger than each day's toil in play. We all need to hear there is a plan, there is some Good. That we are making a difference, if not to the world, then to the people and communities we serve.

Even the most bloodthirsty capitalists speak in terms of impact.

That is a take-away in itself.

Not the cynicism. Just our universal human need for meaning, for the assurance that what we do, leaves a bit of a dent in the world. Even when we just talk about margin, we speak of growth. Motion. Progress. The language we use points to the stars, it's human nature, we can't help ourselves. We all have a need for poetry. We all need to feel the winds of accelerating, intentional, forward motion. We all need to know there is a story unfolding and to feel like we are part of it. And there is value in helping your teams see where they fit into that story, which is why I've been talking about hiring story tellers all along.

But that is not all: there is something even deeper here that your friendly neighbourhood Captain Obvious would like you to be thinking of and acting upon.

Change is mostly disorienting and confusing. The start of a journey may be exciting and full of promise, the end may be exhilarating, heady with the relief of all the things that could have gone kaboom in a terminal way and didn't ... but the middle? The middle is a mess as we have discussed before and the predominant feeling folks have there is stress. Confusion as to whether they are doing the right thing ... as there is no real way of knowing

---

[1] Bips, BPS or Basis Points are a common unit of measure for interest rates and other percentages in finance. One basis point is equal to 1/100th of 1%, or 0.01%, or 0.0001, and is used to denote the percentage change in a financial instrument. It is often how remuneration in the deeper end of financial services is calculated, as advisors, intermediaries and agent functions will get paid in bips.

what *good* looks like, in the detail, when you are doing something for the first time alongside people who are doing their bit for the first time and in a context of resistance and mistrust (which we've described at great length already and doesn't need repeating).

In the heat of battle, so to speak, it's oftentimes hard to know what is working; what isn't; what will work in the long run; what won't; what behaviours will become part of your culture and what will go down in stories as 'those crazy early days'. It doesn't matter if you are a start-up or a behemoth transforming, for the individual this is hard. It's hard no matter where that individual sits. It's not a question of power: this is hard for everyone. And finding it hard doesn't mean you are doing it wrong or are not good at this. It just means you are not delusional.

You are finding it hard because it is hard.

And if you are thinking 'duh obviously' then Captain Obvious says perhaps, when you stop and think about it, it is obvious. But when you are at your desk on a Wednesday afternoon, it is easy to feel that nobody experiences stress like yours, with the weight of the world on your shoulders and everyone's future

> Putting ourselves in a period of sustained and unpredictable change is putting ourselves in a period of sustained stress. As a leader, you need to 'furnish' your transformation journey with predictability. Counter-intuitive as that may be.

hinging on your decisions. Or that nobody feels as crushed as you, working flat-out pursuing someone else's direction, blind as to their reasoning and hostage to their judgement. You may experience imposter syndrome, burn-out, or the low constant throbbing hum of 'what have I missed'.

So obvious or not, it needs to be said: This is hard. It's hard for the decision-maker. It's hard for the order taker. And it's hard for everyone in-between. It's hard for the client. It's hard for the vendor. It's just hard. And despite all our need for uplifting messages and poetry, between the starting gun and the finish line, the reality is that humans need predictability. As much stability as we can muster. As few surprises as can be. So putting ourselves in a period of sustained and unpredictable change is to put ourselves into a period of sustained stress. It drove Frodo half mad and he isn't even real. So the inspirational component of the quest is not enough. And although it may feel counter-intuitive to say that you need to 'furnish' your transformation journey with predictability, as a leader, that is actually what I am saying. That's also part of the call to action.

I did warn you this was not easy.

FURNISH CHANGE WITH PREDICTABILITY

Ironic isn't it?

That we want big change but also want to know that it's all going to be ok? That we want to be brave but also want to be safe and calm? That we want to be worthy of having contributed to the great decisions of our time, but does it have to be so disorienting for so long?

Hard is hard. And if you want to lead teams, if you want to inspire teams, if you want to achieve results, you can't be blind to this conflicting set of human emotions. If you want to help folks navigate the difficulty of the work and the additional challenges we pile on by virtue of being (let's face it) slightly dysfunctional as an industry in ways big and small, you have to do both of these seemingly incompatible things. You have to bring the poetry. You have to bring the uplift on the hard days. You have to inspire and rally and be able to remind folks why we do this. But you also have to manage people's need for predictability, banality, stability and safety.

You know what your client needs most of all, once they have bought into the vision and come onto the journey? They want as few surprises as possible.

You know what your team needs most of all, now they have bought into the strategy and your leadership? Predictability, reliability and consistency. They want to know that on a difficult journey there will be some constants they can rely on. And they need to know that you believe things will be ok. They want to know that the bumps on the road are part of the journey. Hell, they want to know they are part of the plan. They want to know that we are not about to crash, even though it may occasionally feel like it. They want to be reassured. And I know you do, too. And here is the rub. Because they don't want to be lied to. They will know if you feed them empty platitudes. They are not stupid. The stupid ones don't come on this journey. You wouldn't pick the stupid ones for this journey. It's a win–win, strangely.

So how do you reassure people who will see right through a lie, when you are in dire need of reassurance yourself? How do you help a team feel it's all going to be ok when you don't actually know that it is, all going to be ok?

Your clients and your teams want the excitement of progress with as few surprises as possible en route, they want the change, they want the improvement and they don't shy away from the hard work. They want the poetry and they will do their part. But they need you to make it feel less scary than it actually is. They need you to make it feel less unpredictable than it actually is. They need you to manage the bumps on the road. Not just tell them that it will be ok, but make it so. And how do you do that? Part of it is showing leadership. Making decisions with intent, as I keep saying, and not letting things drift. Paying attention to the small things, the everyday things as well as the big things. Part of it is consistency. Doing your part every day like the steady beating of a drum.

But there is more.

Part of it is assembling the right team. Nothing helps navigate choppy waters as well as a good team of sailors. And I won't labour this analogy, partly because we spent most of the last chapter on the team you need, but mostly because I can't. I know nothing about boats, much to my father's dismay.

But you get the point. Leadership, intent and the right team go a long way towards making the middle less scary even though it stays messy.

Transparency helps. Breaking the bad habits helps. And stating the obvious helps. Stay with me here.

People *need* the obvious stated. And the first obvious thing that needs to be stated is that reality is fungible.

I don't mean that we need to argue whether the sky is red.[2]

But we do need to continuously remember that everything people say and do is premised on assumptions about what is real, what is important and what is true. Assumptions. But it is very easy to accept those assumptions without challenge either because you didn't stop to think or because you did stop and think and

> Reality is fungible. We need to continuously remember that everything people say and do is premised on assumptions. And it is easy to accept those assumptions without challenge either because you didn't stop to think or because you did stop and think and where you got to is that you were not allowed to challenge.

where you got to is that you were not allowed to challenge. Or couldn't see a way to challenge. Or you thought you'd be the only one wishing to challenge and your truth when weighed against isolation, didn't burn as bright.

So the first 'obvious' thing to remember to do yourself and, by doing both, remind and allow your teams to do … is … never ever and under

---

[2] Ten points if you recognise this as a line from the English version of the song Poco Loco from the Pixar film, Coco.

any circumstances accept the premise of the question[3] without reflection. If someone gives you a task and you don't understand or indeed accept its purpose and don't ask the question, you have accepted the premise of the question, so to speak. If someone asks, 'what is wrong with you' and you answer 'nothing' and proceed to explain that there is something wrong with the situation not with you, you have accepted the defensive position they put you in. Don't answer them. Challenge them to answer *you* why, after observing you put a stop to a circular argument, point out that a colleague had crossed a line or a line of reasoning was unhelpful, they reached the conclusion that something was wrong with you and they wanted to know exactly what. Do not engage with a flawed piece of reasoning. Not even to refute it.

Is that obvious? Sure when you point it out it is, but in the moment? How often do you challenge the premise of a question asked of you?

___

REMEMBER TO ASK WHY

Our life at work is filled with tasks, questions, asks and pieces of activity that are predicated on assumptions and interpretations that may be benign (and maybe not), that may be flawed or incomplete. How many times does someone challenge their premise? I will tell you how many: not enough. And I will also tell you this. Every time I have asked a senior 'what is the purpose of this' I have gotten a deep sign and rolled eyes because it was experienced as a stalling tactic … and every time I asked a junior the same question they got defensive because they were so used to the question being a passive aggressive way of leading to bad feedback. When the question is literally what is the purpose of the activity? What is it for and how will I know it worked?

And I will tell you something more.

When I was junior I was mostly shut down when I asked this. The idea that knowing the purpose of the work would make me do a better job of it didn't seem to resonate with my bosses. Now I am too senior for people to *not* answer me. And most times, when I ask this question, what I find is people don't actually really know the answer. They were asked for something by someone 'above them', they didn't ask what the purpose of the thing was,

___

[3] This is a West Wing reference. And in case you are not familiar with it, *The West Wing* is an American TV series created by Aaron Sorkin originally broadcast on NBC. It ran from 1999 to 2006 and it is the best TV series ever made. Not the best TV series about politics. The best TV series ever. I will fight you over this.

they went down a rabbit hole of their own making and all they wanted was my bloody sign-off so they could send this thing off to the client, to their boss, to the investors, to the regulator whatever.

It is urgent (because it has an important recipient and a timeline), they have done the work and now here I am making more work for them.

Almost every time I have sent someone back to the original ask to find out what this thing they were working on was in aid of, we found that they had made assumptions that were incorrect, incomplete or, more often, *huge* compared to what was needed, overproducing to no effect. So, Captain Obvious: ask. It may save you effort.

It may also help deal with a lot of the insidious effects of the bad behaviours we have discussed at length so far. Because, let's think about it ... How many of the tasks, questions and asks we are faced with hourly in the workplace are a little jarring? A little annoying? A little out-of-focus? Because they feel out of whack or because you know they are leading you down the garden path but feel you can't call it out. Or because you realised they were leading you on too late in the day and got really annoyed with yourself for not stepping out of the dance and resetting the conversation, for letting the power of the context someone forced you into suck you under. When it was, frankly, obvious what they were doing. It was obvious that there was more to this. It is obvious to you that there is a bigger picture here. That there is a bigger question. It is obvious, now you think about it. And yet. They were so confident and nobody else spoke, so the obvious remained unspoken and here you are now doing work whose purpose is not in the slightest obvious.

If you think about it, how many times have you been in a situation where you doubted your own perception? Because something transpired that you found jarring but nobody in the room flinched. Something was said that is blatantly untrue but nobody in the room spoke up. Something was glossed over that had never been mentioned before and nobody shouted 'hold up now: what was that'. And here you are thinking 'that's not right' but nobody else is speaking. Are they sitting there wondering the same as you or are they happily moving on with the conversation because nobody else thinks this (whatever it is) is odd? Are you the only one to be missing something here? Will you sound stupid or argumentative if you speak up?

> From gaslighting to pig-headedness, there is a broad avenue of intent to cross, but for those at the receiving end of it, it doesn't much matter what the intent is when someone acts like what to you is obvious isn't even there.

Have you found yourself in a situation like this and doubted your own perception? Because I can tell you that your teams are living through this every day and it is neither obvious nor easy for them to pull the emergency break. Especially in the context of nuanced and hierarchical human interactions, commercial relationships, the zoo and jungle that is the workplace.

From gaslighting to pig-headedness, there is a broad avenue of intent to cross, but for those at the receiving end of it, it doesn't much matter what the intent is when someone acts like what to you is obvious isn't even there. Are they manipulating you? Are they blind? Is your perception all screwed up? Or is this the way of the world, which, given everything we have said so far about the realities created by the bad habits of the industry, frankly, it may have been for a long time.

For many reasons, your teams may not know that they can reject the premise of a question. They may have never seen someone stand up to a jarring moment. They may have never seen someone stand up and survive without ridicule or worse.

Or they may have seen it and realised that someone challenging the premise of the question is in itself jarring, as I have described before, and uncomfortable, so you can't expect people to always be brave and get on with it. You have to lead by example. You have to normalise challenging the premise of things. You have to make it ok. Because what happens currently is your team finds themselves in situations where what is obvious to them is treated as *not* obvious by others or so the silence (or indeed resistance) suggests, so they nod and everyone nods and hey presto here we all are having accepted the premise of a question or a set of assumptions that we don't agree with, do not believe in, or maybe don't understand. And now the world is on its head. And what next? We have to make do? And how do we do that, back at our desks, in the context of all the other things that were hard enough before this new curveball was added to the mix?

It is important to stress that for the most part of most people's careers that is exactly what happens. And it is particularly poignant when transformation is ran as a side show inside an organisation mostly holding onto its past. So you, as the agent of change, will be given highly contradictory direction and it will look and sound as gospel at the strategy level but when it all comes down to it, it won't work in the reality you operate in. But you didn't say that during that executive briefing, because nobody else did, and now you are tearing your hair out because there is no way of doing the Thing everyone agrees is the Plan, other than maybe on PowerPoint.

That explains a lot, by the way, if you think about it. But the PowerPoint warriors are not our concern. Our concern is the people who do and build and find this experience crushing.

But what can you do?

Putting your head above the parapet can be dangerous from a career perspective because the people who expect their assumptions to define our collective reality are powerful, senior, loud and often all of the above. But imagine someone asks the question that is on your mind. Imagine someone says that is not right. That is not true. That is not obvious. That is by no means the only answer here. Imagine someone says this calmly and with conviction and causes the conversation to pause, unpack itself and maybe take a different direction. Imagine you, in the shoes of your team member who was beginning to question their judgement and now they see someone vocalising exactly what they were thinking. They take heart. Now they can say 'yeah, it's obvious that this has flaws in it'.

Obvious, now someone else has had the courage to break the silence. Obvious now someone else admitted they can see what you are seeing.

It is powerful stuff. Doubly so, in a world of self-perpetuating demographics and deep-rooted bad habits including passive aggression in almost every interaction, when it is never obvious that you are on the same page as everyone else, especially when there is no blueprint or precedent for what you are doing. And there is no guarantee that challenge won't be met with ridicule as we have discussed before. So don't expect people to be brave when you haven't led by example. Take it upon yourself to state the obvious for your teams. To help them normalise doing it for themselves. And when you do, the team around you will sit forward a bit. They will nod. Yes, yes. It is obvious to us all, we were going down a random path here. Captain Obvious to the rescue.

And look, there are days when you will point something out and you will be greeted with a jeer of 'yes thanks Captain Obvious, where would we be without you' because what you flagged may indeed have been an option that was already thought through and eliminated. No matter. There is a reason why IT support asks you to turn the blasted thing on and off again when you call with a problem. Because not everyone remembers to try it.

Also, there is the other thing. The line between Captain Obvious and a profoundly irritating smart Alec needs to be navigated carefully. Because you don't want to be the person to constantly point flaws in other people's homework. You are not here to embarrass anyone. You are here to help us as a team collectively think together. Everyone is to be challenged, to be questioned. You, as a leader, very much included.

And when you do it to others it has to be done in a way that is constructive, respectful and never personal. Being Captain Obvious doesn't come with a crown or cape. Challenge should never become about power. It is profoundly important to help your team learn how to surface gaps, uncomfortable truths and human silliness. How to face into our collective fallibility with the willingness to acknowledge the size of a challenge or the mess we got ourselves into.

AINT' ABOUT LOOKIN' COOL

The call to action here is effectively twofold.

Firstly, put yourself in the difficult, awkward position of truth-teller, do it often, do it consistently, do it with panache. Ask the questions. For the second part to happen: for your team to know they can too.

And even if there is no conflict or tension to be resolved: state the obvious.

There is power in the telling. In acknowledging a shared reality. In helping people not feel isolated in what they are seeing just because it may be embarrassing to admit.

Putting words to what some folks may be struggling with, or challenging a mistruth you know everyone else is chafing at, may not solve the problem in the moment. And it may put the speaker in a rather awkward spot but, and this is important:

> Always challenge mistruth or obfuscation.
>
> Teach those trying to skate over the hard stuff, silence objection with bravado or dominate the discussion through gaslighting that this is not how we do things around here.
>
> Say the words and make it ok for your team to do the same.
>
> It matters.

Firstly, it starts creating a valuable precedent and a good habit for the future where the team feels empowered to voice the challenge and learn how to challenge the premise of the question and not the person asking it and that means that you are building good habits, profoundly good deep-rooted, constructive habits for the future. The second reason is more straightforward. Do it because the alternative leaves us stagnant. Do it again. Teach those trying to skate over the hard stuff, silence objection with bravado or dominate the discussion through gaslighting that this is not how we do things around here. It matters. So do it.

Putting words to those jarring moments, learning to constructively deconstruct the assumptions underpinning tasks and asks in the workplace is of great value not just as a culture exercise but also as a risk-mitigant. It may save you from going down dead-ends, over-indexing or under-estimating.

Group-think is de rigour for a reason. It is dominant because people are conditioned to avoid discomfort. And the potential for ridicule or conflict is uncomfortable. Silence is safer. So make it not so. Break that cycle. Make speaking up as safe. Make speaking up *safer* than the alternative: make it a habit.

Especially as group-think and silence don't work when it comes to strategy, change and creativity.

So learning to do this challenge/ask/question thing is good for your business. It will also be so very good for your team. Good habits have long-ranging salutary effects and you will never know how beneficial this may be to someone's mental health and professional growth as they start trusting in their own instincts and their own truth each day a little more. Very often a team member's trust in themselves comes via trust in you, your integrity and courage and level-headedness and ability to say something that they were too scared or embarrassed to say. A team member builds up the courage to do this by being in a team that does this, a team that allows folks to state an opinion, which sometimes will be obvious and other times not, and not get laughed out of town over it. There is immense value in your team seeing you voice a hard truth and stand your ground. You make it possible by making it true.

This may take a dramatic flavour but it doesn't need to be 'high-stakes' to be important. The thing I keep saying about consistency applies here too.

'Heather, you are on mute'.

If that's not the soundtrack of our COVID existence, I don't know what is. But a friend who works in recruitment told me that, in many company cultures, team members would *never* say that to their seniors. Obvious as it was to everyone bar the person speaking, that they are not heard. They would let the boss talk to themselves, trying to lip-read rather than say 'hey boss, can't hear ya'.

If you can't say that, what are the chances of saying 'these assumptions are wrong, we have missed something' or the bravest thing of all 'I don't understand, can you explain this to me'.

So. In a world where we are all trying very hard to seem cool, collected and in control and where, intentionally or unintentionally, errors happen, let's state the obvious. Let's point out the gaps. Let's ask the questions.

The thing that makes no sense to us may be unintentional, bona fide error and, by asking, we just helped everyone move along and avoid costly delays, re-work or embarrassment. Maybe there was something we genuinely didn't know and now we do and isn't it great, this learning malarkey? And if the gap we challenged was intentional, then pointing it out was all the more important for the good of the team and the good of the work. It may not always feel like it but you may have just foiled a saboteur.

If you are reading this thinking 'move on already, I get it', my point is simply to make sure you get it in all its facets and mundane glory. That you remember to challenge it in the small ways it manifests itself, as well as the big ones. But honestly, I rather hope you are reading these pages thinking, largely, 'I've got this. I can do this. I already do this. I can double down but largely, I've got this.' And part of the purpose of the original #LedaWrites column that, years down the line gave birth to the idea for this book, was reaching out to the community of Bankers Like Me, in the hope that they exist. I started writing about these things in the hope of finding my tribe, in the hope of this being my beacon that would help us find each other.

Saying 'I see you, you are not alone'. And look. I know better than any-body that feeling seen is no small thing. Feeling like you are not alone is no small thing. Especially when the road is long and the conditions largely inhospitable. Finding validation in things you instinctively knew to look for (like friends in low places or builders and story tellers to help your team through the darkness of the messy middle) is, again, no small thing. And much like the ocean being made up of drops of water, small things add up to life-altering landscapes through habits, choices and consistent behaviours. And yet. When the message so far has been about the radical nature of the shift needed, and the realisation that the world is moving much faster than our organisations, is all this … enough?

YOU ARE NOT, IN YOURSELF, ENOUGH: IT TAKES A VILLAGE

Is it enough to lead by example?

You know … sadly … No. It is not. It's a start and it is essential and it's key to long-term success, but it is not in itself enough to push the change forward.

And we all know this to be true for the very simple reason that, for a very long time, we have been doing all the things I have been describing here, in our own ways inside the pockets of the industry we each inhabit. We have been doing all these things and more. And although the behaviours we champion have helped us move things forward, they helped us make change happen for our teams, our organisations and the industry as a whole, this effort in pockets has not been enough to transform the industry or we wouldn't be having this conversation at all. It has not been enough to become the dominant way of working. It has not been enough to make the transformation inevitable. It has not been enough to eradicate the bad habits. So we need to do more. We all know it. That's why we keep pulling together our collective wisdom and learnings and experiences. To work out how to get to *more*.

And let us be clear: this is not a question of 'just work harder'. It is not a question of the *effort* not being enough. The effort itself is more than enough. Burnout is a terrible idea and a very real outcome for many of us. So more effort is not the answer. It is also never a question of *you* not being enough. You are enough, that is the only certainty. That's never in doubt. But the small acts of resistance and the consistency we bring in our parts of the world, in itself, sadly don't amount to enough. We still have to do all of it, by the way. Everything I have encouraged you to start doing, so far, everything I have challenged you to start doing so far, is important. And necessary.

Without it, we can't do more. It's the starter pack, if you will. Absolutely essential and none of what needs to come next is possible without it so please carry on doing all those things, start doing all those things, don't give up on all those things. But please also know that they are not, in themselves, enough.

So what is, you may ask. In order to get to 'enough', three things need to happen: we need to find our place, we need to find our purpose and we need to find our stride. Collectively. The remaining few pages are about what we need to do as a community. A community of practitioners, a collection of purposeful teams making up an organisation. A community of humans. It is harder, of course, always harder to coordinate purposeful activity across humans dispersed in time and space. But nobody said this work would be easy. We said it was hard and we said it was essential. So. Let's unpack what the next phase of action, this time collective and intentional, needs to look like.

KNOW YOUR PLACE

Let's take a step back to take a leap forward.

In order to fix the fundamentals, you need to go back to basics. In order to be purposeful, you need to be clear about the purpose you serve and pursue. Not the task or the *stuff* you do of a day. But the fundamental purpose you are trying to achieve.

So. What do banks do, *really*?

I appreciate that is not where you expected me to go right now, but this is not a Self-Help manual for purposeful living writ large. It's a Self-Help manual for purposeful bankers. So. What is the purpose of the thing we work in?

I am asking the bankers among my readers to reflect but if you are here from another industry, please apply the same seemingly simplistic question to yourself as if you were trying to explain your craft to a very smart 11-year-old or a chatty alien. They won't get the jargon, but they will understand a well-thought-through, non-cyclical, non-self-referential explanation, if you can offer it. And that is key: everyone can explain what they do in terms of itself. But can we explain it in non-relativist terms, in a way that can be understood with no prior knowledge?

So. What does the thing you work at all day *do*, in the most basic terms?

Pause and try to explain what you do in terms of *why* you do it. What you are here to achieve and how the things you do each day add up to the thing that defines your purpose. It sounds easy. And it may be. Or not. If you are a cricket lover or have ever asked a cricket lover to explain the game to you, you know it's next to impossible to explain it without reference to the game itself (or, at a stretch, to baseball). People are fantastic at explaining cricket in terms of cricket to people who already get cricket. Which is why, 25 years of living in the UK has not been enough time to work out what on earth is happening during a cricket match.

Don't do that. Do the opposite of that.

Explain your industry's purpose from a zero-knowledge basis. In your own words.

Let me help.

I will use banking as the working example here just because it's my ball-game but if you are visiting from elsewhere in the universe of business, the principle applies so *apply it* and see where it gets you.

There are many definitions of banking, as you can imagine, as finance and banking economics are taught at universities the world over. Some of those definitions are pretty basic,[4] some convoluted. Some mechanical (describing banking in terms of the stuff it does) and some abstract (describing it in terms of its place bridging the real economy and macro-economic policy considerations). Definitions abound and you can take your pick.

This is how I explain banking to people who think they know what it is and then invariably look all confused because what follows is not exactly what they thought they knew: *Banking institutions move things of agreed value* (let's call it money or things that stand in for money[5]) *in time and space.*

A payment is a movement in space: the money goes from my pocket to yours, from your bank account to that of the merchant who just sold you that beautiful, new sideboard. A loan is a movement in time: it allows you to pay for the sideboard at a later time, in the future, at a pre-arranged additional cost. It allows you to transact now and pay later.

An investment is equally a movement in time, just with the surcharge reversed, hopefully.

In a loan situation, you pay for the benefit of *not* paying for your house or your invoices pending right now, all at once. In an investment situation, you are paid for the use of your deposit for a whole host of things (including your own loan). It gets more complex when volatility is taken into account but the fundamentals hold.

That's two things banks do. And there's another two that are derivatives of the first two but equally important to defining a bank's purpose.

They safeguard those things of value in-between moving them, in the shape of transaction and custodial accounts, deposits, vaults and promissory notes. The safeguarding is material (they keep stuff physically safe) and conceptual (even if something goes wrong, they've got you. If the bank is robbed, that money isn't someone's in particular, your money is safe and so is Jonny's money and so is Arthur's). Safeguarding is key and, to achieve that,

---

[4] Penn State, for instance, defines banking as the business activity of accepting and safeguarding money owned by other individuals and entities, and then lending out this money in order to conduct economic activities such as making profit or simply covering operating expenses. https://psu.instructure.com/courses/1806581/pages/introduction-what-is-banking-and-why-is-it-important?module_item_id=26004136

[5] Money is itself an abstraction, a token, a representation of a convention of exchange. We can write a separate book on concepts of value and the evolution of money but doing that is not key to my argument here and, besides, others have written exceptional works on the topic including but not limited to Glynn Davies' *A History of Money* or Dave Birch's *Before Babylon, Beyond Bitcoin*.

banks manage the risk associated with those movements in space and time, and levy fees for each step of associated activity.

And they report on all of the above, because they have to (regulators demand it and clients expect it) and because it helps with tracking movements and fees and whatnot.

That's it.

THE COMPLICATED 'HOW' OF A SIMPLE 'WHAT'

So if banks fundamentally do things that are simple to understand, why is banking so hard to explain?

Because what banks do is simple. *How* they do it is where the fun begins. Financial instruments and complex vehicles fall in this *how* bucket. *What* they do is set. They move value in time and space. That. Is. It.

How they do it – what the triggers, steps, requirements and fee structures are – can be weird and wonderful and often is, but the *what* is set. Investment vehicles have, over the years, gotten so abstract and esoteric (futures and options,[6] for instance, should be the stuff of fiction) but, fundamentally, they allow you to commit to some money now in exchange for potentially more money in the future. The amounts are linked to risk mitigants and fees, directly (but not linearly) tied to how we have all agreed to understand, measure and manage risk. So it gets complicated, but the basics are there.

I repeat: the *how* is tricky. The *what* is not.

On top of this all, complex governance structures, systems and technology, humans and legal entities evolved to serve 'the what'. And as the 'how' became more convoluted, so did the systems and the organisation structures and the governance around it all. Hardware, software, offices, resolutions

---

[6] Futures are literally the contractual agreement to sell or buy assets at a pre-agreed price (to be agreed now) in a future date (to be specified now). It allows for speculation around commodities (you may have reason to believe the price of gold, oil or agricultural goods will shift in a particular direction at a particular time in the future), currencies and more complex vehicles. It is a hedging mechanism to balance portfolio exposure and give optionality because you can also buy options, for a fee. And the option simply buys you the choice of buying an agreed asset at an agreed price in an agreed future date. But not the obligation. You can. But you don't have to. But you buy that privilege.

If that sounds a little mad, you should read Terry Pratchett's description of the Pork Futures warehouses of Ankh Morpork, where unborn piglets run around waiting to come into being. It's a bit like that, without the cute little piglets.

and human toil, all fall into the *how* and acquire complexity in direct proportion to it. And they add complexity, in turn. Because of entropy and occasionally for the sheer fun of it. Occasionally, in the hope of obfuscation. Sometimes because humans genuinely get so carried away with their part of the *how* as to lose sight of what is immutable and what isn't. People get caught up in the beauty, importance, complexity and significance of what they do that they over-complicate their part of their world and lose sight of how it does or should link up to the rest of the world.

> Sometimes humans get so carried away with their part of the 'how', as to lose sight of what is immutable and what isn't.
>
> People get caught up in the beauty, complexity or significance of what they do and over-complicate their work, losing sight of how it does or should link up to the rest of the world.

But you catch the drift and you are now thinking fine, whatever.

The *what* of banking is straightforward. The *how*, less so. Captain Obvious is still with us, it seems. Tell us something we don't know, you may be thinking. But that's the point: there isn't anything you don't know here and the challenge is to remember that what you know is all there is to know, when you find yourself faced with assumptions of reality that don't sound true and you are beginning to wonder what you are missing.

Remember that this fairly simple *what* is what we are here to do: that's our place and our purpose. We are not prisoners here, this is not the Hotel California of careers. If you don't like occupying this space you can go off and be a book-binder, a yoga teacher, an accountant, an astronaut. But while you are *here*, you have a duty to face into what we are here to do and ask yourself: why have we made it so complicated? Does all this complexity help? Does it bring choice? Does it add value to the consumer?

Ask and ye shall find that in some cases it does. And in some cases it doesn't.

In all cases, however, there is a subtext of occasionally, potentially complicating things to feed an ego or to perpetuate a myth of occupying the top of a mystical food chain. And let's agree now that this kind of obfuscation is dangerous witchcraft. Exactly because it has held the world in its spell successfully for many a decade while the Wall Street yuppy was ruling the roost. And we can fall for it, even inside the Citadel. Despite our digitisation rebellion and our irreverent ways, even the transformers inside the banks have spent a decade and a half trying to simplify the *how* of this rather straightforward *what* as if we had no choice.

Reality is always the starting point. So, of course, the way things are at the place and time when you start your journey of change is what you are changing away *from*. But how much of that reality you need to revere is the crux of the matter here.

Because we accepted the *how* as an inevitable part of the *what*. And it is not.

We have deployed technology in a million ways, we have spent billions of your currency of choice, transforming parts of banks and the wider adjunct faculty of financial services firms, whose entire raison d'être has been to vertically support little bits of this *how*. We have somehow managed to lock ourselves into the supremely limiting belief that 'doing their bit a little better' is all these organisations can possibly do, really. And we have at no point challenged the premise of that question. Because it is a big bloody premise and a big question and to challenge it raises the most important question of all: if not like this, then how? And we don't really know how to answer that yet.

But even if you don't have an answer yet, it is absolutely critical to face into the fact (and voice the fact) that the entire edifice of a multi-billion-dollar industry is *optional*. And although this is not (necessarily) a call to arms for revolutionary change, it is absolutely a call to arms for wholesale revision. If all of it is optional, we are not bound to any of it other than as a departure point.

Uncomfortable yet?

TURKEYS, CHRISTMAS AND A DUTY TO IMAGINE

Before you say that what I am speaking of will never happen because the folks I am inciting to rebellion are the very custodians of the system and turkeys don't vote for Christmas; before you say that people can only think in terms of what they know and it is understandable that digital practitioners in banking do the financial services equivalent of building a faster horse, because they can't imagine the car; before you do any of that: please don't.

Because the *how* we are speaking of is so unnecessarily complex that what we are left with is turkeys riding the fastest horse in the conviction that, if they keep going, they will outrun Christmas.

If the analogy seems over-laboured and counter-intuitive, then so should the idea of continuing to deploy the best of human endeavour against tweaking the entirely circumstantial and over-engineered *how* of a rather straightforward and unambiguous *what*. Challenging the fundamentals is never easy and never where you start. I am not naïve.

> It should be counter-intuitive, this idea of continuing to deploy the best of human endeavour against tweaking the entirely circumstantial and over-engineered how of a rather straightforward and unambiguous what.
>
> And yet that is exactly what we keep doing.

But this is not the starting line. We are no longer at the starting line. We have been at this for almost two decades. We are well on our way, we have started, done some stuff, made some changes, had some success and there are some of us mounting sustained resistance in pockets.

It is time for more.

Whether we stayed away from touching the fundamentals because we couldn't imagine a world without them in place in exactly the way they look today ... or because it felt irreverent to even try ... no matter: it is time. Whether it is our imagination that faltered or our courage, it is time to find both. And if you don't have them, hire for them and do it fast. And if you don't know who to hire, leaf back to earlier chapters, the folks you need are described there.

The journey of innovation started with pointing new technology at things that wouldn't break the whole monetary system if they went wrong, while working out whether the new-fangled tech at our disposal was as real as the nerds said it was.

That was the right place to start. It's not cowardly, it's actually sensible. It is fine, but it's done. We have the tech. It's here, we tested it and tested it and tested it again. It works. It scales, it's robust, it's secure. It's awesome. Let's get going.

It's ok if you are experiencing a little bit of vertigo, you know.

If you stop to think about it, we are fortunate enough to occupy a singular moment in history where technology is having a renaissance moment the likes of which we have never seen before. There is so much of it, in generational terms, more than any single organisation can consume. It's scaling and maturing rapidly and across multiple verticals and it's there to solve whatever problem we point it at. And it will create some problems without a doubt. Or rather the way we deploy it will. Historically, the human race doesn't have a stellar track record in deploying technology in a way that doesn't create socio-economic disaster in its wake, even when it creates growth and creativity in one place, it always creates a dark underbelly too.

But that's the humans, not the tech.

It's what *we* do with it, not what *it* can do. And although that human aspect is something we should be thoughtful and intentional about, and I will come back to before the end of the chapter (so please keep reading), the point for now is that it has *not* been *concern for our fellow man* that has slowed us down. We have been looking for constraint in the technology itself in the hope that we, as an industry, will be spared the hard work and uncertainty ahead.

> We, as an industry, have been looking for constraint in the technology itself in the hope that we will be spared the hard work and uncertainty ahead.
>
> But alas, no.
>
> The technology is not where the constraint is. The humans are where the constraint is.

Every innovation centre across the globe was deployed in the unspoken hope that the emergent digital avalanche would be found 'immature' or 'too early to scale' or 'small enough to contain'.

But alas, no.

The technology is not where the constraint is. We are where the constraint is. The humans, collectively. Because we are reluctant to face into what our place in this equation is and ask ourselves some hard questions. Again, whether a failure of imagination or courage, it almost doesn't matter after all this time. It is probably a bit of both. Because we know now that we have the tools to move away from what we've always known and what we've always done, to radically depart from the familiar shapes and say 'OK, if this is *what* I need to do and these are the tools I now have to do it with, I should not try and tweak what I inherited but rather wonder at what is possible'.

To do that, we need to know our place in the grand scheme of things and solve for it. So a little bit of self-reflection is key. And that is where the team composition we have been discussing before comes into its own: the right bankers who can look at the behemoth and 'see the matrix' so to speak, the people who understand the business enough to unpick it without unravelling it and navigate from where we are to *where we could be* without breaking systemically important things. The people who have the courage and ability to ask the hard questions, do the hard work and stay the course. This is where it all comes in. There was method to my madness all along.

So once we've dealt with the egos and the habits and the complex organisations we have erected around what I insist is a simple function, a simple function of storing and moving things of value in time and space and keeping records of all actions ... are we done then?

Sort of.

The fact that we got complex and creative with the *how* of our business is not incidental. This complexity and creativity is how we made a big and profitable business out of all this. It is how financial services has become a huge vertical in the global economy. It is why some of the best and brightest seek to join its ranks. Because it's interesting. It's simple work but the doing of it isn't simple. And it is easy to become its own end-game, this pursuit of complexity, when it is a driver for lucrative deals and (separately but not independently) exclusive, hard-to-access careers.

You can see how something becomes self-perpetuating, when it develops its own self-contained parallel purpose.

And if you watched the film Wall Street or lived through a financial crisis or two, you know that can happen rather easily and when it does happen, it ain't pretty. So in a business that has a simple function with complicated execution, if the *what* is simple and the *how* is a complex maze of our own making, the only way to untangle the two with any hope of success is working out our *why* and trying to tie that back to what we do and how we seek to be remunerated. Because this is a business after all and there is absolutely no reason that it can't remain a thriving business with a stronger sense of purpose.[7]

━━━━━━━━━━

FINDING OUR PURPOSE

Although we are in the money business and many of us absolutely do it for the money, the business itself is an intermediary step for life.

Money is the gateway to experiences, access, subsistence, survival or folly. But, unless you are Scrooge McDuck or Gordon Gecko, perhaps, money is not an end-game. And neither are financial instruments. Having money is a motivator and a comfort because of what it can secure for you: shelter, safety, a wonderful holiday, an urgent operation for your mother, labour-saving devices or services, a square meal, a private jet. All of this needs money. What differentiates them is the amount. That's a hard thought to stomach but in its bare bones it is true.

---

[7] If you like that sort of thing, then you will love 'Beyond Good: How Technology Is Leading a Purpose-Driven Business Revolution' by my wonderful friends Theodora Lau and Bradley Leimer.

Money is the business we are in.

The problems money solves come in all sizes and although it doesn't solve all problems, it provides comfort that options can be reached, for most things, through monetary vehicles. Those may be cold hard cash (which is why folks who can, invest and save, to have more of it in the future) or lending vehicles and bridging finance for humans, families, businesses and governments. And the point I am trying to make may be obvious, but it is important to say it out loud because we will need to follow it to its logical conclusion which becomes less obvious with every logical mental step we take.

So back to the obvious point: nobody gets a loan for want of something better to do on a Saturday night. Mortgages aren't an end in themselves. Invoice financing is not a hobby. A financial instrument is always a stepping stone to something else, something separate and independent to the money that gets you there, be it a personal aspiration, a business challenge or a government infrastructure project. The money is sought, borrowed and leveraged 'so that' something completely unrelated to the possession of money can materialise.

So.

As bankers and financial services professionals and FinTech nerds, we are in the 'so that' space. Nobody's journey ends with us.

This is extremely important and although I know you know, I also know that the way we have set up our business is wilfully blind to the fact that we are mere intermediaries and the fate of the intermediaries is to be cut out where possible. And to avoid that 'disintermediation' effect as we openly called it for many years, we sought (the finance industry, the banks and financial services institutions) to increase client touchpoints, in the misguided belief that higher touchpoints increase awareness and dependency (that is not the misguided part) and that those would, in turn, increase stickiness, loyalty and share-of-wallet penetration (that's the misguided part). When all they increase in a digital world is friction and a front-of-mind awareness of how much of a pain your bank is.

So back to the obvious but overlooked point: even the most complex trading instruments are usually a means to an end. Yes wealth. Of course wealth. But usually there is a steppingstone before that. Financial services are about access to money for an activity or purpose, not the money itself. They are about leveraging money to do stuff. The stuff may be about building railways, expanding your business to a new geography or buying a new set of skis for personal enjoyment. It may be personal enrichment also but even then the money is a pathway to security, luxury, choice.

In itself, it's just paper in your pocket and digits on a screen.

Don't you 'duh' me.

This is important so I will say it again. Money is needed just before the phrase 'so that' in the syntax of life. It is a step to *something* people, businesses and communities need or want to do. And banking, as an industry, is the way we have organised to standardise and facilitate that 'step before'. So it is the *so that* before the *so that*. Doubly removed. I consume a financial product *so that* I can have the funds *so that* I can do the thing I want to do. That is our place, just before a double 'so that'. The 'how' of it all, as we have already said, is complex, diverse and occasionally bordering on the occult. But the mechanics of it are blatant and need to be spelled out. Our industry is never at the end of the equation. Even when wealth is the end-game, the financial instrument isn't.

It's important to labour this point because it is important to know our place, especially in a changing world. And it is very much my assertion as you have already deduced, that part of the problem we have had in the last two decades is that we have tried to negotiate digital transformation with a keen eye on maintaining a dominant position that was circumstantial to the way we had delivered services up until now (the how) and not fundamental to what we are here for (the what).

It was a good gig, why would you not try to keep it?

Totally get it. Lucrative, respected, feared a bit. Top of the career food chain. And it lasted long enough to explain why many thought it was the natural order of things. So when the digital transformation journey started, the pre-existing bad habits we have already discussed went into overdrive to protect a world that was both familiar and very comfortable. But human foibles aside, nobody owes anybody else a living, and nobody owes anybody else a continuation of privilege. And yes I am very much saying that the focus on digitising the 'how' rather than focusing on the 'what' is absolutely, in part willingly or unwittingly, an attempt to perpetuate the world as we know it. Whether the driver was greed, insecurity or lack of the ability to imagine anything different (or all three, frankly). We are where we are and to get to where we need to get to, knowing our place is important or we will continue chasing our tails. And our place is this: we are a 'so that' business. We are an intermediary step. We are a facilitator on a good day, a dreaded obstacle on most others. We are a necessary evil, an enabler or a stepping stone but we are never, ever the end-game. So if we are honest with ourselves and look hard at the work we do, there is only one 'why' in our business: to serve.

WE ARE, ABOVE ALL ELSE, A SERVICE INDUSTRY

I am not being mock-deferential here. It's the truth. I don't need to labour the point of how each instrument we sell is a means to an end any further. I think I made my point. But I can imagine two possible objections here so let me tackle them before moving on. Those are (1) it's the function, not the instrument, that makes us systemically significant and (2) some financial activity is indeed an end in itself.

And to that I say: nice try.

Although the sum total of all financial activity, all financial instruments across retail, SMB and corporate banking and sovereign lending makes banks and financial services firms *systemic* in every sense of the term, that does not alter the fact that they are an intermediary service that allows us to store, transport and transpose value. The scope and scale of the activity doesn't make it any less of a 'so that' business. It underlines its importance but that was never in doubt. What I am knocking here is the position the industry has assumed for itself. So the scale and ubiquitous nature of banking is not in question. And it doesn't challenge its purpose. If anything it underlines the importance of reflecting on that purpose. And serving it with intent.

So. There goes that.

The second question around the more creative instruments is a little more challenging to the premise but frankly I will take it head on and if you are a trader or a quant, you may not like where I will take this.

As you start travelling down the road of more complex trading instruments, somewhere around derivatives,[8] the 'means to an end' starts being a lot less linear, admittedly. These vehicles are absolutely used as a means of wealth-creation, which supports my point above. But they are also largely used as a way of managing, mitigating and 'hedging' business risk. If you recall, the complex art of risk management was a part of how I defined what banks do, so yes, you got it: there is a whole host of instruments that banks make money selling you (and you make money buying them so don't feel too hard done by, here) that are essentially a perfectly balanced self-contained circle. Whether it is virtuous or vicious is a matter of perspective. What is definitely not up for debate is that it is unbroken and self-perpetuating.

---

[8] A derivative is an instrument that derives value from something else (hence the name) so essentially it is a contract that allows you to benefit from the performance of an underlying entity which could be an asset, index or interest rate.

Does that mean that it is a chink in the armour of my point about our purpose? *Au contraire.* It is a further proof point that the 'how' of this business has become a little thriving civilisation of its own. And good on it. But just because you spent a lot of time building something doesn't mean that it is universally valuable. Or that it changes the original purpose of things.

Now, before I return to my point, it is important to say that this is the side of the business that politicians liked to call 'casino banking' during the various crises we have navigated. And although I get why it is often called that, as there is a big crossover between gambling and trading and anyone who tells you otherwise is either lying to themselves or you. *But.* There is more to it than that and, if anything, the term and the urge to 'ring-fence' banking that was *for* consumers away from banking that wasn't, shows that politicians, at the time at least, didn't fully understand how the world they were trying to 'fix' interconnected and interacted.

Because the way a derivative is used by investors is indeed a cyclical and rather self-referential exercise, and this is key, the activity it is *derived* from and the volatility it helps regulate by allowing hedging of risks through an extended time horizon is actually directly linked and directly beneficial (or not) to the real economy. Whether we would be better off with greater simplicity or not is a conversation for another time. I am not sure that I care to go for simplicity for its own sake necessarily but I would say *understanding* is key and non-negotiable. And when you understand how things fit together and how they derive from and connect back to the economy, you will find that some instruments (such as cash) are very linear and easy to grasp and others (such as derivatives) take you on a rather circuitous route of many steps and many lateral benefits and inter-dependencies along the way. But back to the economy they lead. Every single one of them.

So I stand by my point.

Banking is a 'so that' business. That's our *why.* We are here to help keep assets safe, to provide liquidity for business and financing for infrastructure projects. We are here to provide children with access to the means to secure an education; their parents with access to the means to

Money makes the world go round and that 'going round' part is the so that of our business. The reason we exist. Yet it is never referenced when we measure the success of projects, digital or otherwise, in this industry.

access healthcare; and the owner of the corner-store opposite the school gates with access to bridging loans and invoice financing that secures their livelihood. Even in countries where education and healthcare are free, money helps with access, not to mention helping the state with the funds to build the school and hospital through sovereign bonds, syndicated lending and investment vehicles.

So the monetary system gives access to the means to buy an ice cream, but let's face it, it's all about the ice cream.

I guess what I am trying to say is money makes the world go round and that 'going round' part is the *so that* of our business. The reason we exist. I know it is repetitive but it is important. It is the whole point. And the least referenced point when we measure the success of projects, digital or otherwise, in this industry. So one more time for the people at the back: our entire industry exists so that money can move in space and time to enable living, commerce and growth. And we do it in a way that allows the doing of it to be a business, i.e. we do it for money. Are we aligned?

I am ready to move on if we are, but I won't be moving far.

WE ARE IN THE MONEY BUSINESS

If we agree that our industry's purpose is to allow money to move in space and time to enable living, commerce and growth then the purpose of financial services is largely fulfilled by what we do today. Inefficient as we are and cynical as that is.

So if the *what* is on point, then the last 20 pages go against themselves and transformation did the right thing focusing on the *how*.

Digital overhauls should indeed focus on the means we use to do our work. If the conclusion we draw here is that, as things stand, we fulfil our purpose (albeit inefficiently and often with pricing that is confusing and predatory, access being a problem for people, businesses and states alike) then going against my own point of focus on the *how* over the *what* was a mistake. But actually I am not. Stay with me.

Banking is a so that business. The 'so that' is important. The business bit is important too. It was a greedy business for a while and it doesn't sit well with people when you talk about profit and bankers in the same sentence.

Why?

Because people think of fat cats (remember Amazon used to flag the 'fat cat charge' back in the day, for cards that came with a processing fee?) and slogans like 'greed is good'[9] that are, in most people's mind, synonymous with banking.

Greed is not good.

Predatory fees are illegal and immoral.

But. Profit is not the same as extortion and when we are thinking about transformation we need to allow for the fact that, actually, banking is not a charity. It is a business and one that needs to be profitable to stay solvent and keep everyone else solvent in the process. It is a business and actually that's the point.

The transformation we keep saying is needed, is not required in order to help finance find its purpose but in order to help us fulfil it in a changing economy. And the difference is subtle but, when it comes down to brass tacks, not at all hard to see what

The transformation we keep saying is needed, is not required in order to help finance *find* its purpose but in order to help us *fulfil* it in a changing economy.

falls where. If you followed the above, it is hard to argue with the simple fact that we know our raison d'être. We may not like it and wish we were more fundamental to society but, if that's our wish, we can all go off and become teachers or physicians. Do jobs that actually enhance people's lives directly. While you stay in banking, you have to accept that we are an in-between step.

Our role is to facilitate and it is an important one even if it is not glamorous. Debating the why and trying to find an alternative purpose is just a stalling exercise. We know what we need to do. We just need to get better at doing the doing. That's where the digital revolution comes in. Allowing us to align a sense of purpose and ethics with a business that can do good and do well at the same time. For the avoidance of doubt, the choice to be ethical was always available to us and some, indeed, made it. It's just that the digital revolution gives us both a moment and a reason to think again. A moment because we need to make choices and in so doing examine all our options. And a reason because the technology at our disposal permits us to reduce obstacles to access and fairness without compromising on the need to stay business-relevant. The tech allows us to do good while also doing well for ourselves.

---

[9] Which is often attributed to Gordon Gekko in Wall Street but actually what Gordon Gekko says is 'greed, for lack of a better word, is good'. Greed is Good is an episode of Doogie Howser though, randomly enough, and it's referenced so often in common parlance as to not matter if it is accurate. Because it is ubiquitous.

Making money is a given. We need to make money. It's business. *How* you make money is a choice.

So what? Well. So a lot.

If we agree that financial services is a 'so that' business, there to enable lives and businesses and civilisations *while* making a profit, then that's our purpose and *how* we do it becomes our mission. How we do it becomes our differentiator ethically as well as operationally. It also allows us to draw a line and look at all activity that doesn't fall in this category separately and say: ok, you there are not part of this. I don't know what your purpose is, but it isn't this. And that doesn't mean you don't have a place and a purpose. You may very well do. But it's not this.

As mentioned above, legislators tried to apply similar heuristics to this on the aftermath of the latest financial crisis. They tried to separate what felt abstract and predatory (the aforementioned 'casino banking') and forced banks to separate it from the banking that has a direct impact on people's lives. Or so they thought.

The idea is noble. Why should a reckless trader in Honk Kong lead to a family in Nebraska losing their home? Creating geographic and organisational separation seemed like a good way to protect consumers. Noble cause but it would help to understand how money flows before trying to draw lines that separate good from bad. Because the reality is, we live in global economies with rather complex financial infrastructure and what happens in one side of the world affects what we consume on the other. It affects what we build, watch or buy, when and how, not to mention how much it costs: from lettuce to computer processors. Moreover, the highly layered and interdependent instruments that politicians put in the 'sin bin' were directly accountable for why the family in Nebraska could afford a mortgage in the first place. So maybe let's start by regulating sub-prime mortgages (it's done now, obviously) and then pausing to trace those lines of dependence. And in the process, let's have a long hard think about which of those instruments allows for some prosperity to flow back into communities and which are just hijacking stability. It's an exercise in risk-reward and one that banks are very good at (remember the definition at the very beginning?).

The how of the what is complex, I believe I have made my point.

And blunt instruments don't cut through complexity very well. So what we have found is that *some* ring-fencing is futile. Money flows across borders, consumer loans are backed by money coming from capital market accounts (credit card debt appears in Repacks and asset-backed securities may very well include your house) and often affordability of consumer instruments is premised on trading revenue downstream. And that also applies to the instruments traded to make sovereign debt investable. The way money flows is highly integrated. Right or wrong. I am not saying don't change it. By all means, dear policy makers, do. But just as I say to bankers that to change the industry's technical make-up, you have to understand it in the first place, and the same applies to policy makers. To change anything, you need first to understand it. There isn't a direct line connecting bond issuance to dams or schools but the line is there. We need to remember it. We need to understand it and then we need to actively keep it in mind: bankers, techies and policy makers alike.

WOULD YOU MOVE ON, ALREADY?

If you are wishing I would move on, I'm afraid I need to stay with this a bit longer because the implications of it are far reaching and profound. We have some seriously obscure investment vehicles. We absolutely do. So before consigning them to the sin bin, do the work of figuring out how they link up to the economy. If you really can't trace a line of how an activity pumps liquidity into commerce or underwrites mortgages or … or … or … then put it in the sin bin by all means. But do the work. You will find connections. And then you may need to reflect on whether those connections are helpful, healthy, understood (they are not) and whether they could be replaced by another way of achieving the same end. Which is where I've been going with this all along. There is no easy path to this, I'm afraid. The easy stuff was already done by our predecessors.

And if you are thinking 'there are people and businesses who trade for the thrill and profit alone in closed circuits that are only loosely connected to the real economy', you have read Flash Boys[10] and I totally get your discomfort. That sort of behaviour happens and the way the industry is set up has historically if not consistently enabled pockets of

> This is the hard part of the call to arms in this volume.
> But you knew that.
> It's not about how you apply technology. It's about how you apply technology *so that* we can re-baseline an industry that had grown apart from its purpose.

conduct such as described in the book or the films we love to hate. Treat

---

[10] Michael Lewis, 'Flash Boys: Cracking the Money Code'.

them as a thing apart, because they are. And regulate the hell out of them, I am with you all the way.

Everything else is part of the 'so that' business. The business that is there precisely to serve life, commerce and development. And yes make a profit doing it. But *doing it* is the non-negotiable part. If that's not what you are here to do, you are in the wrong business. Please leave.

It isn't that simple, but it should be. And that's the hard part of the call to arms in this volume. But you knew that. It's not about how you apply technology. It's about how you apply technology *so that* we can re-baseline an industry that had grown apart from its purpose.

And the new economy forces a return to it.

And that comes with letting go of privileges and power. And it's all non-negotiable. All of it.

How you get there is leadership. And it's hard. For all the reasons we have already discussed.

And for all the reasons we have already discussed, we have not progressed as much as we could have down this path. So despite being two decades on this road, we have a lot of work ahead of us still. Most of the work, in fact.

We need to use what we have learned and the technology we have built to make this 'so that' better: more robust, more scalable, profitable and affordable, as digital connectivity reduces cost allowing you a bigger, more nourishing pie. You won't have it and eat it and yet you will eat some of it and others will eat too and some of the pie will still be left to be had later. So that's the why, as far as I see it, to do better at the thing you are here to do.

The 'so what' of us being a 'so that' business is that we are here to serve.

And that means that when we are not of service, we are just in the way.

You are nodding now and finally feeling good about where this chapter was going and about to reach for another biscuit.

Not. So. Fast.

I want to make sure we understand each other here. I want to make sure we are aligned as to what *being of service* looks like, when it's at home. This is not about corporate social responsibility and tax-deductible employee socials that allow companies to generate proof points of doing the right thing alongside same old.

This is about transforming the business.

So let's talk about inclusion for a minute. Because that's usually one of the 'initiatives' folks hide behind, almost as a givey-get, a non-profitable nod towards doing the right thing so we can talk about purposeful banking while carrying on unchanged across the rest of the board.

FINANCIAL INCLUSION: A MUCH-USED, MUCH-MISUSED AND LITTLE-UNDERSTOOD TERM

Financial inclusion became the 'little black dress' of our industry for the best part of a decade. Everyone was expected to have one, everyone felt they ought to have one.

I am not jesting.

It was seen as a topic that *everyone* needed to at least talk about and a topic everyone needed to be seen to care about. Businesses would justify their existence in terms of assisting financial inclusion in ways that, sometimes, entailed suspension of disbelief, and we all nodded solemnly. No Captain Obvious interventions, there. And yet we all thought it and the proof that this pudding was an empty gesture and a feel-good factor or high PR and low real value is, as ever, in the eating.

Ten years on, the excluded are still on the outside and the poor are still poor. In fact, if I had a penny for every time someone heralded a momentous financial inclusion conversation across the industry and then immediately and exclusively talked about getting the unbanked onto the system by giving them a current account, I would be one rich woman and the financially excluded would be as excluded as ever. Only this time with bank accounts. Empty ones.

And this facile way of attempting to tackle, address or window-dress (take your pick) a very complex subject with deep socio-economic implications and dependencies is not used here as an anecdote but rather as a use-case that can help us highlight what really tackling the problem could look like. If we are going to do the hard work of going deep into the questions to address them properly without baulking at the hard stuff and without losing sight of the fact that we need to be profitable in the process, this is as good a test case as any because, historically, the industry's approach to financial inclusion has been under the guise of a corporate social responsibility agenda. This means that initiatives under this banner specifically did *not* seek profitability, keeping them by extension to the side of the business. It was more a case of inviting poor Cinderella to the ball. An act of charity, perhaps, but not imagination as, arguably, there were many things Cinderella needed ahead of a night out. Which is not too dissimilar to giving bank accounts to those without.

And look, for the avoidance of doubt or misunderstanding, I am not suggesting having a place to safely store a hard-earned wage is not important.

It is.

I am a migrant myself. I am still a banker at heart. I have worked in countries that are remittance hubs. So I know, from all angles as well as both personal and professional experience, that having a safe, accessible and cheap way of storing and sending a wage home is, for migrant workers, as valuable as the wage itself. That's why they put themselves through the hardships of exhausting, manual, often unsafe labour. To send money home. So yes. Mobile-first remittance money corridors at low prices are vital. And using digital means to improve the way we provide current accounts and remittance services is great. But it is also a perfect example of the industry focusing on deploying digital means to improve the 'how' of what we've always done. We deliver something we can shout about, without challenging ourselves to *do* better but allowing ourselves to *feel* better because we have done a small thing that was neither complex nor time-consuming and now we get to talk about inclusion to the press and in our annual report and in our employee literature. Having actually achieved precious little.

Stand on the tarmac of Tribhuvan International Airport in Kathmandu, watching the coffins of workers killed in industrial accidents far-away being shipped home to a country that until recently had not seen a coffin (they are not immortal, they just don't use them, traditionally) and then tell me about how having a way to cheaply send wages home achieved inclusion.

Bleak, but true.

And sobering.

It got your attention. Because the thing that took a Nepali farm boy away from home to an unsafe scaffold on the other side of the world was poverty. And giving him an e-wallet did not help him get access to the system. Not in a real way. And if you want to talk about inclusion, the challenge is to address it in a real way.

The issue is poverty. And that's no easy fix. But it demands our attention. And deserves it. And this is part of what I meant when I said that the collective call to action from hereabout is harder than ever before.

DEMOGRAPHIC REALITY CHECKS

So, now that I have your attention, I want to talk about infrastructure. How is that for a segue? Stay with me though because this highlights what knowing our place and leveraging the tools to improve the what of the business not just the how looks like. It also allows us to marry the hitherto straining opposite poles of doing good and making money. So, let's unpack this.

Poverty is real and so is financial exclusion. But the biggest reason for financial exclusion is not lack of access to banking. Banking, as we have explained at some length already, is a 'so that' business. A step in-between. Exclusion is not describing being left out in the cold because you can't access banking. It's lack of access to money. The bank is just a step in that process. Now that lack of access isn't down to the banks, but it can be alleviated by them. Us. Stay with me here.

I have worked with a bank that wanted to ensure they offered attractive remittance products *but* kept the immigrant workers out of the main product sets. Not to mention their branches. The immigrant manual labourers were deemed incompatible with that particular bank's brand image and, on the whole, unprofitable as a segment. So the remittance product offering was limited, contained and very public in the right fora.

PR, check. Inclusion, check. Bank accounts, check.

Real transformation, not so much.

I have also worked with a different bank that was trying very hard to 'palm off' the elderly to a competitor with as little noise as possible. Because you don't want them on your books: they are high-touch as they make extensive use of the most expensive contact points (branches and call centres), they rarely if ever self-serve and they almost never provide profitable up-sell opportunities as the vast majority of the elderly subsist on a pension that hardly makes it to the end of the month. They won't invest, they won't amass wealth any more, they won't start a business or get a mortgage. They are a high-cost/low-value customer segment and this particular and very-well-known high street bank wanted nothing of them. But they knew that you don't want to be seen not wanting them. So there was some interesting horse-trading with a competitor to try and hand over this part of the business without actually admitting that is what was happening.

I have worked with several banks that have agonised over how long the young take to become profitable and how that 'wait' is getting longer and longer for the bank. A burgeoning demographic with low credit scores, subsistence wages and crippling debt. Who wants to carry *that* on their books? Bring me their parents any day, thinks the high street bank. I even had a conversation with a bank *designed* for the young, not so long ago, and behind a closed door the leaders of said bank said something along the lines of: the proposition doesn't matter, the millennial attention-deficit disorder gets worse the younger they get, we just need to get them now and get them cheap, in anticipation of when they become the sort of customers we want.

Meanwhile, the actual youth this is meant to be in aid of is struggling to reach financial independence in a world made inaccessible by the plenty of others.

But facts be damned.

What is the point I am trying to make?

That all the bad behaviours I have been speaking about so far show themselves in ways that affect our customers, just as above.

That it is despicable to start with such patronising disregard for the customers that keep your business running. That I have worked in and with (too) many banks that look at their client segmentation in terms of profitability.

And look, banks do look at profitability, as they should. They have a business to run.

But I am also saying that inclusion has always been looked at through that profitability lens and approached as a de facto loss-maker, done for corporate citizenship or as a necessary value-neutral step towards a different endgame. A bit of charity. Something the bank finances out of the part of the business that is actually profitable and the goodness of its heart. That's the point I've already made. The point I am *about* to make is that that is not good enough. In fact, it's not good at all.

We are committed and able to do better and so we should.

And the way we do that is twofold: first we need to look at why the poor are poor and what we can possibly do about it, and then we look at why they are unprofitable. Duh because 'they have no money' is a facile answer and actually not the right one. The profitability of customers has very little to do with what they have in their pocket and more to do with how you set your shop up and how you construct your cost to serve. If anything, customers who need access to financial products are better customers than the ones who can do fine without you, you being the bank. So making the exchange profitable is on you.

Observe.

I started off this book by declaring that I am an immigrant and that undeniably colours my perceptions in a lot of things. Some of us leave home and hearth because we have dreams bigger than our circumstances permit us to pursue and that's hard enough, let me tell you. But others are driven by poverty and desperation and a hope to do better, not for themselves, but for their children at home, their parents, and cousins and neighbours. Immigrants who risk and often sacrifice their lives, immigrants who write themselves out of their own story to provide for their loved ones. Do you really tell me these people deserve your charity rather than your admiration? Someone this determined to survive doesn't need a hand out. But imagine what they could do, if you re-thought the system. Yes, leaving

> Immigrants risk and often sacrifice their lives, they write themselves out of their own story to provide for their loved ones. They deserve our admiration, not our charity.
>
> Someone crossing the earth in pursuit of work and opportunity should be a bank's dream customer.

home is triggered by poverty and desperation but it is also an act of bravery and determination. Surely the capitalist ideal shines bright here in more ways than one. A segment that crosses the earth in pursuit of work and opportunity should be a bank's dream customer. Just saying.

But of course, the cost to serve is high and if these guys live hand to mouth and since there are no deposits, no credit cards and home loans, then the traditional ways a bank monetises its consumer relationships don't add up.

A major consumer bank I worked with a few years back had worked out that in order for a retail customer to not be a net-loss for the bank, they needed to sign up for at least three products: a current account, a credit card and a loan or a mortgage. That's a lot. You can see why immigrants aren't even on the radar. You can see why the young or the elderly are seen as a burden. Because in many places on our hyper-civilised earth, even in its shinier corners, there are old folks who have to choose between turning the lights or the heat off to afford their food before the next remittance or pension check. And that was before the latest energy crisis.

The bank didn't make it so. But the way bank services customers makes it impossible to do even the basics here. Their hands are tied.

And the young? The pesky snowflakes who have the moon on a stick and ask for sprinkles? The generation we love to vilify for reasons I don't entirely understand, especially when we and the generation before us have saddled them with an explosive combo of overpopulation, climate disaster and a long-drawn-out economic contraction that means they won't ever know middle-class security unless they call Jeff Bezos Daddy ... what about them?

Thirty years ago, a family could subsist on a single income in most European and North American cities. In the UK, house prices are rising at twice the rate of salaries.[11] And those salaries are harder than ever to get because people are living longer, there are more people around and the shifting economy makes skills-matching a highly elusive game that is often forbiddingly difficult to break into if you can't afford an education.

So yes. The vast majority of the world's population is extremely unprofitable for banks. Because they don't bring deposits. They don't make investments. They need access to loans and can't afford the collateral securities. So. If you want to talk about inclusion, let's talk about money.

WE HAVE THE TECHNOLOGY TO BE BETTER BANKERS, AND BETTER HUMANS. ALL WE NEED IS INTENT

Let's talk about money. Not where you put it. But how you access it.

I am a banker by trade and a political scientist by background. I have a PhD in political reform *and* I know how capital markets work. I know how universal banking works. I know how policy works. And I know how technology stacks work. I am not saying this to brag (though my mum is very proud, thank you for asking). I am telling you to highlight that despite me being a bona fide expert in this here thing, a day doesn't pass when someone doesn't look at me in an 'oh, sweetheart' manner when I say that *we can fix this.*

And it gets worse. I've been called naïve many a time. A few years back, I got a bunch of death threats on Twitter because I publicly and unashamedly expressed admiration for the intentions behind India Stack,[12] a public good infrastructure that tried, among other things and among many reversals, to enable *access* for those without. That doesn't mean current accounts. It means easier access to social security for those who need it with greater transparency and reduced risks of manipulation and corruption. It means access to meagre pensions without disruption. It means a lot of things. And of course it was not perfect. Far, far from it. Genuine mistakes were made. Big ones. Miscalculations that had a real impact on people's lives. And of course it was

---

[11] https://www.newstatesman.com/politics/2021/05/how-uk-house-prices-have-soared-ahead-average-wages and if you have questions about how that plays against a backdrop of rent vs buy and post-war house building and population variations and all that jazz, there's some excellent detail here: https://www.schroders.com/en/uk/private-investor/insights/markets/what-174-years-of-data-tell-us-about-house-price-affordability-in-the-uk/

[12] For a highly readable albeit one-sided account of this work, see *Rebooting India: Realizing a Billion Aspirations* by Nandan Nilekani & Viral Shah.

politicised. And of course it was divisive. But what is the alternative? To leave the poor to their fate until we can get things perfect?

Not on your life.

Besides. Every time we tried and didn't get things 100% is a cue to do better. Not stop.

IT'S BEEN DONE BEFORE

The first time I read about Muhammad Yunus, it felt like a Cinderella story, complete with a dashing daring prince. But it is not a fairy tale. Grameen proved that a bank that enables access to credit for the poorest of the poor, allowing them the dignity of believing that their ability to repay is not just possible. *It is profitable.* If you haven't heard of this before then it is my gift to you: tackling poverty can be good business. Don't take it from me. Take it from someone who did it. In his autobiography,[13] professor Yunus describes the *what* and the *how* of the Grameen project. He also describes that the biggest challenge to scaling Grameen was *not* getting the poor to pay back their loans. It was getting the establishment locally and globally to believe that they would. Even, and this is the most important part, even after they consistently had. Even after the Grameen project had proven in rural Bangladesh that the poorest of the poor could be given dignity through access to microloans and in their absolute majority would pay back, making the system sustainable and, in the medium term, adequately profitable, *even after that*, the established wisdom ranging from the World Bank to journalists and global businesses to local bankers, said it will never work and it will never make money and we are not a charity.

Even when it had, they said it wouldn't.

So spare me.

Vulnerable customers are not poor because they are vulnerable. They are vulnerable because they are poor. And of course, access and financial education matters. But an empty current account ain't gonna solve nothin'. And for the avoidance of doubt: we *can* fix this. Through initiatives like Grameen now rendered even easier to deploy exactly through the application of the technology we have, to serve the purpose we would know we need to serve if we knew our place. We have technology that allows us to distribute and

---

[13] *Banker to the Poor: The Story of the Grameen Bank.*

disseminate services faster and cheaper than ever before through the incredibly high market penetration of smartphones, the availability of cloud infrastructure and the new ways we can process payments and loans at unit costs small enough to make micro-loans and micro-payments possible. Not because in the past they were not. They've always been possible. But the cost outweighed the fees so they weren't done. We could but chose not to because it would lose us money. Now that equation is gone. We can and we have the technology to sustain unit economics that make us money while also giving access to the poor. We can. We just haven't.

Is this getting uncomfortable now it is specific?

It should.

Because the reality is we *know* how to fix this and we have the tools to fix this and we are still not fixing this. Because we are collectively choosing not to. By erecting boundaries of bad behaviour and established wisdom that hinge on this not being our problem to solve, the economics being impossible to reconcile or the small gestures of charity being 'a start'. We have addressed each of those behavioural issues in this book already, albeit in a different context but the issue of banks generating their own short-sightedness is consistent. And all I have to say is 'nice try'. But no. Part of this *is* ours to solve, the economics are absolutely possible to reconcile and small gestures are not enough. So. To work.

I am not, for a moment, suggesting fixing world poverty is quick or easy, by the way. Just that it is possible. It is man-made and what man made, man can un-make. So if we are going to talk about inclusion, let's start about talking about it properly. Staring into the extent of the problem and the depth of its roots. If you

> I am not, for a moment, suggesting fixing world poverty is quick or easy, by the way. Just that it is possible. Poverty is not a natural occurrence. It is a sociological construct: man-made. And what man made, man can un-make.

do that with honesty, you won't talk to me about current accounts. You will instead talk to me about money. Because what we are talking about is people who have none, and the things they need to do to make it, store it, transport it or borrow it safely, without falling prey to manipulation, predatory arrangements, loan sharks and pawn brokers, people traffickers and human bondage or the exclusion and subsistence poverty we are seeing the world over. That middle bit is what we said the purpose of banks is, right? Our purpose? Our current function? And our duty, to serve? To make the 'so that' a little less difficult?

The world is not bountiful enough for everyone to get a mansion. No arguments there. But that's not what we are talking about and 'where would it stop' is a grade-A Neo-con argument that I won't even bother to dismiss. Mansions and private jets are not the issue. You can keep yours and the vast majority of the world can actually comfortably live without. I am not going to go full communist on you, have no fear. I have no issue with wealth. None at all. But the world is not binary. Eradicating poverty should be our expectation, our mission and our North Star. No matter how hard it gets or how long it takes. We are in the money business after all. Just because the problem is too big, we have no excuse to consider it inevitable. At the end of the day, poverty is a societal construct. We did this. And we should be fixing it.

Also. We live in a moment of great transformation. If you really allow yourself to face the question of what can and should we be doing with the things that are now possible the answer is glaring: do better.

So. Back to my point. Financial plumbing.

That is how we make the economics work. By reducing the cost to serve. And how do we do that? By leveraging digital capabilities that are infinitely cheaper and more effective to run and reduce what we spend to keep the lights on, allowing us to do it cheaper and still maintain a margin. And how do we do that? By allowing transformation to happen, deeper in our organisations, where its impact will be felt by reducing the cost footprint and complexity of what we do, to make it possible to do more things, differently, faster, at a lower cost. See? It all comes together.

It's beautiful, isn't it? And it's not the stuff of science fiction. This is the very same infrastructure that enables open banking, BNPL or the cute little tooth icon that appears on your mobile banking app next to the payment you just made to your dentist: that very same technology actually enables faster, safer and 'lighter' connectivity between systems.

So?

So.

Banking becomes cheaper to run. Easier, safer and cheaper to scale. It becomes faster to parse data. We become able to plough through more data for more nuanced decisions. It means micro-loans become financially viable because the cost of service goes down and credit scoring is nuanced and dynamic so more accurate. It also means alternative credit scoring becomes possible because there are multiple real-time data points now. Things that were too small or too complex for our old systems to cope with are now the right size. We can service the poor without losing money. And this matters. Banks are businesses. They can't run the ship aground, cold as it sounds.

But it's OK. They no longer have to make that choice, assuming (for the benefit of the doubt's sake) that this is what held us back before. Alternative credit scoring with robust informed data-sets underpinning it and lending products, repayment schedules and access-points tailored for the poor are technically possible and financially viable. This may not be sexy or dramatic. But it can change lives. It is here. It is real. It is robust, scaled and available. We have the tools. We know how to do it. All we need to do is choose to actually fulfil our purpose as a 'so that' business and serve.

I told you that this chapter's call to arms was deeper than the small changes we can each make in our daily lives. And that it would take collective action and intent. The voicing of hard truths is no easier to do for being, when you come down to it, obvious.

This is what it looks like. The work we need to do.

It is not going to be easy. But it is important and it needs to be done and we are the ones standing on the pitch right now and this is the game.

I AIN'T GONNA BREAK MY STRIDE: MAINTAINING INTENT THROUGH DISCOMFORT

Talking about a mission and purpose and doing the right thing is much easier in the abstract, isn't it?

Many years back, I went to see a spectacular performance in London's St James' Theatre. It was called the Pianist of Willesden Lane.[14] A lone woman on stage, a piano and her mother's story (also a pianist). It was moving. It was life-affirming. It was heart-breaking. It was riotous. The theatre was weeping and roaring. And at the end of the performance, Mona Golabek stood up and said this was the story of my mother. Who wouldn't have lived if it wasn't for the people of this country who took in the Jewish children brought into the UK, escaping Nazi Europe on what has become known as the *Kindertransport*, saving the lives of young Jews as the Holocaust loomed ever-nearer.

Riotous applause. Yes this is us, the London audience basked in the inherited glory of the ancestors who did the right thing.

So I ask you, she said, to give generously as you leave the theatre for the children whose lives are cut short by another war, today, right now: in Syria.

---

[14] Based on the memoir 'The Children of Willesden Lane' by Mona Golabek & Lee Cohen.

The applause petered out. The wallets mostly didn't materialise. This was different. This was 'here and now and me'. This was not just a story where we got to side with the good guys at no personal cost or discomfort. This was something that commanded choice and action, even if it was simply to part with a tenner.[15]

Why am I telling you this?

Because I know people like the idea of purposeful banking much more than they like the idea of cheaper banking, or the idea of delving into the politically contentious and murky waters of poverty, discrimination and socio-economic tension. But that is where the problems live. You don't get to tackle that problem without going there. It is not a choice you get to make, hard as you may try to deflect. Because inclusion is not a pink credit card or a little more choice for the already well-served. The discomfort will have to stay I'm afraid. We will have to work through it to get to where we are going. And frankly, the discomfort will do us good. It's time we remembered, as an industry and as a species, a few home truths.

Once upon a time we were all little. Once upon a time we were anything-and-everything-in-waiting. And our mama told us, we could be anything we put our mind to. Because we are special. And although our mama didn't lie to us, what she told us isn't exactly the whole truth either, what she told us doesn't actually bind the world. It doesn't create a cosmic obligation that it should be so. We are not that special. We are not that different. We can't be everything. And although we can still be anything, time is running out and the way there is neither simple nor linear. Mama didn't say it would be this way, perhaps, but there you have it.

I am not saying this to be upsetting but neither you nor your organisation is that special. Exactly because we are talking about digitisation and the new economy, it is relevant and important to stress this. It is important to say that, in order to stay the course, you need to remember you are not that special. And I feel compelled to stress that both because, as the song goes, ordinary people do extraordinary things all the time[16] and being special is not a requirement but, also and more significantly, because feeling special has long been an excuse for inaction. Frankly, realising we shouldn't be feel-

---

[15] If you are reading me from outside the UK, hello. A tenner is a £10 note, at the time of writing that is approximately USD 14, EUR 12, QAR 49 or NOK 129 – just throwing currencies at you to keep it interesting.

The important thing is, it's not a lot of money. Especially if you can afford a London theatre ticket that would probably cost a minimum of 6× and an interval glass of wine that would cost at least 2× that.

[16] Ok Go, What to Do 'Sweetheart you'll find, mediocre people do exceptional things all the time'.

ing special for our industry (and any industry that is a little bit full of itself) will be a much-needed liberation.

Exhibit A: a few years ago, at an industry event in Madrid, three unconnected people came up to me separately after my talk to tell me how brilliant I was *but* how none of what I had said applied to them. One felt they were exempt from disruption because they were in investment banking, the fluffy fears of retail did not touch them. Another because they operated in a country where the regulator still raised barriers to entry for challenger of any kind, shielding them from having to face into the hard questions plaguing others. And one because he would retire soon. None of them were the first of their kind, to tell me how they were different. How their situation was special. And how their special status would shield them from the challenges I spoke of forevermore.

To all I say: pah.

You are not that special. You are not exempt. The future with all its change is coming for everyone so it is also coming for you. Axiomatically. And if you see other people's disruption as other people's problem because you are special and different, then you are just like the proverbial god-fearing man in the flood who berated god for not giving him a sign that he needed to evacuate, after news crews had beamed the coming deluge and rescue crews had knocked on his door trying to get him out of his crumbling house. No said the man. I am special. My faith will save me from the flood. Missing every warning sign and opportunity to be indeed both special and, most importantly, safe and also missing, along the way, what *special* may look like, what shape a message from god may take. Because in the same way the news crew and the rescue workers are god's way of saying 'don't die', having options and resources and the chance to make changes in order to survive in a changing world is what 'being special' looks like. It's not guaranteed survival and it may not be exactly as you would have wished but it is better than oblivion and it is a chance to have a go at it.

> Our industry has been so busy looking for a locked-in happy ending, we have been squandering the time and energy and resources we had to build one.

And yet we have been so busy looking for a locked-in happy ending, we have been squandering the time and energy and resources we had to build one.

So if you think you and your sliver of the industry are special and different and somehow exempt from everything I have been saying here, because of the incredible complexity you have brought to your craft that is *so hard* for common mortals to navigate or untangle. If you think that your hands are tied because of the price tag of previous IT investment that makes change so painful and hard to champion, because who can write another check? Or if you think that the greyness of your suits and the belief that the devil you know will always win the day; if you think your *special* status means you are blissfully exempt from the onslaught of change, I have to ask you to go back to the beginning of the book and this time maybe take some notes?

I'm afraid I have bad news for you. Mama didn't lie exactly. You are special. But special is as special does. It wasn't a hall pass. It was a call to action.

CONTRARY TO WHAT YOUR MOTHER TOLD YOU

At the beginning of a journey, you could go in any direction you like. But you can't go in every direction at once. When you were little your mama told you you could become anything you put your mind to. But you can't become everything. And as your business stares down its choices in an ever-shifting macro-economic context, you could do anything but you can't take every path and hedge every bet. You can't beat uncertainty. And you need to stop trying. Because in putting so much energy in protecting the option to potentially be anything, you may end up with nothing.

As a species and as an industry we like optionality. We like knowing we are not trapped. We like knowing we have options and choices and avenues ahead. *Hedging* is a whole cottage industry inside banking. Hedging risk is how we do our investment and how we run our businesses. Betting against ourselves, sometimes, just in case we were wrong. Opting for smugness and diluted attention spans instead of conviction and the risk of having to start again as we showed in earlier chapters.

So when it came to digital transformation we, as an industry, did everything in our power to retain the option of being everything and doing everything … potentially … perhaps. Pilots and POCs running in parallel with no market-readiness roadmap or real intention. Conferences attended with the fierceness of an addict. Events hosted. Small investments made. Research commissioned on what technology we should be looking at. And then again the following year. And again and again. Meanwhile the actual question of what business opportunities should be understood and pursued played second fiddle to the search of a silver bullet. What tools, what tech, what stuff do we need so that we can at all times be there, ready and informed, triumphant against the most basic form of corporate FOMO.

But as you were signing off on the travel expenses of an army of team members boarding planes for events the world over, as you were signing off on an AI pilot, the latest blockchain pilot, a machine learning pilot on top of your chatbot and an RPA implementation for cost reduction; as you hired design thinking coaches and agile coaches and UX folks to sit alongside the newly arrived Kafka team, *surely* you were registering that it's all getting rather expensive. Expensive and exhausting as more activity doesn't translate to more progress. Especially when you don't point your teams in the same direction. You may find that their respective progress clashes against each other creating tension, frustration and laughing in the face of your hedge.

And of course all this dilutes focus: the attempt at being everything leaves you exactly nowhere, compromising business drivers and creating an army of people who are de-skilling themselves while playing with the coolest stuff. The *how* over the *what* again and again. That's what we've been talking about throughout these pages. And now what I am saying is

> Your mama didn't lie when she told you that you can be anything you put your mind to. She thought you would take it in the spirit in which it was intended: don't feel that you have to make a certain, specific choice. You can choose anything.
> But choose, already.

that to do the hard work of focusing on our shared purpose and actually do that with purpose and on purpose, part of the journey is accepting you can't be everything. Not you and not your organisation.

Your mama didn't lie. She thought you would take it in the spirit in which it was intended: don't feel that you have to make a certain, specific choice. You can choose anything. But choose, already. That choice is the point. You have it. So make it. In trying to preserve most of what we know of the world around us despite every indication that change is inevitable, we have tried to hold onto everything. Well you can't have everything and you can't be everything. But not all is lost.

Perversely, you *can* be anything. It just doesn't come as an epiphany. The road there will get messy because you will have to make choices on incomplete information. And making choices in a changing environment is hard. There are no guarantees. There are no fail-safes. You could be anything but you may also get it terribly wrong and fail. That is part of the deal and what makes it all scary.

Plus the rules of the game are also constantly changing. And that is uncomfortable on a foundational human level. It is also counter-intuitive, because we are saying that to do digital well, you have to go against the fundamental measures of power in our industry. You have to play this game by breaking its rules, the rules that used to lead to victory and now may not. But we don't have new rules yet and it's all very fluid and uncomfortable … What I mean is that, in banking as in many other hierarchical fields, authority was historically tied to experience and expertise. With new things coming at us at an unprecedented pace, what we know is fast becoming obsolete. We have the choice to become enthusiastic polymaths, curious amateurs soaking up new knowledge, but mostly we allow our executives to react to new stuff on the basis of reduced executive summaries targeted at feeling and instinct. What I know and how I feel are the proverbial rock and the hard place. Between them lies the only place that matters. The place where you start not knowing enough of anything but resolutely decide you don't want to stay there. It's that conviction to not stay in the 'not knowing' that makes this place of confusion and discomfort a learning space. The awkward phase of a wallflower learning to dance. That's where we maintain this much-needed stride I am talking about.

Too abstract?

How about this: imagine you are someone reflecting on their own behaviour for the first time, part of a dev team trying to capture requirements using new tools for the first time, or working in a bank trying to launch its first data-driven product. You will mess it up. You are meant to. Until we accept that, we don't stand a chance of learning from it and moving on. I know banking executives are shocked at how chaotic and disorganised some design phases feel, how many times you scrap stuff and go back to the beginning. So we tend to conceal that from view. For their peace of mind and ours. But it's time we stopped. If we all agree we want to dance, then learning to dance is essential. You can do it with a teacher or in front of your bathroom mirror. You can trial and error behind closed doors or iterate with your customers. You can reflect on your own or get reality checks from friends, colleagues and industry partners. Whatever you do, your software and your character will improve if you accept that learning is essential and while it takes place it is awkward, messy and non-linear.

That's what your mother was talking about. When she said you were special. That you could make it through the messy phase and do and be anything you like, on the other side. So get going. And keep going. It will be difficult and uncomfortable, that much is clear and unavoidable. But the journey is also unavoidable: both because it's happening across geographies and industries so we can't opt out even if we wanted to. But also because all the dabbling, half-hearted though it was, brought some grudging progress and the place we are in now is even more tenuous and untenable than if we had done nothing: legacy systems and shiny experiments, precariously stacked on top of each other. Hard truths voiced but not addressed. A future discussed but not pursued.

Finding and keeping our stride for the rest of the journey isn't just a choice to do and be better. It's also an urgent need, because the halfway house of half-baked experiments, contradictory business imperatives and systems spanning five decades is just not great for anybody. Moving out of this space is the next stage of the journey. And it will take all of us getting into our stride through all the actions of individual and team transformation I have been flagging throughout this book. But maintaining this stride is a collective endeavour. We can't do it as heroic rebels in small pockets here and there. Heroic individualism and small teams going against the grain is indeed how we've come this far, and it has been spectacular but sadly it's not how we go the rest of the way.

WHAT DOES THAT LOOK LIKE, IN REAL TERMS?

If I look back over the last 20 years, every single job I have ever had has involved talking to people about things they didn't want to hear. They knew they had to hear them. And they knew they had to be seen to be hearing them. And in the grand scheme of things they were sure that they would benefit from hearing them. It's just that, in the moment, in the 'right here, right now' of everyday life, they never wanted to hear them. Not ever, you understand. Just not now. And now. And also now. Because they were too abstract, too hypothetical, too big, too hard, too uncertain or didn't feel important enough yet when sharing headspace with the very concrete challenges and demands of the existing business.

Whatever the reason.

They didn't want to listen and often still don't.

The tone of mild exasperation persists whether it is a senior client executive saying to a young innovation lead (me) 'we are not here to play sweetheart, not all of us can think about the future, some of us have a business to run'; or a bank CTO saying to a senior representative of a tech business (also me, just many years later) 'what's wrong with my main frame?'. Both true stories. They both need to listen. They know that. But they would rather they didn't and don't expect to have to do it every day.

If you transpose this to your organisation, you can be sure it happens in many offices and for many stated reasons but essentially boiling down to the same underlying behaviours. Sure, the function that seeks to transform, and not only that, but accelerate that transformation aligns with the direction of strategic vision for the organisation, but in my experience my team and I represented the corporate version of the gym membership before the summer break, the dentist appointment after Christmas. As we said before: we were the insurance policy the corporate's better demons wished upon their future selves. Sadly their present selves had no time for us, at least at first. And often still, despite the way the world has changed and all we should have learned by now. What does it say about me, really, that over the last 20 years I have been getting stuck in, deeper into these transformational functions? The functions the business often treats as time-wasters and dangerous rebels, children at play and nuisances that need to constantly explain and justify themselves or reckless wholesale architects of a new future? Too little and too much all at once … what does it say about you dear reader, that you do it too? What does it say about the industry that it collectively thought 'this works, we can carry on like this'? Taking a difficult problem and making it even harder by getting in our own way.

> Innovation teams often represented the corporate version of the gym membership before the summer break, the dentist appointment after Christmas. We were the insurance policy the corporate's better demons wished upon their future selves. Sadly their present selves had no time for us, at least at first.

But the thing is it sort of did work. And it didn't.

If the unspoken hope was that the tension and tinkering would unearth a magic formula or closely guarded secret that would make digital transformation a cake walk, then we collectively failed.

There were no shortcuts here.

Still, it's ok. As hard work, curiosity and creativity tend to find a way to get things done even if it isn't quite as effortless as we would have originally liked. And as I have pointed out already, the people in these functions found a way to work their magic despite the behaviours and structures and obstacles around them. You know they did. And if you are one of us, you also know how. But if you are new to this game, I want to reveal the tricks of the trade exactly because the change trade has now to become everyone's business and the way we've been sneaking change in can't be the way we work in the future. The future is everyone's business, contrary to my very senior colleague's view all those years back. We should all worry about the future, *sweetheart*, exactly because we have a business to run.

I wonder what he's doing now and whether anyone ever explained what an API was. I joke. I know what he's doing now. He is retired. And in know who explained what APIs were to him. It was me. A good few months after he treated me like I was 7 years old and not before one of his major clients asked a set of questions he had no idea how to answer and he needed my help. And I gave the help because helping is what we do. And because his behaviour is no way unusual. This is how it historically goes. The industry resists and belittles things until they become inevitable or useful and then it's all hands to the pump. Feast or famine and no rest for the wicked.

But the point is, there *is* a better way. And it involves addressing all the dysfunctions we have discussed in the first half of the book.

SMUGGLING THE FUTURE IN THROUGH THE BACK DOOR

So let me tell you how we've been smuggling the future in so far, so we can all come clean and move forward. We've been doing some party tricks on y'all and they work a treat but sadly don't scale. That said, they are where you need to start. We can't carry on working like this. But it is how we begin. And sometimes it is how we nudge the organisation along when it gets stuck. Which it does often.

Picture this: you have a meeting with your sponsors and executives. It doesn't matter if they are your bosses or your clients. The same shape applies. This is the most important meeting of *your* week, but to them it's just another briefing in a week full of meetings about things going wrong. You have spent the last two weeks arguing with your direct boss or your team on what you will share, how you will present information, what you will ask for. You have gone 17 rounds trying to make your PowerPoint deck look grown-up and serious, informative and water-tight. You have assumed nobody will remember what you told them last time. So you recap and start at the beginning. You remind them of the first principles, what you are doing, why they hired you in the first place or why they engaged your firm. You are answering every potential question. Only they haven't asked any. And you may be answering all the wrong questions. They may remember more than you give them credit for. Or even less. And don't ask me how are you to know that. It's your job to know. Or at least try and guess.

So think. Where do your stakeholders come from? Not in life. Where were they five minutes before they came to your meeting? Senior risk committee, an HR disciplinary hearing, credit review board, a terrible vendor pitch, a promising job interview? A call with their kids' school? Junior is sick or in detention. A divorce lawyer. A sick parent. They come into the room and their 30' with you are already laden with the problems of being alive and the pressures that come with working in an industry of bad behaviour and a cult of stress. They come from somewhere deep in the complexity of the 'how' of their organisation (which may also be your organisation and either way is your problem to address) and you have a small window to pitch to them an alternative vision of the 'what'. And there is so much to say and so much to explain and so much you are not sure about and the people you need to convince are not looking excited to see you. They are hassled. Flicking through their emails. Sending a quick text. They may be in the room, but their head isn't.

And you have half an hour of their time, that's it. And you are wasting it oscillating between making what you have to say similar to all the other things they see and hear all day to avoid being branded an imposter while also painting a future that is fresh and new and radically helpful. You are trying to be transparent and update them on challenges and reversals without falling down a rabbit hole of poorly understood questions, recriminations and flaring tempers. You are trying to walk a tightrope of your own making.

Should that even be your job?

You are trying to build a bridge to the future, be it as an internal or an external resource tasked with a part of the digital journey. Surely isn't that the most important job of the collective, inside the organisation? Surely carrying this shouldn't come down to you alone? Of course it is and of course it shouldn't. In the abstract. And yet. In the here and now, mid-morning on any given day, it is not as urgent as anything else. And probably a little less. Because one of the systems we should have replaced by now had a double fail-over (hypothetically speaking, she says with angelic innocence) and now the bank is in breach of SLAs for producing reports, the regulator has been notified and there is a project kicking off to investigate whether what was produced by hand, through other systems, falling back onto previous batches, etc. was accurate or if reparations and embarrassing explanations have to be made. So on that (entirely hypothetical) day and the weeks after it, good luck talking to your stakeholders about the budget you need for your Open Banking programme or the value of your micro-services architecture.

For the last decade and a half bringing the future and navigating the resistance and disinterest – or downright hostility occasionally – has been the task of a small team. Keeping the flame of change and future-proofing burning while the rest of the organisation is constantly distracted by problems that, in their majority, would go away if they focused more on future-proofing has been the task of a small team. It has been their task to get into a room of distracted executives and, first and foremost, try and get them in the room *also*.

For the last decade and a half bringing the future and navigating the resistance and disinterest has been the task of a small team. Keeping the flame of change burning while the rest of the organisation is constantly distracted by problems that, in their majority, would go away if they focused more on the change at hand.

The room you are in. The room where we think about this together. The place where your work matters and gives the organisation what it needs by giving the team what they need to carry on doing the job. 30' to bring the people who hold the purse strings and make decisions into the room and from there into the future. Decision-makers who, as I said already before, may be sitting in front of you but their mind is straying back to the meeting they just came from or think ahead to what comes next. Like the future is your problem and you need to pitch them convincingly to persuade them that it will indeed come. Or, equally worryingly, as if having you and your team is all they needed to do to take care of the future.

And here you are, speaking about purpose and fairness and going back to basics and the need to serve our communities, while someone in the room is thinking about a potential regulatory issue with a fine at the other end, on their watch, and what else can matter more?

In every organisation, decision-makers are worried, they are stressed, they are harried and their attention span is, as we already discussed, highly fragmented.

That has always been so and it doesn't show any signs of dissipating.

And although they really care about what you have to say, in principle, they feel guilty about taking the time away from the stuff that seems to be on fire in practice right now. As if the future itself isn't on fire. And of course they know it is. But that's a problem for their future selves and their present self has enough problems. They know this is important, of course they do. But it is not urgent yet. This discomfort of balancing the important with the urgent hasn't decreased after a decade and a half of doing a bit of this and a bit of that to keep the wolf of becoming irrelevant from the door. And our way of doing it (by giving some folks the responsibility to run the bank and some folks the responsibility to build the bank of the future) isn't working because the chasm they have to cross and the amount they have to do, as we have already discussed, spans systems, business, structure and culture and it can no longer be done as a side project, if it ever could. And frankly with every passing year what was important is now increasingly urgent, alongside all the other things on fire.

I am preaching to the choir here if I tell you that the future is everyone's responsibility. The big decisions around purpose and mission need to be top of mind all the time and across all things. But the point is, this is *not* how it has worked so far and if you do all the individual acts of resistance and active leadership I have highlighted in the book so far you will undeniably help your organisation and the industry get further, faster. But you will not, individually, solve for this. Because, fundamentally, our chosen path of dealing with this new-fangled long-lasting disruption malarkey across the industry has been to carry on doing the old thing (as you were, soldier) while building the new things in parallel with the same metrics of success. And I believe it is patently clear that it isn't working.

Not because the mechanics don't work. The mechanics work fine. But because the low-hanging fruit has been reaped. In short (and despite our best self-sabotaging efforts half the time) we have had some success.

But the work left is more involved and complicated and needs other pieces of the puzzle (including structure and culture) to start shifting. And those changes cannot really coexist with a different version of themselves without driving people mad. Plus. There is another reason why the parallel processing hedging-by-another-name is not really working and that is simply that conviction is still lacking. If you think about the innovation journey starting a decade and a half ago, banks admitted that there was a lot they had to learn. And that the learning covered technology and ways of working. The thing they had to learn and the way they had to learn it was new, so they admitted it had to be approached differently. That was a big leap and I, for one, believed it at the time. So we started. Innovation and transformation programmes and all the jazz we have talked about here. And then we sort of ... stayed there.

The programmes got bigger, but the mechanics stayed the same. Whether I have to 'sell' a bank on the idea that an API is real or the fact that leveraging their licence and reach to launch a Banking as a Service offering, the mechanics are the same. We still come in and need to pitch that the future is real, viable and preferable to the past. And the unspoken argument is that it is not de facto preferable to the past thank you very much. And nobody says your preference is irrelevant, you don't get that choice, when they are pitching.

Captain Obvious is often silent on this one. And yet the truth remains true.

HOLDING ONTO THE PAST IS AN EXTREME SPORT

So we have made the past decade and a half about education, but in all the wrong ways. Teams are continuously deployed to work stuff out, prove them out and then educate decision-makers to make the big decisions. It used to be small teams with small projects. Now it is big teams with ambitious projects but always a proof of concept first. And then another.

And what are we proving? That the tech is real? Actually, almost never.

We are proving that this new thing will not break the things we have and value; or the things we just have because we haven't had the time, courage or conviction to replace. That it can, whatever it is, play nice with what we are holding onto. That it will speed up the boat into the future without taking us too far from our familiar shores.

This has been the way.

And admittedly the work has gotten bigger, we used to agonise over permission to build widgets and now we launch ambitious platforms. We have come a long way. But. We are not going far enough or fast enough. Or, indeed, deep enough inside our organisations. The conviction is still lacking and we don't have that kind of time any more. Especially as the world we need to understand is not standing still and decision-makers in our industry were not historically chosen for their teachability. So there is more to learn, less time to learn it in and the people who have to do the learning aren't great at it. Despite realising we have to learn new things in new ways, we are still desperately trying to fit the new things into the old mental categories we know and love.

How do we break out of this cycle?

Obviously hiring for teachability and then promoting those folks is key as we have already discussed. Breaking the bad habits that make us short-sighted and self-sabotaging would also be nice. And if you haven't been doing enough of it over the past decade and a half, you don't have time to ramp up: it is now urgent. And although we, as an industry, specialise in dealing with urgent things, we are not great at doing so *with urgency*.

Because what we need here is not a series of tasks to be done but some fundamental directional decisions to be made and then carried out. And those decisions need to be made right now with the folks we have and using what we know. There is no time to go off and commission one more report, do one more experiment. Buy some more time. The era of optionality is over.

242 • *Bankers Like Us*

And I don't mean it's coming to an end. I mean it was never an era, it was a small window of time that has already been squandered. Kaput.

The only saving grace is that everyone did it so no single banking institution is truly transformed. Some are leading the pack but mostly everyone is still on the same boat. What has been moving ahead in leaps and bounds is not the competition. It's the economy. It's the world outside your office, using digital capabilities in a way that is rapidly educating your consumers and your regulators and rewiring the world. So I can turn on the heating in my apartment before I board my flight back to London, from my phone while waiting at the airport in Dublin, but I can't set up a euro payment on my high street bank GBP account without logging on from a desktop computer or visiting a branch.

And that is what we get for having behaved the way we have over the past decade and a half.

So.

As I was saying. Decision-time. With what we have, where we are and what we know.

And for that to happen we need to start actually talking about the things we normally side-step. No more euphemisms. We need to collectively face into the questions we have repeatedly discussed here, in this book and in conferences and publications across the industry. It's time we do that in the board room with honesty and urgency.

For instance, we have historically asked each other 'what's your actual, personal appetite for digital transformation if it touches your core competency value chains' and that has felt bold. But the real question should be

> Do you have the stomach for what is ahead, because if you don't, the option is not to not do it, it is for your business to not do it with you.

'do you have the stomach for what is ahead, because if you don't, the option is *not* to not do it, it is for your business to not do it *with you*'. Implicit in the way these decisions have been approached is the fierce holding on to the fairy tale belief that we get to set the pace of change, the direction of change and the depth of change. When in reality all we get to affect is whether we will be a part of it or whether it will happen to us.

A few years back, I did a two-day workshop with the executive committee and board of a large entity. They were nice people. Intelligent people.

They came to the workshop willing to pay attention and participate. A sea of middle-aged white men in suits. The jokes write themselves but there was nothing funny about it. I have never been closer to work-induced tears than I was on the drive to the airport after this session. They came to the room knowing they need to learn this stuff. That's why we were there. That's why they invited us. They knew this was important. And then ... two full days of presentations, exercises, activities: getting them to stare into the realities of the digital economy and the fact that this is happening with or without them. That bit is not up for negotiation. What you do next is the only thing you control.

Two exhausting days of guiding them through the interdependence of the hard questions ahead and, as the second day came to an end, the CEO thanked me and my colleague for our work, our energy, our knowledge. And he said words that branded themselves into my brain. He said we understand. We learned a lot these past two days. And I believe I speak on behalf of everyone here when I say we do not have the courage to do what you say is necessary. So we will not. We will carry on as we are and hope for the best. And his peers nodded. And the board nodded. And he was not fired. And here we are. At least he had the honesty to say 'I won't pretend: I can't do this'. Unlike many others who share the fear and feeling of inadequacy and helplessness and come at it all bravado and bluster, shouting 'what is wrong with my mainframes' (as I already said, true story) and throwing modems at people who dare say the world has changed.

Nobody has thrown a modem at me, truth be told.[17] But my friends Trygve and Martin always used the phrase as a short-hand to describe the people we knew would resist new ideas in life as well as the industry, because they were new. *I know what I know and I like what I like* is an understandable human condition but a limiting one at the best of times. The problem is, the world is moving too fast for an *'e pur si muove'* moment.[18] We can't wait for generations to pass and digest the new ideas. Our societies and our economies are transforming all around us. If we don't act, our businesses will become

---

[17] Hello youngster! For those born this century, a modem is a hardware device (a modulator–demodulator) used to convert data from a digital format into a format suitable for, say, a telephone. It was how we accessed the internet back in the day. The development of radio-based systems means that a modem in your mobile device is invisible, ubiquitous and doesn't make the beep-beep-bip-beep-bip sound we used to wait for, to know we were about to connect to the world. Those were most decidedly *not* the days.

[18] 'And yet it moves'. It is a phrase attributed to Galileo who was forced by the Church to recant the controversial claim that the Earth rotates and not only that but it moves around the Sun and not the other way round. He did. It was the 1600s. You could be executed for less. People knew what they knew and would kill you to stick to their guns. And yet. It moves.

obsolete under our noses. In this context and given this pace, 'I know what I know' lacks both finesse and realism as both what you know and like is changing irrespective of whether you are choosing to pay attention. And that is the call to arms, friends. We need everyone to pay attention. We can't have a band of few dedicated individuals battling against the tide any more. We can't leave this to the social conscience of a few CEOs or the national 'keep the country running' mandate of a few state-owned banks.

The next steps are too big for what got us here to work.

The challenge works across the board, by the way. It's not just banking. We see it in politics and the rise of a certain brand of 'but I don't like it' populism.

For instance, if you refuse to acknowledge the realities of global trade dynamics and population movements because you don't like your brown neighbour and want to have the benefits of global prosperity, accessible travel and affordable goods from all over the world, all year round but none of the components underpinning it; if you refuse to engage with ecosystem economics because you preferred it when you kept the entire profit margin to yourself, no sharing ... if you refuse to engage with the world and learn the detail of what it is you are basing your decision-making on (be it fisheries, tariffs or investing in Environment-as-a-Service) and you defend your right to an uninformed opinion as if that is what democracy and making it to the executive committee was all about, then you *are* a problem to your organisation and your society and part of why they can't find their stride in this rapidly changing world.

THE TECHNOCRATS NEED TO LEARN TO DREAM, OR STAND ASIDE

I came clean right at the beginning of the book that when it comes down to brass tacks the line between 'business' and things that we think of as 'politics' blurs. And I am fine with that and you should be too because, as Thomas Mann put it, '*everything* is politics' but also because the fundamental urges of human nature that drive behaviours are not context specific. Humans are consistent in that they are inconsistent across the board and emotive under a thin veneer of rationality.

Of course I generalise, but the point remains that there is a strong urge across business and politics, across the globe and across our officers defending people's right to be uninformed, be it on immigration, why the things you dislike about the EU have nothing to do with the EU, why the things the Neo-cons say are not even logical enough to be true or untrue or the mechanics of data segregation for compliance. You wouldn't take your car to a mechanic who refused to learn how new engines process fuel or a surgeon who still practised phlebotomy to release the bad humours like a medieval spectre.

So. When people say they are entitled to their opinions whatever those may be and however those have been derived, we are essentially defending a right to be uninformed. Which I will fight you to the end over.

Because you do not have that right, if you then make decisions that affect others. And you do. As a voter and as a business decision-maker and *yes* the mechanics are the same.

So. If we go on treating your claim to a right to be uninformed as valid and defensible and not the entrenchment of a 5-year-old who didn't realise that, now the baby brother arrived, there is another person around and that changes things and doesn't like it so wants to send him back, then we are part of the same problem.

I don't want you to agree with me. Not on politics, not on business trans-formation, not on future-state architecture. But I do want you to acknowl-edge that, if you are joining the dance, you will have to dance. And to do that, you may need to do some learning, a lot of practising and maybe stub your toe once or twice. If this is new to you because you resisted all this time, you may still need to find your feet. Maybe you can't lead the dance on your first day. You can't rush the learning. You need to put in the hours.

And I don't mean the learning you have been doing all this time, perfunctory glances over lengthy PowerPoint decks and signing off budgets for projects and programmes of work here and there. And yes the budgets got bigger but the fear didn't. So. Decision-time, as we said. And to make those decisions you need to turn up prepared to do the hard work. And you need to accept that some of that is the lessons you've been trying to skip all this time. And there is no skipping. The hard yards are not optional. If you want it be part of a key decision, you need to be part of the process. You can't just turn up for 30' and look at the deck. The things that could be resolved that way have been resolved, the world moved on. So should you. And that entails coming to the meeting without an entrenched a priori position and arms tightly crossed at the chest. That no longer counts as participation, whatever you are discussing, be it what movie to watch or whether to invest in a data lineage project.

Getting the rest of the journey right is not a spectator sport and it cannot be driven by a small team inside a big organisation. Not just because they can't (although also because they really can't). But because you shouldn't want them to. I can't explain what an API is on slide 2 of an executive briefing pack and offer you two options for your future-state architecture and monetisation expectations by slide 9 without manipulating you.

And I know that because I have been asked to do it (and let's face it, have done it) many a time. And the implicit acceptance that 'the important choices' will be surfaced for the executive is flawed. The important choices are made by the person holding the pen, making decisions about the things 'the bosses don't need to worry about', the things that are 'way too big for us' or the things that they frankly have no conviction you will have the courage to pursue or patience to understand.

How is that a good outcome?

Please stay with me here and understand this. There are types of activities that can be distilled to salient facts and executive-level options with a clear understanding of cost/benefit and implications but we can't treat everything like it is familiar because we are misleading in the process. And we are leaving so much out of the deck to make it look like you expect it to look or need it to look, given all the constraints we have described at length.

And the things we leave out entail choices you, the decision-maker, will never get to make. Choices that you will never know are choices.

I have sat in so many meetings where my boss or my team or me in some cases thought 'who is this proposal going to, will this confuse them? Keep it simple'. We also think 'how can we get to yes, how can we make the asks small, the risks manageable, the horizons of returns palatable'. Every 'outsourced' strategy deck where you ask us to simplify is a pitch. What did you expect us to do? You hired us because we cared, you tasked us with paving a road to the future and, look we have a job to do and we all come at this with good intentions.

But well-intentioned and universal as this may be, it is still manipulation.

I give you two options. What about all the options you will never see, the options I decided (for valid reasons, perhaps) not to show you? Do you even consciously know that this is happening? Have you stopped to think about what this actually means? Because you, the decision-maker, are complicit in this. You are effectively ok with that implication as the price to pay for efficiency and that we agree to call it 'executive-level briefings'. And that is a problem. Almost as big a problem as reducing law to tweetable sound bites. If you want to be a part of the decision, you need to be a part of the conversation. There is no short-cut that doesn't leave you and the organisation you represent short-changed. And that is part of the call to arms. There is no way around it. And if you look around you, right now, you will see your peers facing into the same challenge. Some with more courage than others.

And this is not quick, hence why it is now urgent.

You need to put in the time to learn what is at stake, what is on offer, what your options are. Across all relevant verticals and to a level of detail adequate to make a choice.

I was recently asked to speak with a very senior cohort of bankers in a huge global bank. Closed door session. Sales opportunity for me, to be honest. So I did it. No dice. They were still at the level of 'should we *do* blockchain or replace our core banking system'.

If I have to explain the difference between a distributed ledger and a general ledger (which I had to do) we are not even getting started here folks. You need to put in the effort. By all means be self-interested in the process, think of yourself, your family, your business first. I am cool with that. But put in the effort. You can't leave the room and expect people to be done by the time you return from lunch. Not just because you may miss out on the best bit. But because by leaving the room you forfeit your seat: if you want to be a part of the decision you need to commit to the process. You need to be present. You need to join the dance. It may be familiar, you may have absorbed more than you think over the past few years. So before you know it you will be twirling and thumping and leading. Or it may be a new melody, unfamiliar steps. Things of greater complexity than you had appreciated. New technology. Complex policy issues. Implications of law, enterprise architecture of go-to market strategies that you had not encountered or paid attention to before. You need to slow down. Learn the steps. Study. Observe. Decide for yourself which of the million moves available suit you. You won't shine immediately. There is grace in learning even though the learning itself is not graceful. You will not be of sound judgement always, although working to a decision without rushing past the hard bits is the highest form of wisdom.

If you want to be there for the finale, if you want to be part of the decision, if you want to share in the pride of getting over the line with whatever it is you are involved in, you need to join the dance.

You don't have to. And this, too, is important. You are totally within your rights to stay away from politics, policy, business transformation, technology infrastructure debates and ethics. It's ok, no matter how disappointing I personally find it, to say like the CEO quoted above 'I see it, I get it, I don't have the stomach for it'. It's ok not to care to dance and leave the dance floor. It's also ok to want to be an awesome dancer without putting in the effort. Without the blistered feet, the sweat, the sprains, the effort. To be lazy about it. It's ok to want it, it's human, this laziness. But it's not realistic. You can want it but you can't expect it. You can want it, but you can't buy it. So you can't have it.

And we are doing nobody any favours by encouraging the view that people can make complex decisions by virtue of where they happen to sit at the time the decision is needed. The world is changing. New things appear every day. The dance is changing. Join it, learn it, lead it if you will. But if you want a hand in the choreography you need to learn to dance first. And if you want to share the applause for the finale, you need to stay dancing till the end. I have said this before and I will say it till the day I die to everyone, from toddlers learning how to ride a bike to senior decision-makers managing billions in budgets: the hard yards are non-optional. For anybody. That's it. It's not easy but it's simple and clear, albeit hard to do with intent and consistency. Find your place. Find your purpose.

Find your stride.

THERE IS ONE MORE THING, YOU WILL NEED FOR THE JOURNEY: COMPANIONS

Actually. I lied. That was not the last thing.

There was one more thing we need to find and hold onto, to navigate into the future. To successfully complete any quest of this magnitude. You know it from the stories, fairy tales and heroic quests and Star Wars. You know it from life. You can't do long-drawn-out, hard work alone. You need to find your place, sure, and purpose and stride. And you need to find your tribe. Ah this is a lonely path, I hear you say. Leadership. Being a change agent. Being at the forefront of this work. Dealing with the uncertainty in your own head and the hostility and resistance all around, mainly from the people you are doing it for. It is lonely work and it feels like thankless work. Be it because it's lonely at the top, or it's lonely at the front: it's lonely. I hear it a lot and from many quarters, often unexpected quarters, that *this* is lonely work. And I agree that it is. Or that it can be. Not that it has to be. But it is, undeniably, lonely work, to be driving change against the grain.

How many times a week do you get asked 'how was your day'? By friends, your partner, the waitress at your favourite bar. Man alive. I'd rather be asked to do some complex mathematics. I always hesitate. I am tempted to ask 'how long have you got'. I know you don't actually want to hear it, but I want to tell you all about it. *How was your day?* My day was awesome. You know what I do for a living? I get to see people's ideas take shape, I get to see businesses and tech before it's market-ready, before they take the world by storm, when they are nothing but a bunch of dreamers with battered laptops. I get to see them at the dawn of success, at the start of life. I get to marvel, I get to learn, sometimes I get to help. I get to work with people who long thought that nothing can change in our organisations. I get to watch them sit up straighter, talk louder, get animated and push through. I get to watch them do the very things they told me can't get done. Sometimes I even get to help. I get to watch decisions get made, I get to see learning get done. I get to see ideas take flight. I get to start these conversations, keep them going, shield them while they are too young to withstand an avalanche, let them soar when they are ready. My days are amazing.

How was your day? My day was terrible. You know what I do for a living? I push against closed doors and run into walls. All day, every day. I get to defend other people's dreams against cynics and often let both sides down. I get to beg for favours, time and access. I get to break big ambitious things into nonsensical proof points to navigate emotion while all the while talk about facts and figures. I get tripped up by a million random things. Policies nobody knew existed. Policies everyone knew existed and all agreed should change. But not now. Not yet. I get to fight tooth and nail to bring someone to the table only to find that the people I bring them for have lost interest or, worse, never meant for me to bring these guys over. They didn't think I would succeed. I get a deployment signed off but access to the environment denied. I get the use-case signed off, but the data set, not. I bring the client but lose access to the resource because of policy cut-off dates. My days are an endless chain of unexpected small-scale man-made frustrations and showdowns with men of little faith.

How was your day? My day is not over. You know what I do for a living? I ask people to believe and try and work harder than their contract demands and put their head above the parapet. And although I've left the office my head is still there. I am still refreshing my email in the hope that the approval, the sign-off, the user acceptance testing (UAT) report, the night owl dev will be coming through. I am home, but I am still fuming about the information that was promised 11 days ago and is still nowhere to be seen and I am trying to figure out who I may know in the far-away office who can go stand by that other person's desk until they give me what they promised me (thank you

Matt for once doing just that, you legend). I am home but my head is full of noise, frustration and hope. My days are long.

How was your day? My day is never how I think it will be. You know what I do for a living? I am paid to force organisations to do things for the first time. They hire me to force them. They hire me to partner them so they won't lose heart. They hire me to resist me. They hire me to help build something that will prove their fears were wrong. So although we all know everything we do is new, we all try to pretend it will behave in familiar ways. When it doesn't, we either have jubilation or despair. I spend days squaring circles, trying to figure out what the hardest thing will be and getting it wrong. Every. Single. Time. Sometimes that's a good thing. That's how you learn. That's how discovery works. Some of the things, some of the times turn out easier than expected. The corporates continue to surprise me. I prepare for every eventuality apart from the one that occurs.

How was your day? You ask, and I am dying to tell. But a little voice reasonably reminds me that most people don't go to war, they don't go to school, they don't go to the races, they don't go exploring and fighting and striving and dreaming and hoping and seething with silent rage and the opportunities missed, when they go to the office. Most people just go to work. So they ask: how was your day and pause and I say yeah not bad, yours?

And if they are just another corporate body, they tell me just how hard their day was. But if they are of the tribe, they say nothing with a look that says it all. Because they recognise the pause. Because they recognise themselves in it and they see you for what you are: one of them. So find them. This may have been lonely work thus far but it needs be lonely no longer. Plus it won't work if you keep doing it alone. You will go mad and you will never have the impact you need. Find the people you belong with, the friends in low places, the bankers who hack the system, the dreamers and doers and story tellers. We are legion. Just find us. Find the ones still standing despite how hard we have made all this for ourselves all these years, for no real reason. Find them. And if you don't know how, ask.

IT TAKES A VILLAGE

I grew up in Athens in the 1980s. Small compared to London where I now live but already an anonymous and faceless city. However, I clearly remember visiting my grandmother's village, a place called Temeni in Achaia as a small child. Temeni had just over 1,000 inhabitants at the last census. It was half that when I was a child and every visit came with a heady feeling of openness. There I was in a *village*, relishing in the freedom of being allowed out onto the streets without a supervising adult, trying this sense of safety on like a new coat and finding I liked it. And then one day a grown-up I had never seen before stopped me and asked me the most baffling question, 'Whose are you?'. When I told my nan later that day she chuckled. Of course, she said. This is a community, he wanted to know where you belong. Not if. You are here, you are welcome. They don't doubt you fit, you belong, you have a place. They just want to know where that is. And the rest will come.

Is it because this is a small village, I asked, ready to deploy all my storybook knowledge to tackle this new riddle. No, said my nan. Location and size has nothing to do with this. You don't live here and you are part of the community. AM NOT, I thought, proud of being able to say I am from the capital. You are, she said. Because I was her grand-daughter, and my favourite great uncle Ilias' lookalike and because now the village knows whose I am, I *belong*. I belong here. And 'here' is wherever I go. Community is not about geography, said my grandma.

And off I went to grow up, travel far and wide, study sociology with people who used terms such as 'glocal', and nationalism with people who described nationhood as a state of 'imagined community'.[19] And then came social media. Connectivity became easy, cheap and ubiquitous. After the early excitement of finding long-lost friends and remembering you lost them for a reason; after the early heady joy of hyper-connectedness and visibility, you found yourself immersed in noise. Building community in a virtual world became harder than doing it in real life and, for most, much less fulfilling. And yet here it was. Communities of online writers, thinkers, activists reach out. Isolated youths found they are not alone. They are not freaks. There is another hand stretching out to them and geography be damned. Social movements from Belarus to Egypt emerged, glued together and morphed with deliberate determination through and despite a web of noise and randomness.[20] Community as a word took a brand new meaning for some and simultaneously got banded about a bit too much.

At a time when I get approximately three LinkedIn messages per day calling me Paul (why always Paul, seriously?), an average of five in a language I don't speak, at least one opening with 'as the CEO of [insert name

---

[19] Benedict Anderson 'Imagined Communities'.

[20] If you are interested in this, incidentally, read my friend David Patrikarakos' exceptional book 'War in 140 Characters'.

of company I don't work at]' or as 'the CFO of [insert the name of the company I do work at but thankfully has a highly competent CFO who is not me]', the concept of digital community-building seems a bit moot. What do you say to the complete strangers who get your name wrong, get your job wrong, don't even do some fact-finding work before riding the wave of cheap communication to arrive, uninvited, at your digital doorstep?

I mean frankly I mostly say 'be gone'.

Ubiquitous connectivity and facile connections never yielded fruit, in the physical or digital worlds. And ultimately the metaverse be damned: we live real lives with real constraints and opportunities and humans – whether we see them in the flesh, on screen or reach out to them asynchronously – are what make the difference. They form communities.

I call my community a tribe because I am a lapsed sociologist and I like the implication of it being a social grouping that may include sub-communities linked through a variety of ties, with common cultural behaviours and a shared system of meaning (in our case it is not so much a language as a set of values). It is not formal and you don't need a passport. You belong because you choose to (admittedly traditional tribes don't always operate that way, but ours does). This is a community that demonstrates the power of being helpful and present. The power of defaulting to always seeking for a way through rather than a reason to stop. You need these people around you for this journey. And frankly you need them physically around you. You need them in your team and in your office and in your life. You need to be able to reach out to them for advice and help. For a rant or a moan. Whether the world is open enough for you to walk up to their desk or drag them out to the pub or not. You need these people. Not in an abstract imagined community but in a real band of warriors. Around you. Every day. Even if you don't need them the same way every day, you might. And they might need you. The people who will read this book and go 'oh I do that already' or 'actually, I can do more of this'. The people who are still standing.

This is a hard journey ahead.

Find your tribe. Find a community that feels bound by values. There is such a community out there. It is dispersed throughout our industry, they defy national borders and cross

Find a community bound by values. Such a community exists. It is dispersed throughout our industry, they defy national borders and cross verticals. Mostly they do great work even though they are neither supervised nor structured to that effect. That is actually how you discover them.

verticals. Mostly they do great work even though they are neither supervised nor structured to that effect. That is actually how you discover them.

So find them and enable the structure and offer the leadership. There are people out there who step up to the challenge and volunteer to form a web of reciprocal obligation, be it inside your organisation or across organisations enveloping our industry. All I am saying is: I know there is a global community out there that chooses to support each other for no other reason than they want to. In real life. In the office. Over social media. Across the globe. Creating connectivity and connections, never thinking 'me first'. Never selling each other short. It's a network in the truest sense. So. Build a team of people like that. From that community. So you don't feel alone any more because you won't be.

Don't hear network and think 'lukewarm white wine and forced conversation at a corporate mixer'. Think again. If you thought, 'social climbing careerist cut-throats', also think again. This tribe can be made of individuals in different parts of the world, different stages of their lives and different measures of what the world would outwardly call success. Some are soaring. Some are only just getting started. Some are stuck. Some have no interest in going further than they are.

They are not all in one place. They do not all know each other. So don't think that 'well that's all good and well but I am not in London, I am trying to do this from Mumbai or Rome or Melbourne or Bogota' I say so? You are looking for a type of person not a specific person. And they are everywhere even if they are outnumbered. So find them.

That's your last call to action, I promise.

But in some ways it's the most important one and the point the entire book was coming to all along and I am sure you sort of knew it.

This is hard complicated work. And we, as an industry, make it even harder for ourselves.

You can't do this alone. It is not possible for any one person to do it alone. So build your team. And then, when you realise that it is actually impossible for a team to do it alone, reach out more widely. To other teams like yours in your organisation and across the industry. Find your tribe.

Ok, you say, getting either tired or excited by now. Fine. I will find my tribe. I think I know where to start. Then what? What do you do with the tribe once you find them? The answer is exactly what you thought it would be. Nothing and everything. Mostly: you have them. You can hire them and build teams united by purpose. Or they may hire you. You may seek their advice and guidance. Learn from them or learn together. Learn from their mistakes so you don't repeat them and share your learnings so they can accelerate their journey. You will hold each other accountable when it gets a bit hard to stay focused on changing the what, or when you meet the resistance of those who would like you to fix the future and wake them up when it's over.

#MYTRIBE

Once you found your tribe they will give you energy and help and support and ideas and advice. They will join you and join in the work. So the hard question is not what you need them for but how you find them. If you are looking for them in the wild you will know them from three tell-tale signs:

First, they are knowledgeable. They have battle scars and stories galore. They have seen things, they have learned things, they have built things. Second, they are helpful. They put in the time. They invest in each other. They invest in people. Even strangers. Even people who don't turn out to be worth it. They don't prejudge and don't give up on the next one because the last one didn't work out. They believe in people and ideas the way cartoon inventors keep coming back with childish enthusiasm and relentless determination. They don't rush to an outcome, an ask, a sale. You may interact with them for years before you even get a glimpse of what they do for a living.

Third, they are unfettered. They are enthusiastic, optimistic and unfazed by how hard the work gets.

Oh. One more thing. They share. And share. And by sharing, they augment. They learn and evolve. They don't put a price on what they have to give and in doing that they make it priceless.[21]

You notice, perhaps, that none of the things you are looking for are technical or business aptitudes. Not because they are not needed. They are very much needed. But because they are both teachable and a hygiene factor. We talked about needing to find the right bankers already. I am not shying away from that. I am just saying that within the group of folks who have the right skillset for the work, you need to find that attitude that drives with consistency and integrity towards results that are arrived at with humility and purpose.

---

[21] Don't take my word for it, read the excellent book by Adam Grant 'Give and Take: A Revolutionary Approach to Success'.

It's not all airy-fairy kumbaya stuff.

If you have ever sat opposite me at a negotiating table you will know there is nothing soft and fluffy here. Being teachable and values-based and putting people first doesn't make you a hippie. I would argue it makes you an altogether hardier flower, it makes you more likely to survive in inhospitable surroundings and god knows we've made this habitat a hard place to flourish.

Ultimately, you may value things differently. You may need a group of people bound by different values to mine. That's ok. That's the point.

Find your tribe whatever it is. This is mine and you are welcome to join us: a group of people who actively, riotously, embrace the power starting from a place of openness, acceptance and wonder. Starting from a place of believing in others and expecting them to amaze you means they may well just do exactly that. And if they don't? We move on. We don't live with problems. We stay with them and fix them. Be it a system failure, a policy shortfall or a person who is destructive or distracting. And that is also important. Being people-focused doesn't come with letting people run riot. This is not playtime at kindergarten where everyone gets to sing some and dance some and put orange finger paint all over the furniture. Everything we have spoken about in this book needs to be true at the same time. And that's the bit that we haven't managed to even address let alone do as an industry. All the things: human, structural, technical and societal need to be true at the same time. And that time is now. And the road ahead is long because we haven't really found our stride yet. So chop chop.

There is nothing that will make the work ahead less in size, scope or complexity. Nothing that can make the uncertainty less daunting. Other than, perhaps, not going it alone. So, in a global village filled with noise and people trying to get a free ride, an industry still seeking to hedge and find shortcuts that don't exist, find the people who can cut through the noise and face the hard questions and can do that with determination, courage and empathy. All at the same time. You will know them when you meet them, you will know them by the way they tilt their head when you tell them how your day was, by the way their eyes blaze when you describe the wall you just banged your head against, the idea that died in the hands of procurement or the micro-aggressions that made your day feel 10 times as long as it actually was.

You will know them immediately but if you feel you still have to check, just ask, 'whose are you'. And they will tell you, in their own words but without a moment's hesitation: each other's. They will joke about why on earth we keep doing this to ourselves and why we haven't moved on to something less thankless by now. They will share battle scars. They will look fiercely ahead.

Not for a moment satisfied with how far we've come, even though it was their effort and determination that dragged us all this way in the first place. They will only talk about how we can make it further, faster.

You will know them on sight, so make yourself known to them.

Pull up a chair. You are home.

We've been expecting you.

FINAL CALL TO ACTION (I PROMISE)

1. Ask the hard questions: of yourself, your team and the industry.
2. State the obvious. There is power in the telling and it empowers people to do the same so that we can start moving away from the sacred cows and established wisdom of yesteryear.
3. Take on big problems. We have navigated change so far by taking on the smallest challenges, taking small cautious steps. We've gone as far as that will take us. Take on the big problems next.
4. Find your tribe. You don't need to do this work alone.
5. Remember that we are a service industry: if we are not being of service, we are just in the way.

Printed in the United States
by Baker & Taylor Publisher Services